D1141691

Sikh Nationalism and Identity in a Global Age

Sikh Nationalism and Identity in a Global Age examines the construction of a Sikh national identity in post-colonial India and the diaspora and explores the reasons for the failure of the movement for an independent Sikh state: *Khalistan*. Based on a decade of research, it is argued that the failure of the movement to bring about a sovereign, Sikh state should not be interpreted as resulting from the weakness of the 'communal' ties which bind members of the Sikh 'nation' together, but points to the transformation of *national* identity under conditions of globalization. Globalization is perceived to have severed the link between nation and state and, through the proliferation and development of Information and Communications Technologies (ICTs), has facilitated the articulation of a *transnational* 'diasporic' Sikh identity. It is argued that this 'diasporic' identity potentially challenges the conventional narratives of international relations and makes the imagination of a post-Westphalian community possible.

Theoretically innovative and interdisciplinary in approach, it will be primarily of interest to students of South Asian studies, political science and international relations, as well as to many others trying to come to terms with the continued importance of religious and cultural identities in times of rapid political, economic, social and cultural change.

Giorgio Shani is Associate Professor in the Faculty of International Relations, Ritsumeikan University, Kyoto, Japan. He holds a doctorate from SOAS, University of London, and is co-editor of *Protecting Human Security in a Post 9/11 World* (2007).

Routledge advances in South Asian studies

Edited by Subrata K. Mitra
South Asia Institute, University of Heidelberg, Germany

South Asia, with its burgeoning, ethnically diverse population, soaring economies, and nuclear weapons, is an increasingly important region in the global context. The series, which builds on this complex, dynamic and volatile area, features innovative and original research on the region as a whole or on the countries. Its scope extends to scholarly works drawing on history, politics, development studies, sociology and economics of individual countries from the region as well as those that take an interdisciplinary and comparative approach to the area as a whole or to a comparison of two or more countries from this region. In terms of theory and method, rather than basing itself on any one orthodoxy, the series draws broadly on the insights germane to area studies, as well as the tool kit of the social sciences in general, emphasizing comparison, the analysis of the structure and processes, and the application of qualitative and quantitative methods. The series welcomes submissions from established authors in the field as well as from young authors who have recently completed their doctoral dissertations.

Sikh Nationalism and Identity in a Global Age

Giorgio Shani

Routledge
Taylor & Francis Group

LONDON AND NEW YORK

First published 2008
by Routledge
2 Park Square, Milton Park, Abingdon, Oxon, OX14 4RN

Simultaneously published in the USA and Canada
by Routledge
270 Madison Ave, New York NY 10016

Routledge is an imprint of the Taylor & Francis Group, an informa business

Transferred to Digital Printing 2010

Typeset in Times New Roman by
RefineCatch Limited, Bungay, Suffolk

British Library Cataloguing in Publication Data
A catalogue record for this book is available from the British Library

Library of Congress Cataloging in Publication Data
Shani, Giorgio, 1970–
Sikh nationalism and identity in a global age / Giorgio Shani.
p. cm.— (Routledge advances in South Asian studies series; 9)
Includes bibliographical references and index.
1. Sikh nationalism. 2. Sikh diaspora. 3. Sikhs—Political activity.
4. Sikhs—Social networks. 5. Globalization. 6. Punjab (India)—History—
Autonomy and independence movements. I. Title.
DS432.S5S395 2007
320.540917'646–dc22
2007022117

ISBN10: 0–415–42190–X (hbk)
ISBN10: 0–415–58610–0 (pbk)
ISBN10: 0–203–93721–X (ebk)

ISBN13: 978–0–415–42190–4 (hbk)
ISBN13: 978–0–415–58610–8 (pbk)
ISBN13: 978–0–203–93721–1 (ebk)

To Dharam Singh Sahni, who lived his life according to the universal and egalitarian values of the Sikh faith, and to his great-grandchildren, Milena and Arjun, so they can discover them.

He is without colour, mark, caste and lineage.
He is without enemy, friend, father and mother.
He is far away from all and closest to all.
His dwelling is within water, on earth and in heavens.
He is Limitless Entity and hath infinite celestial strain.

(Guru Gobind Singh, '*Akal Ustat*', *Sri Dasam Granth Sahib*, verses 4–5)

Contents

Figures

Tables

Preface and acknowledgements

He is the One in many, countless are His shapes and forms.
He pervades all that exists: wherever I look, He is there.
(Namdeva, Raga Asa, SGGS; cited in Dass 2000: 29)

This book, which is a substantially revised version of my Ph.D. thesis presented at the School of Oriental and African Studies (University of London), attempts to account for the construction, demise and persistence of a Sikh national identity within India and the diaspora. It is also a highly subjective account of how the central values and ideals of Sikhism can be adapted to our contemporary global age, characterized by increasing interconnectedness between societies and the establishment of transplanetary social networks. Written by someone of mixed Punjabi–Italian parentage who is certainly more 'at home' in the 'diaspora' than in the Punjab, it argues that the ideals of Sikhism, as embodied in the *Khalsa*, are universal and should not be confined to a Punjabi *ethnie*. Consequently, the book makes no attempt at 'objectivity', and no apologies are offered for not providing a definitive portrait of Sikh identity in the twenty-first century (although I take full responsibility for any factual errors). However, it is hoped that many Sikhs – as well as scholars of South Asian studies, sociology and international politics – will find the book of interest and not revoke my 'permission to narrate' (Said 2000) on the grounds of religion or ethnicity.

Indeed, the book is written with two different audiences and objectives in mind. The first objective is for scholars working within the discipline of political science and international relations in particular to take Sikhism and Sikh identity more seriously. Sikh nationalism first emerged as a 'problem' in Punjab studies in the early 1980s. Punjab's 'problem' subsequently became a 'national' one after Blue Star and the assassination of Indira Gandhi. Finally, militant Sikh nationalism became an international one – at least for India – with the mobilization of Sikhs in the diaspora under the banner of 'Khalistan'. Since the crushing of the militancy in the early 1990s, there has been a declining academic interest in Sikh identity within South Asian studies and political science – although this has been countered by the development of 'Sikh studies' as a sub-discipline of religion and history in some Western academic institutions. There has also, as far as I am aware, been no attempt to theorize international relations from a transnational Sikh perspective, and it is hoped that the last chapter of this book goes some way towards doing so.

The second objective I share with Nikky-Guninder Kaur Singh and many others: I would like the Sikh community to be (even more) *self-reflective* (2005: 175, emphasis mine). Specifically, I would like more Sikhs in the diaspora to question whether a sovereign state is really needed to preserve the transnational ideals of the *Khalsa* in a time of globalization and regionalization. Perhaps, given the continued 'Hinduization' of Indian society, it still is, but I believe that further debate on whether *Khalistan* is, in fact, desirable will – if allowed by states – be beneficial for Sikhs everywhere. If, as I conclude, *Khalistan* is not needed, then how else can these ideals be maintained and articulated both nationally and internationally?

Although, unlike Kaur Singh, I am unable to claim this community as my own, it was unquestionably my grandfather's, and it is to him – and his great-grandchildren – that I dedicate this book. Dharam Singh Sahni embodied the ideals of the *Khalsa* and lived through many of the formative events of twentieth-century South Asian history, including *Jallianwallah Bagh*, anti-colonial nationalism and the 'holocaust' of partition. This book would have never been written without his inspiration or the support of my extended family: principally my father and mother; my Uncle Charanjit and Aunt Tavinder; my 'brother' Raju and his wife Sumiti; Nirmal and Jawant Singh Chowdury; Jagjit Singh Chaddah and his family; and, of course, Akiko, Milena and Arjun.

Special mention must also go to my Ph.D. supervisors at SOAS, Professor Sudipta Kaviraj and Professor David Taylor; to Professor Subrata Mitra and two anonymous reviewers for their helpful and critical comments on four draft chapters; and to Helly Chalal in the UK, Surinder Singh Sawhney in India, and Dr Swaranjeet Singh in the US for their invaluable help in arranging interviews across three continents. Research for the thesis was initially carried out in India over a decade ago and in the UK between 1998 and 2001. This has been supplemented by further research at a post-doctoral level with the financial support of the Japanese Ministry of Education (MEXT) and Ritsumeikan University.

I am, furthermore, very grateful to the following people for making the time to be interviewed by me: Mejindarpal Kaur, Tejinder Singh, Patwant Singh, Ajit Singh Khera, Bhupinder Singh, Surinderpal Singh, Amardeep Singh, Rajinder Singh Magoo, Dr Balwant Singh Hansra, Dr Amarjit Singh, Dr Jasdev Singh Rai and the late Dr Jagjit Singh Chauhan. I would like to thank Dorothea Schaefter, Tom Bates and the editorial team at Routledge for their patience; and the following people for comments made on my work at various stages of preparation: Professor Pal Ahluwalia, Professor Brian Keith Axel, Professor Partha Chatterjee, Dr Stephen Hopgood, Dr Virinder Singh Kalra, Ms Harvind Kaur, Professor Richard King, Professor Kristina Kinvall, Professor W.H. McLeod, Professor Arvind-Pal Singh Mandair,

Professor Mustapha Kamal Pasha, Dr Bobby S. Sayyid, Professor John Sidel, Professor Ian Talbot and Professor Peter van der Veer. Finally, I wish to especially thank Professor Gurharpal Singh for his constant encouragement, support and advice as well as his pivotal role in pioneering Sikh studies in political science.

Earlier versions of Chapters 2 and 3, 5, 6 and 7 have been published in *South Asia Research* (Shani 2000b), *Studies in Ethnicity and Nationalism* (Shani 2002), the *International Journal of Punjab Studies* (Shani 2000a) and *Sikh Formations: Religion, Culture, Theory* (Shani 2005), but all have been substantially revised, updated and rewritten for this volume.

Giorgiandrea (Giorgio) Dharam Singh Shani
Kyoto, Japan
April 2007

Abbreviations

AIADMK	All-India Anna Dravida Munnetra Kazhagam
AISSF	All-India Sikh Students' Federation
ASR	Anandpur Sahib Resolution
BJP	Bharatiya Janata Party
BK	Babbar Khalsa
BKI	Babbar Khalsa International
BSP	Bahujan Samaj Party
BT	Bhindranwale Tigers
CKD	Chief Khalsa Diwan
CPI	Communist Party of India
CPI (M)	Communist Party of India (Marxist)
CRE	Commission for Racial Equality
CSDS	Centre for the Study of Developing Societies
DK	Dal Khalsa
DMK	Dravida Munnetra Kazhagam
DT	Damdam Taksal
EIU	Economist Intelligence Unit
EU	European Union
FRY	Federal Republic of Yugoslavia
GOI	Government of India
HRAG	Human Rights Advisory Group
HYV	high-yield variety
ICCPR	International Covenant on Civil and Political Rights
ICHRA	International Civil and Human Rights Advocacy
ICT	Information and Communications Technology
IMF	International Monetary Fund
INC	Indian National Congress
IR	international relations
ISYF	International Sikh Youth Federation
IWAs	Indian workers' associations
KAC	Khalistan Affairs Center
KCF	Khalistan Commando Force
KLF	Khalistan Liberation Force

MEPs	Members of the European Parliament
MLAs	Members of the Legislative Assembly
MNC	multinational corporation
MPs	Members of Parliament
MTA	Metropolitan Transit Authority
NDA	National Democratic Alliance
NGO	non-governmental organization
NYPD	New York City Police Department
PRC	People's Republic of China
RSS	Rashtriya Swayamsevak Sangh
RTT	Right to the Turban (United States)
SAD	Shiromani Akali Dal
SAD (Amritsar)	Shiromani Akali Dal (Amritsar)
SAD (Badal)	Shiromani Akali Dal (Badal)
SAD (UK)	Shiromani Akali Dal (UK)
SALDEF	Sikh American Legal Defense and Education Fund
SAPs	structurally adjusted policies
SDGS	Sri Dasam Granth Sahib
SGGS	Sri Guru Granth Sahib
SGPC	Shiromani Gurdwara Prabandhak Committee
SHRG	Sikh Human Rights Group
SMART	Sikh Mediawatch and Resource Task Force
SWAN	Sikh with a Need
TDP	Telugu Desam Party
UAD	United Akali Dal
UK	United Kingdom
UN	United Nations
UNDP	United Nations Development Programme
UP	Uttar Pradesh
UPA	United Progressive Alliance
USA	United States of America
VHP	Vishwa Hindu Parishad
WSC	World Sikh Council
WSC-AR	World Sikh Council – America Region
WSO	World Sikh Organization

1 Introduction

Rethinking Sikh nationalism in a global age

The appointment of the first Sikh prime minister of India, ironically one instigated by the daughter-in-law of the woman who ordered the infamous storming of the Golden Temple complex in Amritsar in June 1984,[1] provides an opportune moment to reflect upon Sikh national identity. The twenty-odd years since the military action, codenamed 'Operation Blue Star', designed to eliminate a band of armed Sikh militants taking refuge in the holiest shrine in Sikhism have seen the rise and fall of a separatist movement dedicated to the achievement of an independent Sikh state: *Khalistan*. Although this movement was unsuccessful, there is evidence to show that it enjoyed the support of a significant number of Sikhs in the Indian state of the Punjab (Pettigrew 1995; Gurharpal Singh 2000) and in the 'diaspora' (Tatla 1999; Axel 2001). What then can account for first the strength and then the 'strange death of Sikh ethno-nationalism' (Gurharpal Singh 2004)?

Generally speaking, four or five different approaches to this question may be identified. The first approach attributes the rise of Sikh nationalism to the coherence of a religiously and culturally defined *ethnie* (H. Deol 2000; Gurharpal Singh 2000) and accounts for the decline of Sikh militancy in the Punjab as primarily a traumatic reaction to the 'crescendo of state led violence' orchestrated by the Indian state (Gurharpal Singh 2004). The second approach considers Sikh identity to have been 'invented' in the colonial period (Kapur 1986; Oberoi 1994) and Sikh nationalism itself to have been primarily a reaction to state-led violence and to the ruthless centralization of political power in India by the then prime minister, Indira Gandhi (Brass 1991). A variant of this approach sees Sikh ethno-nationalism essentially in socio-economic terms as an ideology propagated by rich, capitalist farmers to unite the rural Sikh masses under their hegemony (Purewal 2000). The 'death' of Sikh ethno-nationalism is attributed to the readjustment of relations between central and state governments and the liberalization of the Indian economy. A related approach sees modern Sikh identity as a 'construction' of colonial Orientalism (Fox 1985) and Sikh nationalism, in Partha Chatterjee's words, as 'derivative discourse' (Chatterjee 1996 [1993]) or even a 'pathology' of modernity (Fox 1996). Finally, many scholars have followed the Indian state in considering Sikh nationalism to be primarily a 'long-distance' phenomenon (Anderson 1992). Sikhs settled overseas, particularly in advanced capitalist societies such as Canada, the US and the UK, are seen to constitute a 'diaspora', mobilized for the achievement of sovereign statehood (Tatla 1999; Axel 2001).

It will be argued that all of the approaches outlined above are problematic: the first essentializes Sikh identity; the second 'reduces' identity to a single causal principle and is, furthermore, unable to account for continuity within the Sikh tradition; the third reproduces the Orientalist discourse it is attempting to critique, whilst the final approach conflates the concepts of 'nation' and 'diaspora'. It will be argued, instead, that a more comprehensive approach is needed: one which accounts for both *continuity* and *change* in Sikh narratives and, furthermore, takes into account the *global* dimensions of Sikh identity.

Ethno-symbolist approaches

The first approach attributes the strength of Sikh ethno-religious nationalism to the coherence of a religiously and culturally defined community and accounts for the decline of Sikh militancy in the Punjab as primarily a traumatic reaction to the 'crescendo of state led violence' orchestrated by the Indian state and the Indian National Congress (INC) in particular (Gurharpal Singh 2000, 2004). From this perspective, the Sikh community or *qaum* corresponds to A.D. Smith's definition of a politicized *ethnie*, or nation. For Smith, an *ethnie* is defined as a 'a named human population with myths of common ancestry, shared historical memories and one or more elements of a common culture, including an association with a homeland, and some degree of solidarity, at least amongst elites' (A.D. Smith 1999: 13).

The Sikh *ethnie* share common ancestry myths dating back to the founding of the *Khalsa* in 1699 and historical memories of martyrdom and persecution under successive Mughal, British and Indian rulers. Although Punjabi is spoken by Sikh, Hindu and Muslim in East and West Punjab alike, the Sikh scriptures are written in the *Gurumukhi* script particular to Sikhs. Sikhs following the edicts of the tenth Guru, Gobind Singh, are enjoined to keep their hair, including facial hair, long (*kes*); carry a comb (*kanga*); wear knee-length breeches (*kach*); wear a steel bracelet on the right hand (*kara*); and carry a sword or dagger (*kirpan*). Those who hold these five symbols of Sikh identity are known as *Kes-dhari* Sikhs. Those who don't are known as *Sahajdhari* Sikhs: 'slow adopters' who would eventually progress towards full participation in the *Khalsa* (McLeod 1989: 96). Finally, for the Sikhs, the Punjab may be equated with what A.D. Smith terms the ancestral land where, 'in the shared memories of its inhabitants, the great events that formed the nation took place' (A.D. Smith 1996: 383).

This ethno-symbolist view of the Sikh nation is reflected in the recent work of Sikh scholars as well as in the nationalist narratives in the Punjab as articulated by actors operating within the Sikh political system. In *Religion and Nationalism in India: The Case of the Punjab* (2000), Harnik Deol illustrates how the origins of modern Sikh national consciousness (1947–1995) lie in the historical roots of Sikh communal consciousness (1469–1947). For Deol, a specifically Sikh ethnic identity based upon the Sikh religious tradition and Punjabi language pre-dates colonial rule. Consequently, the introduction of print capitalism in the colonial period merely 'energized' the existing tendencies towards differentiation between the diverse religio-linguistic communities of the Punjab rather than, as in Benedict Anderson's formulation, created a radically different consciousness (H. Deol 2000: 90). Like Deol, Gurharpal Singh believes modern Sikh identity to be 'remarkably cohesive' (Gurharpal Singh 2000: 87), having its roots in a *Jat* Punjabi *ethnie*, 'a sacred text and religious tradition dating from Guru Nanak' (Gurharpal Singh 2000: 78). Central to this ethno-nationalist narrative is the *territorialization* of Sikh socio-political identity in the homeland of the Punjab. As early as 1946, the SGPC committed itself to the 'goal of a Sikh state' and, therefore, the territorialization of the Sikh *qaum* or 'nation'. The Sikh people needed a state of their own to 'preserve the main Sikh shrines, Sikh social practices, Sikh self-respect and pride, Sikh sovereignty and the future prosperity of the Sikh people' (SGPC 1946).

However, it is argued that this approach, although convincing in its analysis of the strategies of violent and hegemonic control adopted by the Indian state, *essentializes* Sikh identity and ignores the voices of those in the Sikh *qaum* critical of territorialized nationalist narratives. Identities are multiple, subjective and infinitely contested. Communal identities are not ascribed at birth but are adopted, rejected, reinterpreted, negotiated, imagined and, in certain circumstances, invented. In multiethnic states, 'new' identities, such as Black, White, European, Asian or Indian, coexist with 'older' identities based on language, religion and culture (S. Hall 1997). In such circumstances, identity becomes, in Stuart Hall's words, a 'moveable feast' which is 'formed and transformed continuously in relation to the ways we are represented or addressed in the cultural systems which surround us' (S. Hall 1992: 277).

Identification may be understood, following Lacan, as the 'transformation that takes place in the subject when he assumes an image', to which Lacan gives the term *imago* (Lacan 1977: 2). Lacan argued that identification first takes place when the child is between six and eighteen months and first recognizes a reflection of itself in a mirror. This image, however, is *alienating*. The 'specular' image of the child does not correspond to the identity of the child but comes to the child 'from the outside'. The mirror-state 'situates the agency of the ego, before its social determination, in a fictional direction' (Lacan 1977: 2). Thus, for Lacan, identity is not inherent within the subject but comes into being 'from the place of the other'. It is, therefore, a 'fictional' construct: all identities are 'imaginary' based on the fundamental misrecognition (*méconnaissance*) of the child with its *imago*. The subject and the social order in which the subject finds a place are both in a continuous process of becoming. Both are always in a process of formation.

It follows that the identity of the *collective* subject, the community, society or nation, cannot be *fixed* by a 'primordial attachment'[2] such as language, religion or ethnicity, but is too in a process of becoming. Although ethno-symbolists are correct to point out that 'religious' traditions pre-date coloni-alism, *ethnicized* religious communities in South Asia are relatively recent phenomena and their claims to primordiality are based upon an appropri-ation and reinterpretation of colonial categories. As will be argued later, the religious and cultural homogeneity upon which ethno-symbolists based their claims for Sikh 'nationhood' is itself of recent origin, a product of elite manipulation (Kapur 1986; Brass 1991), a reflection of colonial Orientalism (Fox 1985; Dusenbery 1999) or both (Oberoi 1994).

Instrumentalist approaches

The second approach considers Sikh identity as it is known today to have been 'invented' by Sikh elites during the colonial period. Particular attention has been paid to the activities of the *Singh Sabha* movement in the late nine-teenth century and their elucidation of a *Tat Khalsa* discourse which became hegemonic in the twentieth century (Kapur 1986; Oberoi 1994; Barrier 2004a, 2004b). By far the most impressive account of the rise of a *Tat Khalsa* discourse is provided by Harjot Oberoi's *The Construction of Religious Boundaries* (1994), which despite its sophisticated use of constructivist and post-structuralist theory appears to support the instrumentalist thesis. For Oberoi:

> In the late nineteenth-century a growing body of Sikhs took part in a systematic campaign to purge their faith of religious diversity, as well as what they saw as Hindu accretions and as a Brahmanical stranglehold over their rituals. The result was a fundamental change in the nature of the Sikh tradition. From an amorphous entity it rapidly turned into a homogenous community.
>
> (Oberoi 1994: 420–421)

However, for instrumentalists, it is post-1984 Sikh nationalism, and in particular the movement for a separate Sikh state, which, to paraphrase Ernest Gellner, engendered the Sikh nation (Gellner 1983: 55). Sikh militancy itself is seen to be primarily a reaction to state-led violence and to the ruthless centralization of political power in India by the then prime minis-ter, Indira Gandhi (Brass 1991). There are two variants of the instru-mentalist position which purport to account for the emergence of a Sikh nationalist movement within India. One school of thought has stressed the primacy of the centralizing tendencies of the national government in Delhi and the post-Nehruvian leadership in alienating the Sikh community (Brass 1991). Another complementary approach has emphasized the role of eco-nomic factors and, in particular, the effects of the Green Revolution in making the emergence of a new type of politics possible (Narang 1983; Purewal 2000).

The 'death' of Sikh ethno-nationalism is attributed to the readjustment of relations between central and state governments which followed the decline of INC hegemony within the Indian political system and the rise of a loose federation of regional parties, including the Badal faction of the SAD, which has helped keep the centralizing tendencies of the centre in check. A variant of this approach sees Sikh ethno-nationalism essentially in socio-economic terms as an ideology propagated by rich, capitalist farmers to unite the rural Sikh masses under their hegemony (Gill and Singhal 1984; Gopal Singh 1984; Narang 1986; Purewal 2000). For Shinder Purewal, Sikh ethno-nationalism is a by-product of the struggle between the Sikh 'kulaks' and the predominately Hindu commercial and industrial bourgeoisie of India. Sikhism had become 'an ideological weapon of the *kulaks* to build a "common" bond among Sikhs of all classes and to build them under their command' (Purewal 2000: 73).

> In the name of Sikhism, the Kulaks seek to strengthen their domination over the home market of Punjab either by demanding the transfer of all jurisdictions except communications, currency, defence, and foreign affairs to the provinces, or by asserting complete independence of India.
>
> (Purewal 2000: viii)

Since the demands of this new Sikh elite were primarily material and centred on greater access to the world market for their mainly agricultural produce, it follows that the decline of Sikh ethno-nationalism can be explained in terms of the transition to a market economy which followed on from the economic reforms which the then finance minister and current prime minister, Manmohan Singh, inaugurated in 1991.

It is argued that both the instrumental approaches outlined above are *reductionist* in that they seek to reduce the complexity of Sikh ethno-nationalism to a single causal principle: the internal dynamics of the Indian political system or the impact of the 'Green Revolution' upon agriculture in the Indian state of Punjab where most Sikhs live. Furthermore, 'instrumentalist' approaches are unable to account for the *persistence* of Sikh nationalism today and for its continued salience for, in many cases, wealthy young Sikhs settled in Western, capitalist societies. No attempt is made to account for what Walker Connor termed the 'irrational' nature of the ethno-national bond: the strength and depth of feeling of belonging to an ethnic or national community which cuts across different classes (Connor 1994). Nor is there a concerted attempt to explain just how the consciousness of belonging to a *religious* and cultural community which included adherents from many different classes and 'castes' was constructed over time and developed into a *political* consciousness. Finally, there is no explanation of how Sikh elites were able to exert hegemony over followers of the Sikh faith and redefine a religious tradition which has stood, in one form or another, for almost half a millennium, long before the transition to 'modernity' in the Punjab. The contributions made by people *'on their own, that is, independent of the elite* to the making and development of' nationalism are conveniently ignored (Guha 1988: 3, author's emphasis). Instrumentalist approaches, therefore, do not provide us with an adequate theory of how political identities based upon religion and culture are constructed but merely with a description of the conditions under which *existing* ethnic and religious identities may be politicized.

Constructivist approaches

For constructivist approaches, colonial discourse prescribes limits to elite manipulation of ethno-cultural identity. Colonial power, Edward Said persuasively argued, was supported and made possible by the development of Orientalist scholarship which had the effect of distorting indigenous narratives about their own societies (Said 1978). The purpose of Orientalist scholarship, 'Indology' in the case of South Asia (Inden 1990), was to render the 'Orient' an object of colonial knowledge, and Orientalism in turn deeply influenced the self-perception and identity formation of indigenous elites. Whilst Romilla Thapar, Ashis Nandy and Chetan Bhatt amongst others consider the development of a Hindu national consciousness to have been profoundly influenced by Orientalism (Thapar 1989; Nandy 1998a, 1998b; Bhatt 2001), Richard Fox comes close to arguing that the very notion of a distinct 'Sikh' identity itself is an Orientalist construction. Fox follows Said in considering Orientalism a totalizing discourse, and has argued that contemporary Sikh identity is a re-appropriation of the colonial stereotype, or *imago*, of the Sikhs as a 'martial race' (Fox 1985).

As the British believed the Singhs to constitute a separate race, possessing a distinctive physiognomy, habitat, behaviour and appearance, the colonial state strove to treat the *Kes-dhari* Singhs as a distinct community. 'British rulers, in pursuit of their colonial interests through means directed by their own cultural beliefs, foreshadowed the reformed Sikh, or Singh identity, propounded by the Singh Sabhas' (Fox 1985: 10). The myth of the 'Lions of the Punjab', like that of other 'martial races' in the subcontinent, was functional in that it served the interests of the Indian army. Between a quarter and a third of all soldiers from the Punjab were Sikhs at a time when Sikhs barely made up a tenth of the Punjab's population. The military authorities tolerated and moreover encouraged the Sikh initiation ceremony, the *khande ki pahul*, since British officers believed that the valour and even loyalty of their Sikh troops were closely linked with their religious identity. In return, the British expected the Singhs to fight and die for king and empire. However, when the Punjab's rural economy deteriorated after the First World War, the demobilized *Jat* soldier-peasants, imbued with the Raj's image of a Singh, joined the urban religious mainly *Khatri* reformers in the movement for *gurdwara* reform.

In a more recent work, Fox has extended his conclusions to a general theory of 'communalism' and modernity. For Fox, colonialism was merely the mode by which modernity came to South Asia. Although colonial modernity may have differed from Western modernity in the degree of coercion used to implement its policies, it had similar consequences: namely, following Weber, disenchantment brought by bureaucratic rationality and capitalist alienation, and the 'hyper-enchantment' of pre-existing ethnic and religious identities (Fox 1996). 'Communalism' in South Asia is therefore merely a local instance of how modernity builds new forms of identity once it has disenchanted the pre-modern world. It is not specific to a particular geographical area, South Asia in this case, as much as it has been assigned to one by modernity.[3] Sikh 'nationalism' is, for Fox, an example of a communal identity produced by the institutional embodiment of modernity: the bureaucratic state (Fox 1996: 239). The bureaucratic state is characterized, on the one hand, by its rationality, secularism and efficiency, and on the other by its intrusions upon the autonomy of local elites. Fox claims that the autonomy of both Sikh and Welsh local elites was compromised by the development of the bureaucratic state in India and Britain respectively. As with the Sikhs, Welsh ethnic identity was initially infused with a religious dimension. Chapels, like Sikh temples, conserved Welsh identity and became centres for communal politics. However, whereas the post-colonial British welfare state, because of its greater efficiency and competence, was able to placate local elites by institutionalizing a Welsh linguistic identity, the Indian state was less successful. Fox implicitly, like instrumentalists, relies upon a distinction between the Nehruvian and post-Nehruvian state which tried to exploit factional divisions within the sectarian movement, leading to Sikh 'hyper-enchantment' under Bhindranwale.

Fox's account, however, reproduces the hegemony of the Orientalist discourse which it appears to be critiquing. Sikh identity appears to be a mere reflection of a colonial discourse which, in Said's words, reduces the Orient to silence.[4] As Peter van der Veer has pointed out, this is in itself an 'orientalist fallacy that denies Indians agency in constructing their society and simplifies the intricate interplay of Western and Indian discourses' (van der Veer 1994: 21). Sikh identity, as Harjot Oberoi argues, 'cannot be explained by referring to the British policy of divide and rule, or the compulsions of elite politics' but 'resulted from a complex evolution' (Oberoi 1994: 424). Colonial discourse did not reduce the Orient to silence but stimulated a search for an 'indigenous' *modernity*: a modernity which could *speak for* and on behalf of the colonized. Furthermore, Fox does not make a distinction between modernity as it is experienced in the modern West and *colonial* modernity. His comparison of Sikh communalism to Welsh ethnic nationalism not only empties the Sikh tradition of any religious significance, regarding it as little more than a 'sect' of Hinduism in the same way as Methodism was a branch of Protestantism, but also ignores the very different cultural contexts in which both arose.[5]

Long-distance nationalism

This final approach assumes Sikh nationalism to be a diaspora-led phenomenon. Sikhs settled overseas, particularly in advanced capitalist societies such as Canada, the US and the UK, are seen to constitute a 'diaspora', mobilized for the achievement of sovereign statehood. According to Darshan Singh Tatla, 'the Sikh diaspora, through its location and involvement in Punjabi affairs, has helped in providing an ideological framework . . . redefining Sikh ethnicity in terms of an ethno-national bond' (Tatla 2001: 185). Arjun Appadurai goes so far as to claim that *Khalistan*, the 'land of the pure' or Sikh homeland, is 'an invented homeland of the deterritorialized Sikh population of England, Canada and the United States' (Appadurai 1990: 302).

It is argued here, however, that this approach ignores the depth of nationalist sentiment in the Punjab, which led between 1984 and 1992 to an undeclared war of national self-determination between armed militants and the Indian state (Pettigrew 1995), and is, furthermore, unable to account for *why* the nationalist discourse is so strong in the diaspora. Other attempts to conceive of Sikh nationalism as a primarily *diasporic* phenomenon ignore the transnational linkages between the diaspora and homeland (Anderson 1992, 1994) and/or unwittingly silence the voices of those critical of the nationalist narrative by equating nation with diaspora (Axel 2001).

What all explanations have in common is their treatment of Sikh nationalism as what Kenneth Waltz terms a 'unit-led' phenomenon and not a 'systemic' feature of international relations (Waltz 1986). Sikh nationalism has been regarded as a distortion of South Asian political and economic development (Fox 1996) and even as a product of multiculturalist policies in the West based upon 'western ethno-sociology' (Dusenbery 1999) but it is primarily analysed *within* the parameters of the nation-state, through the disciplines of political science, history or anthropology. The international and global dimensions of Sikh identity are ignored, making it easier for the theorists and practitioners of the notoriously 'state-centric' discipline of international relations (IR) to ignore the Sikh *qaum* completely. It is suggested instead that an engagement with critical theories of international relations may prove productive, as it forces us to re-examine the statist assumptions of conventional narratives of IR and those of the movement for *Khalistan*. It is argued that globalization has created space for the articulation of a deterritorialized Sikh identity which, in its desire to move beyond *Khalistan*, challenges the territorialized narratives of the Westphalian international order upon which the modern discipline of international relations is based. Both 'homeland' and 'diaspora' may be regarded as indivisible parts of a global Sikh *qaum* which sees the establishment of an independent sovereign state as merely one strategy used to secure recognition of its cultural and religious particularity.

Globalization, sovereignty and national identity

Since the events of 11 September 2001 (hereafter 9/11), it has been common-place on both right and left to talk of the end of globalization (Ferguson 2005; Rosenberg 2005). While transnational economic transactions stalled (albeit temporarily) in the wake of 9/11, the US-led 'War on Terror' has heightened nationalist sentiments throughout much of the world through the (re)deployment of the doctrine of national – at the expense of human – security (Shani *et al.* 2007). In Held and McGrew's words, 'borders and boundaries, nationalism and protectionism, localism and ethnicity appear to define an epoch of radical de-globalization: the disintegration and demise of globalism' (Held and McGrew 2006). This rapid process of *de-globalization* has led some to definitively claim that 'the age of globalization is over' (Rosenberg 2005: 2). In doing so, this perspective builds upon the sceptical view which cast doubt on the extent to which the contemporary world was 'globalized' and upon the degree to which the economic trends towards internationalization and regionalization were historically unprecedented (Hirst and Thompson 1996; Krasner 1999). For Niall Ferguson, there lies a very real danger that the contemporary era of globalization could be 'sunk' by 'another, bigger September 11' and that 'we seem no better prepared . . . than were the beneficiaries of the last age of globalization, 90 years ago' (Ferguson 2005: 76–77).

Certainly, much of the optimism which accompanied the collapse of the Soviet bloc and the expansion of capitalism in the 1990s seems to have dissipated in a post-9/11 world characterized by a 'clash of civilizations' (Huntington 1996) and increased global inequality (Shani *et al.* 2007). The 'borderless economy' predicted by Ohmae (Ohmae 1990) has failed to materialize and it would seem that the demise of the 'nation state' (Ohmae 1995) seems, at best, premature. However, the contemporary world does appear to be more 'global' than that of previous epochs. The world we live in is characterized by greater interconnectedness between societies and enmeshment of economies so that 'events in one part of the world more and more have effects on peoples and societies far away' (Baylis and Smith 2001: 7).

Globalization may be defined as:

> a process (or set of processes) which embodies a transformation in the spatial organization of social relations and transactions – assessed in terms of their *extensity, intensity, velocity* and *impact* – generating trans-continental or interregional *flows* and *networks* of activity, interaction and the exercise of power.
>
> (Held *et al.* 1999: 16)

Viewed in such a light, globalization is hardly a new phenomenon and has its origins in the rise of a world capitalist economy (Frank 1969; Wallerstein

1974; Marx 1977), imperialism (Biel 2000; Hardt and Negri 2000; Harvey 2003) and 'organized violence' (McGrew 2006). However, many theorists have identified the post-Cold War world in particular as marking a new stage in the history of globalization (Held *et al.* 1999; Giddens 2000; Held and McGrew 2000, 2006; Scholte 2005). Whilst some have located the dynamics of the contemporary intensification of the processes associated with global-ization in the 'impersonal forces of the world market' (Strange 1996), others have pointed to the emergence of new technologies (Castells 1996; Giddens 2000). For Castells, the deregulation and restructuring of world capitalism, combined with the information technology revolution, has induced a new form of society: the network society (Castells 1996). This society is character-ized not only by the erosion of the power of the nation-state but also by 'the widespread surge of powerful expressions of collective identity that challenge globalization and cosmopolitanism on behalf of the cultural singularity and people's control over their lives and environment' (Castells 1997: 3). Thus, for Castells, the intensification of economic globalization is accompanied by greater political fragmentation: a view in stark contrast to hyperglobalist orthodoxy.[6]

For hyperglobalists, particularly of the liberal variant, the intensification of economic globalization erodes the sovereignty of the nation-state, usher-ing in a new 'global age'. The nation-state, in the words of Kenichi Ohmae, 'has become an unnatural, even dysfunctional, unit for organizing human activity and managing economic endeavour in a borderless world' (Ohmae 1993: 79), whilst, for Albrow, the nation-state is a 'timebound form, which no longer contains the aspirations nor monopolizes the attention of those who live on its territory' (Albrow 1996: 170). The universalization of a human rights discourse dating from the United Nations Universal Declaration of Human Rights in 1948 and guaranteeing property rights throughout the world, or at least in the developed North, forms the foundation of a 'global political culture'[7] or 'global civil society' understood as 'the space of unco-erced human association' (Walzer 1995: 7). However, this 'global civil society' has yet to emerge from the shadows cast by late-twentieth-century ethno-national conflict and the contemporary 'War on Terror'. The global resur-gence of politicized collective religious identities points not only to an absence of a liberal 'global civil society' (Kaldor 2003) outside of the UN and, by implication, state system, but also to the existence of multiple trans-national civil societies questioning and challenging the legitimacy of a system or society of territorialized nation-states.

What then can be said about the impact of the contemporary phase of globalization on the nation-state and, by extension, on the Westphalian international order? In contrast to the claims of sceptics like Steven Krasner that 'sovereignty is not being transformed fundamentally by globalization' and that to claim so is at best 'exaggerated and historically myopic' (Krasner 1999: 34), it is argued here that the contemporary phase of globalization has transformed, or, more accurately, is in the process of transforming, the

Westphalian conception of territorialized sovereignty. Although the state remains the 'principal actor' within the global political order, it is no longer the unique centre of authority and governance. Held *et al.* argue that 'a "new sovereignty" regime is displacing traditional conceptions of statehood as an absolute, indivisible, territorially exclusive and zero-sum form of power' (Held *et al.* 1999: 9). Similarly, Sassen argues that although 'sovereignty remains a feature of the system ... it is now located in a multiplicity of institutional arenas' (Sassen 1997: 29) and that this 'reconfiguration of space may signal a more fundamental transformation in the matter of sovereignty' (Sassen 1997: 14).

Finally, in its cultural dimension, globalization, driven by a technological revolution which has made communication instantaneous over large distances, breaks down the barriers of territorial identity, facilitating the development of new kinds of 'imagined community' or, rather, the *re*-imagination of existing cultural communities based on ethnicity, language and religion. Information and Communications Technologies (ICTs) 'offer new resources and new disciplines for the construction of imagined selves and imagined worlds' (Appadurai 1996: 3). However, these new 'imagined' identities remain communally defined, understood and experienced primarily in terms of language and religion (Castells 1997). They *coexist* with – but are not replaced by – newer, hybrid identities (Pieterse 2004: 59–83). Furthermore, the globalizing world has witnessed a pluralization of national identities. Instead of the previous effective monopoly of the state over the articulation of national identity, national identit*ies* have come increasingly to take sub-state, transstate and supra-state forms. Indeed, many individuals have acquired 'a plurinational sense of self' (Scholte 2005: 231).

Globalization, or rather the globalization of liberal-capitalist modernity, has thus not resulted in the *erasure* of localized, communal identities, but rather in their *transformation*. The growth of the Internet and linked technologies in particular has facilitated, and often enabled, the formation of 'transworld' (Scholte 2005) networks among individuals and groups with a shared cultural or religious background. These may be termed *digital* or, following Cohen, *global* 'diasporas' (Cohen 1997). Using Anderson's conception of the nation as an imagined community (Anderson 1991), it is argued that, just as the convergence of capitalism and the printing press – print capitalism – made it possible for readers of the same language to imagine themselves to be members of a nation in an earlier age, the convergence of computing and telecommunications underlying the Internet – digital capitalism – makes the imagination of deterritorialized, *diasporic* identities *on a global scale* possible.

Rethinking Sikh nationalism

The approach taken in the subsequent chapters is based upon a critical reading of two modernist assumptions. Firstly, following Anderson (1991 [1983]), it can be argued that the Sikhs *imagine* themselves to be a 'nation' possessing their own separate religion, history, institutions, territory and martial traditions. This is not to deny that the Sikh nation is 'real' in the sense that it exists in the eyes of its members, but simply that it is *imagined* as a finite and sovereign political community (Anderson 1991). Secondly, the need to constantly re-imagine communities, particularly that of the nation, leads to the invention and reification of traditions (Hobsbawm and Ranger 1983).

However, neither Anderson nor Hobsbawm and Ranger are able to account for the continued salience of 'imagined *religious* communities' (Thapar 1989, emphasis mine) or invented *religious* traditions in South Asia or elsewhere. Indeed, the persistence of communal attachments can be explained by neither instrumentalist nor constructivist accounts alone. It is suggested instead that Sikh nationalism, in common with other religious nationalisms, arose as a result of a dialectical relationship between the Sikh religious tradition and the colonial state. Following Peter van der Veer, it will be argued that religious nationalism in the nineteenth and twentieth centuries was built upon forms of religious identity which pre-dated the colonial encounter and modes of religious communication that were themselves in a constant process of *transformation* (van der Veer 1994: xiii).

At this point, a distinction should be drawn between religion as an ideology, where it is used for political purposes, and religion as faith (Nandy 1998a). For Nandy, religion as faith refers to religion as a 'way of life, a tradition that is definitionally non-monolithic and operationally plural' whilst religion as an ideology refers to a 'subnational, national or cross-national identifier of populations contesting for or protecting non-religious, usually political or socio-economic interests' (Nandy 1998a: 322). Nandy cites two examples of the difference between the two concepts. For Nandy, it was 'religion as faith' that prompted 200,000 Indians to declare themselves Mohammedan Hindus in the 1911 Census, yet it was 'religion as ideology' that prompted Punjabi Hindus to declare Hindi as their mother tongue in the 1951 Census. The state, as Nandy points out, prefers to deal with 'religion as ideology'. While the colonial authorities were at a loss as to which category to place the 200,000 Mohammedan Hindus in, the post-colonial state used the Census to 'communalize' the Punjab by using it as a pretext to eventually partition it along 'linguistic' lines, conveniently creating Hindu-majority (Haryana) and Sikh-majority (Punjab) states.

Since the two categories are not mutually exclusive, it is possible to conclude, following Nandy, that 'religion as ideology' is constrained by 'religion as faith': that, in other words, the ability of religious and political elites to use religion for material ends is limited by the beliefs of their followers. Nandy, however, does not elaborate upon the *ideological* nature of modern religious identities in South Asia beyond recognizing that contemporary religious identities in India are often viewed through the eyes of post-medieval European Christianity and this has contributed to the reification and 'fixing' of previously more fluid identities. This perception reproduces the 'Orientalist fallacy', outlined by van der Veer (1994), which regards modern South Asian identities as little more than reflections of colonial discourse.

For a more comprehensive understanding of 'ideology', it is suggested that we turn to Althusser. For Althusser, ideology was all encompassing; there could be no 'reality' or 'authentic' tradition outside ideology, for it is ideology which creates 'subjects' through 'interpellation' (Althusser 1971: 170–172). Applying Lacan's concept of the 'mirror-stage' to the development of *political* identity, Althusser argued that the duplicate 'mirror-structure' of ideology ensures simultaneously:

1   the interpellation of 'individual' as subjects;
2   their subjection to the Subject;
3   the mutual recognition of subjects and Subjects, the subjects' recognition of each other, and finally the subject's recognition of himself;
4   the absolute guarantee that everything really is so and that, on condition that the subjects recognize what they are and behave accordingly, everything will be all right: Amen – '*So be it*'.

(Althusser 1971: 180–181)

Religion as an ideology when territorialized and largely confined to an ethnic group, as in the case of Anglicanism, Calvinism, Methodism, Judaism, Shintoism, Daoism, Wahabbi Sunni Islam in Saudi Arabia and Shi'ism in Iran and, in South Asia, Hinduism, Sikhism and Islam, may be seen as a form of nationalism. The autonomy for elite manipulation of this ideology of nationalism, however, remains heavily circumscribed by popular interpretations of the religious tradition. In other words, the success of what Nandy refers to as religion as 'ideology' is dependent upon its ability to 'interpellate' subjects in terms that they can understand. The story being told must be familiar to them in order to be convincing. For that to occur, the 'national' story must be narrated in the vernacular using idioms which chime with their lived experience. Agents act within socially constructed ranges of possibilities which are inscribed within them as well as the social world in which they move. Their actions are *improvised* but at the same time constrained by the *universe of possible discourse*: the range of options, not necessarily expressed in language, available to them (Bourdieu 1977: 169–170). The range of options, or *sense of limits* (Bourdieu 1977: 164), is itself the *product of history*, of the past choices accepted and legitimized by 'tradition'.

This perspective differs from instrumentalist (Brass 1991) and other constructivist (Oberoi 1994) approaches in the degree of autonomy accorded to elites. Although successive Sikh religious and political elites have played a crucial role in this process of imagination, they have not *consciously* done so. Contemporary Sikh political elites, whether moderate Akali or separatist, are seen as 'unconsciously' subject to the past cultural choices of their forefathers in the *Tat Khalsa* movement who helped to define the 'tradition' which they are now endeavouring to defend. The 'unconscious' in this sense may be seen as nothing other than the *forgetting of history*. This forgetting of history is itself produced by history through the internalization and incorporation of social structures. This corresponds to what Pierre Bourdieu termed the *habitus*. For Bourdieu, 'the *habitus* – embodied history, internalised as a second nature and so forgotten as history – is the active presence of the whole past of which it is a product' (Bourdieu 1990: 56). Sikh religio-political elites have *unconsciously* helped redefine Sikh identity in the light of new challenges to the Sikh 'tradition' by attempting to construct an *orthodox* understanding of what it means to be a Sikh. This orthodoxy emerged during the colonial period and was *embodied* in the external symbols of Sikh identity which gave the Sikhs a distinctive appearance, enabling colonial administrators to classify them as both a distinct 'religion' and a 'race' or 'nation'. Colonial modernity constituted a break from the past and, unable to rely upon a Guru for guidance, Sikhs were forced to consolidate and redefine their 'faith', which, contrary to instrumentalist and constructivist claims, pre-existed the colonial encounter, through organizations such as the Singh Sabhas and, later, the Chief Khalsa Diwan (CKD) and Shiromani Gurdwara Prabandhak Committee (SGPC). The SGPC institutionalized *Tat Khalsa* orthodoxy through the *Rehat Maryada*, a code of conduct considered binding on all Sikhs, and in the twentieth century, along with the various factions of the Akali Dal, it has constituted a Sikh 'political system' (Wallace 1981) which coexists with, and potentially challenges, the state power.

It is argued here that the SGPC and Akali Dal have played a central role in the articulation of a *national* discourse. Nationalism may be understood, following Althusser, as an *ideology*: a particular discursive articulation which constructs subjects as being of a particular nation and thereby having certain distinctive characteristics and political needs and interests. Sikh nationalism, as opposed to the Sikh 'faith', may be seen as relying on the interpellation of people as Sikhs, rather than as Indians, Punjabis, *Jats, Khatris, Mazhabis* or members of a particular class or gender. For Althusser, all ideology 'hails or interpellates concrete individuals as concrete subjects' (Althusser 1971: 170–172). We are thus constituted as subjects through a process of recognition. To be hailed is to become a subject. This interpellation may be seen to have first taken place in the colonial period and continues today.

The structure of the book

Chapter 2 will examine the construction of a Sikh 'national' identity. Sikh nationalism, it will be argued, relies upon the 'interpellation' of Sikh communities as members of a Sikh *qaum* or nation with the Punjab as their homeland or place of origin, rather than as followers of a religious tradition, a *panth*, or as Punjabis or Indians. This interpellation first took place in the colonial period, which saw a redefinition and reinterpretation of what it meant to be Sikh. There existed by the end of the colonial period a more homogeneous, *modern* conception of Sikh identity as *internal* religious boundaries between 'orthodox' and 'unorthodox' Sikhs and *external* boundaries between Sikhs and other religious communities were institutionalized first by the colonial state's project of classification and enumeration and subsequently through the creation of Singh Sabhas and the CKD and finally by the establishment of the SGPC.

Chapter 3 will examine the further development of Sikh nationalism in post-colonial India. After independence, the SGPC continued to define Sikh identity and together with the various factions of the Shiromani Akali Dal (SAD) a Sikh 'political system' emerged which both co-exists within and potentially challenges the Congress 'system' that has dominated Indian politics for much of the post-independence period. It will be argued that the SAD leadership's use of ethno-religious symbols to mobilize the Sikh masses behind the creation of a linguistically defined Sikh 'homeland' within independent, secular India and the subsequent 'communalization' of the demand for a restructuring of relations between the central government and the states by the Indian government under Indira Gandhi created space for a *nationalist* challenge to both the Sikh 'political system' and the Indian state by armed militants seeking to create an independent Sikh state: *Khalistan*.

Chapter 4 will account for the demise of armed Sikh separatism in India. It will be argued that, although the movement was initially crushed by a reassertion of state and central government power using a strategy of 'violent control' as Gurharpal Singh suggests (Singh 2000), the erosion of Congress hegemony afforded Sikh elites an opportunity to articulate Sikh demands to the Indian political system from *within* the democratic system. The economic reforms which Dr Manmohan Singh initiated as finance minister in Narasimha Rao's government in particular facilitated a structural transformation in Indian politics, economics and society resulting in both regional and Hindu 'nationalist' challenges to the Congress 'one-party dominance' system. Moreover, the failure of the BJP to 'rebrand' India as a homogeneous Hindu nation-state based on 'One Nation, One People and One Culture' (BJP 2004) and the appointment of Dr Singh as prime minister have convinced many Sikh former militants to suspend, at least temporarily, their 'struggle for Khalistan' and to focus on securing recognition of INC complicity in the systematic human rights abuses carried out in New Delhi and the Punjab during the 1980s.

In Chapter 5, the focus shifts from India to the 'diaspora'. This chapter considers the rise of Sikh nationalism outside of India after the storming of the Golden Temple complex by Indian troops in June 1984. Based on empirical research of 'Khalistani' organizations in the UK and North America, it is argued that, whereas the military solution preferred by the Indian state to the 'Punjab Problem' may have succeeded in reducing the Sikhs of the Punjab to silence, it has opened up an alternative site for nationalist activity in the 'diaspora'. The nationalist discourse as articulated increasingly through the Internet in the diaspora is then examined. It is argued that the violence of partition and the storming of the Golden Temple complex in 1984 are central to the imagination of *both* the Sikh 'nation' and a specifically Sikh 'diaspora'.

Chapter 6 will examine the uneasy transition from a nationalist 'politics of homeland' to a diasporic 'politics of recognition' in the wake of 9/11. Recently, a plethora of groups have emerged in the diaspora committed to representing the interests of Sikhs in their places of settlement, and their activities will be analysed in detail. It is suggested that these groups, such as the Sikh Federation and Sikh Agenda group in the UK and Sikh Coalition in North America, are in the process of articulating a 'new' counter-hegemonic *diasporic* Sikh identity: an identity made possible by the nationalist project but opposed to its territorializing, reifying imperatives. However, both 'nationalist' and 'diasporic' political projects have a common dynamic: the rift between location and identity in places of Sikh settlement.

The possibilities opened up by globalization for the articulation of a post-nationalist discourse are examined in Chapter 7. By asserting the sovereignty of the *Khalsa panth*, Sikh transnational religious actors such as the World Sikh Council (WSC) and UNITED SIKHS *potentially* interrupt the closure of the nation-state and thus, it is argued, the Westphalian order of territorialized nation-states. Interviews with Sikhs in India and the diaspora, together with an empirical analysis of Sikh discussion groups on the Internet, suggest that the Sikh *qaum* has indeed, on the whole, gone beyond *Khalistan* in considering the establishment of an independent, sovereign Sikh state unnecessary for the continued survival of a distinct Sikh identity in a globalizing world.

Finally, in the Conclusion it will be argued that Sikh identity has been, and is being, *transformed* by 'globalization' and its forerunner, colonial modernity: from a *panth*, a 'religious' community, to a *qaum* or 'nation' during the colonial period and, finally, to a global 'diaspora' as a result of the latest phase of globalization. Furthermore, it is argued that the transformation of Sikh identity – and those of other transnational ethno-religious communities – will have profound implications for the theory and practice of international relations in the new millennium, since the sovereignty of the territorialized nation-state over the religious community as established in the aftermath of the Peace of Westphalia in 1648 can no longer be assumed in our 'global age'.

2 From *panth* to *qaum*

The construction of a Sikh 'national' identity in colonial India

The search for descent is not the erecting of foundations: on the contrary, it disturbs what was previously considered immobile; it fragments what was thought unified; it shows heterogeneity of what was imagined consistent with itself.

(Foucault 1991: 82)

The Sikhs are an ethno-religious community originally from the Punjab region of North-West India. Although a multiethnic, secular state, India is an overwhelmingly Hindu society. Hindus make up approximately 80 per cent of the Indian population, whilst Sikhs, regarded by some Hindus as a sect of Hinduism, make up just 2 per cent (see Table 2.1). As Table 2.2 makes clear, the majority of Sikhs in India continue to live in the state of Punjab, where they form a majority of the total population.

As a religious tradition, Sikhism is open to all those who are prepared to accept its doctrines and practices. Indeed, there is a thriving 'white' Sikh community in North America. In practice, most Sikhs are Punjabis and the Sikh community has a strong regional identity. Sikh elites within India have frequently used a religious vocabulary and symbols to champion ostensibly regional demands such as the creation of a Punjabi-speaking state and

Table 2.1 Indian population by religion (adjusted percentage), 1961–2001

Religion	1961	1971	1981	1991	2001
Hindu	84.4	83.5	83.1	82.4	81.4
Muslim	9.9	10.4	10.9	11.7	12.4
Christian	2.4	2.6	2.5	2.3	2.3
Sikh	1.8	1.9	2.0	2.0	1.9
Buddhist	0.7	0.7	0.7	0.8	0.8
Jain	0.5	0.5	0.5	0.4	0.4
Other	0.3	0.4	0.4	0.4	0.7
Total	100	100	100	100	100

Sources: Census India (2001); GOI (2001); Sikh Pride (2001).

Table 2.2 Sikhs in India

Code	State/union territory	Total population	Sikh population	Proportion of Sikh population	Sex ratio	Sex ratio (0–6)	Proportion of child population in the age group 0–6 yrs	Literacy rate	Female literacy rate	Work partici- pation rate
	India*	1,028,610,328	19,215,730	1.9	893	786	12.8	69.4	63.1	37.7
01	Jammu and Kashmir	10,143,700	207,154	2.0	809	773	10.6	85.4	77.6	36.4
02	Himachal Pradesh	6,077,900	72,355	1.2	898	827	12.1	83.0	76.2	38.7
03	Punjab	24,358,999	14,592,387	59.9	897	780	12.8	67.3	61.2	38.2
04	Chandigarh	900,635	145,175	16.1	910	781	9.1	92.0	88.5	33.1
05	Uttaranchal	8,489,349	212,025	2.5	898	844	14.8	73.1	64.2	33.6
06	Haryana	21,144,564	1,170,662	5.5	893	742	13.0	68.9	62.2	37.4
07	Delhi	13,850,507	555,602	4.0	925	796	10.8	92.1	89.1	31.4
08	Rajasthan	56,507,188	818,420	1.4	892	828	15.1	64.7	53.8	42.3
09	Uttar Pradesh	166,197,921	678,059	0.4	877	831	14.1	71.9	63.8	32.7
10	Bihar	82,998,509	20,780	0.0	879	919	14.2	79.8	73.3	31.3
11	Sikkim	540,851	1,176	0.2	108	1556	2.0	97.2	87.1	85.8
12	Arunachal Pradesh	1,097,968	1,865	0.2	264	808	7.6	92.4	79.2	71.0
13	Nagaland	1,990,036	1,152	0.1	488	1000	8.3	82.8	72.7	56.9
14	Manipur*	2,166,788	1,653	0.1	515	932	8.5	88.5	79.8	58.2
15	Mizoram	888,573	326	0.0	299	2200	9.8	91.8	88.7	72.4
16	Tripura	3,199,203	1,182	0.0	101	710	4.5	98.4	89.5	86.6
17	Meghalaya	2,318,822	3,110	0.1	718	896	12.3	74.7	64.1	39.5
18	Assam	26,655,528	22,519	0.1	667	818	9.9	90.4	83.8	42.2
19	West Bengal	80,176,197	66,391	0.1	807	852	10.1	87.2	82.0	33.7
20	Jharkhand	26,945,829	83,358	0.3	838	879	11.1	87.8	82.3	30.8

21	Orissa	36,804,660	17,492	0.0	851	860	10.8	90.5	86.1	31.7
22	Chhattisgarh	20,833,803	69,621	0.3	899	845	12.3	89.0	84.7	31.0
23	Madhya Pradesh	60,348,023	150,772	0.2	882	849	12.9	82.9	76.7	34.9
24	Gujarat	50,671,017	45,587	0.1	824	782	12.7	85.1	79.7	33.5
25	Daman and Diu	158,204	145	0.1	576	600	11.0	93.0	89.4	49.0
26	Dadra and Nagar Hv	220,490	123	0.1	281	750	11.4	91.7	95.2	65.0
27	Maharashtra	96,878,627	215,337	0.2	829	849	11.6	88.9	84.5	35.8
28	Andhra Pradesh	76,210,007	30,998	0.0	796	864	12.4	78.7	72.7	37.2
29	Karnataka	52,850,562	15,326	0.0	739	882	11.9	83.7	77.3	38.4
30	Goa	1,347,668	970	0.1	644	1021	10.0	95.5	94.9	45.2
31	Lakshadweep	60,650	6	N	–	–	0	100	0	100
32	Kerala	31,841,374	2,762	0.0	714	865	10.0	92.4	89.1	43.3
33	Tamil Nadu	62,405,679	9,545	0.0	731	854	10.4	83.7	77.2	43.6
34	Pondicherry	974,345	108	0.0	543	2000	8.3	90.9	78.1	40.7
35	Andaman and Nicobar Is	356,152	1,587	0.4	818	858	12.4	94.1	90.7	34.8

Source: The First Report on Religion: Census of India 2001.

Note: *Excludes Mao-Maram, Paomata and Purul sub-divisions of Senapati district of Manipur.

greater state autonomy within India. Following Roger Ballard, three dimensions of the 'Sikh tradition', encompassing both religious and ethnic elements, may be identified: the *panthic, dharmic* and *qaumic* (Ballard 1996: 16–31; 1998: 5–9).

A *panth* may be seen as a term particular to Northern India, where it is used to identify the devotees of a specific spiritual leader. It consists of those religious ideas and practices concerned with spiritual experience and with the way in which followers tend to gather around a charismatic spiritual master. One of the most central aspects of spirituality in the *panthic* tradition is the quest for gnostic awareness: the union of the separate personal being with the universal being. *Dharma* in a South Asian context both refers to the notion of coherence at all levels in the cosmic framework and also provides the foundation for the local moral order. Although the founder of the Sikh religious tradition, Guru Nanak, may be seen to have been preoccupied with the *panthic* domain, the very task of preserving his teachings drew his successors into the *dharmic* or social domain. The more the followers of the Sikh religious tradition became an organized *panth*, the more complex the social order which they constructed became. Nanak's teachings were collected and eventually transformed into the *Adi Granth*, a sacred text which was subsequently to be endowed with the status of a holy book, or a status equivalent to that of a Guru. Similarly, physical pilgrimage sites came into existence and there was a move towards the codification of religious rituals and manuals of correct behaviour, *rahit-namas*, after the death of the tenth and last Guru, Gobind Singh.

Most importantly, Sikhs define themselves, and are identified by others, as a *qaum*, a community in a socio-political sense. Unlike *panth* and *dharm*, a *qaum* is not primarily a religious term and has Arabic rather than Sanskrit roots. This suggests that the term became incorporated into the political discourse of the Punjab as a result of the interaction between its Islamic Mughal rulers and the guardians of the various panthic traditions. British colonial administrators and scholars writing in the nineteenth century understood a *qaum* to refer to a specific 'race' or 'nationality' and treated the Sikhs accordingly. The institutionalization of the principle of national self-determination as the legitimizing principle of the post-colonial state and, as will be discussed later, the Westphalian international order may be seen to have added a territorial dimension to the idea of a *qaum*.

It is argued here that, although the Sikhs, like Muslim and Hindu communities, may have constituted a *panth* after the institutionalization of the *Khalsa*, the development of a *qaumic* dimension to the Sikh faith can be seen as the outcome of a historical process with its origins in the colonial encounter (Fox 1985; Kapur 1986; Oberoi 1994; Barrier 2004a, 2004b). The British introduced new arenas of competition that encouraged a different kind of thinking about politics, such as the need to form associations, to communicate effectively across these associations, to focus opinion on particular issues and to mobilize support. Ian Talbot has seen the colonial era as having made three key contributions to the emergence of a 'communal' consciousness in the Punjab. Firstly, the colonial state, associated in 'native' Punjabi minds both with a superior technology and organizational system and with an alien Christian faith, challenged the world-view of its subjects. Secondly, the British provided the means for the transmission of reconstructed Punjabi identities to a new mass audience. Thirdly, colonial rule created new arenas of political competition, including the granting of separate electorates (Talbot 1996: 26–27). Furthermore, colonial and Western assumptions about the 'primordiality' of ethnic and religious identities influenced the intellectual development of political identities on religious lines (Fox 1985; van der Veer 1999; Bhatt 2001). The colonial state, in short, created the mechanisms by which the *Tat Khalsa* movement could imagine a Sikh religio-political community with a cohesive *Kes-dhari* identity. The *panthic* and *dharmic* dimensions of Sikh identity, however, were already in place before the encounter with colonial modernity.

The Sikh *panth*: from Nanak-*panth* to *Khalsa panth*

The term 'Sikh' refers to the learners or disciples of the first Guru of the Sikh *panth*, Nanak (1469–1539). Nanak differed from the other *sants* of northern India in two respects. Firstly, Nanak developed, during the course of his life, a religious and social philosophy which, although deeply influenced by both Hinduism and Islam, was distinct from both. Declaring that 'there is no Hindu, and there is no Musalman', Nanak drew a sharp distinction between what following Nandy (1998a, 1998b) may be termed as the 'faiths' of Hinduism and Islam on the one hand, which he broadly accepted as legitimate, and the 'ideologies' of Brahmanism and Mohammedanism on the other hand, which he vehemently rejected. Brahmanism was unacceptable to Nanak, given his belief in caste and gender equality, as the system of *varnashramadharma* restricted the possibility of *mukti* (liberation) for the lower castes, whilst Nanak regarded the Islamic insistence in the finality of the Prophet Muhammad's revelation as recorded in Arabic as precluding the vernacularization, and thus universalization, of the Lord's message. For Nanak, there was 'only one Lord, and only one tradition', which encompassed both Hinduism and Islam but which could not be reduced to either. The Sikh faith was, therefore, from its very inception monotheistic and unitarian. The Sikh concept of God, *Vahiguru*, is as the omnipotent and omnipresent transcendent creator and sovereign of the universe who lies beyond human understanding and, in contrast to Islam and Christianity, does not take human form. The *Vahiguru*'s intentions were, however, revealed to Nanak, who is assigned the title of Mahala 1 or the 'first body in which the divine voice resided' in the Sikh scriptures (Mann 2004: 15). As in other faiths indigenous to South Asia, the goal of human life is to attain liberation, which is defined as being united by the *Vahiguru* by having a respectful place in the divine court (Mann 2004: 81). Liberation, however, could not be sought individually by withdrawal from the world but by active engagement within it, as part of a community. Nanak defined the ideal person as a *gurmukh* (one oriented towards the Guru) who practised the threefold discipline of *nam dan ishnan*, which encompassed the cognitive, social and personal aspects of Sikh identity. *Nam* referred to 'the divine Name' and prescribed the individual Sikh's relationship with the divine, *dan* ('charity') prescribed the individual Sikh's relationship with other Sikhs, while *ishnan*, the pursuit of 'purity', prescribed the Sikhs relationship with the self (Pashaura Singh 2004: 78–79).

Secondly, Nanak organized his followers in a community in Kartarpur (Creator's Abode) on the right bank of the river Ravi where they could live in conformity with his teachings. At Kartarpur, Nanak's Sikhs[1] were able to combine a life of 'disciplined devotion with worldly activities, set in the context of normal family life and regular *satsang* [true fellowship]' (McLeod 1968: 228). Central to this life of true fellowship was Sikh participation in the *sangat*, a spiritual fraternity or fellowship, through communal worship in a *dharamsala* and dining together, after prayer, in the *langar*. The *langar*, in particular, encouraged a sense of communal solidarity, as Sikhs were required to sit together in status-free lines (*pangat*) to share a common meal. Thus, 'the institution of the *langar* promoted the spirit of unity and mutual belonging, and struck at a major aspect of caste thereby advancing the process of defining a distinctive Sikh identity' (Pashaura Singh 2004: 80).

Nanak's decision to anoint one of his disciples, Lehna, as his successor in preference to his own son, Baba Sri Chand, established a lineage of Gurus where succession was based upon piety rather than blood relations. Lehna took the name that Nanak gave him, Angad, meaning 'my own limb', and attempted to consolidate Nanak's *panth*. The term 'Sikh' was bestowed upon those who venerated Guru Nanak and accepted Guru Angad (1504–1552) as his legitimate successor. Those who followed Nanak's son, Baba Sri Chand, became known as *Udasis*. Angad helped distinguish the Nanak-*panthis* (McLeod 1989: 21) from dominant Hindu religious practice by claiming that the *bani*, the 'divine Word', was able to liberate all people from the shackles of *karma*, irrespective of caste. The *bani* thus assumed a significance parallel to the *Vedas* and were recorded for posterity, neither in the *devangari* script of the Hindus nor in the Arabic or Persian scripts favoured by the Punjab's Muslim rulers, but in the *Gurmukhi* script. The use of the *Gurmukhi* script to record the message of Guru Nanak made the *bani* intelligible to the *Khatri* merchants of the Punjab who constituted the majority of Nanak-*panthis* yet limited its appeal to those outside the Punjab. For Pashaura Singh, the use of *Gurmukhi* added 'an element of demarcation and self-identity to the Sikh tradition', one which has become 'the cornerstone of the religious distinctiveness that is part and parcel of the Sikh cultural heritage' (Pashaura Singh 2004: 81–82).

The third Guru, Amar Das (1479–1574), further institutionalized the Sikh community through the establishment of the city of Goindval on the banks of the river Beas, and the festivals of *Diwali* and, more importantly, *Vaisakhi*, which provided an opportunity for the Guru to meet his followers. Further-more, it was during Amar Das's time that the Goindval *pothis* (books or volumes) which recorded the compositions of the Gurus were undertaken and a system of attracting new converts established (Pashaura Singh 2004: 82). Amar Das added his own hymn of *Anand*, 'divine bliss', to the emerging Sikh liturgy, providing the Nanak-*panthis* with distinctive ceremonies for birth and death. The city of Goindval was to be eclipsed by the establishment of the city of Amritsar by the fourth Guru, Ram Das (1534–1581) and the construction of the Golden Temple of *Harimadir* as the central place of Sikh worship by Guru Arjan (1563–1606). The Sikhs now had their Mecca or Vatican, and Arjan further facilitated the institutionalization of the Sikh faith through the compilation of the *Adi Granth*, the 'original book', which would come to acquire as great, or an even greater, significance for the Sikh faith as the Qur'an for Islam or the Bible for Christianity. Although Gurinder Singh Mann has traced the formation of the Sikh canon to Guru Nanak himself, the dominant narrative which continues to be hegemonic today attributes this to Arjan (Mann 2001: 10–24). For Pashaura Singh, Guru Arjan created an authoritative text for the Sikh community whereby it could understand and assert its unique identity. By doing so, he 'affixed a seal on the sacred word to preserve it for posterity, and also frustrate attempts by schismatic groups to circulate spurious hymns for sectarian ends' (Pashaura Singh 2000: 283–284). Arjan's assertion that 'we are neither Hindu nor Musalman' established the Nanak-*panthis'* claim to be a separate religious tradition. This claim appeared to be well supported. According to McLeod, by the time of Guru Arjan's death, the *panth* possessed a line of Gurus, a growing number of holy places, distinctive rituals, and its own sacred scripture. Consequently, there 'could no longer be any question of vague definition or uncertain identity' (McLeod 2000: 51–52). Such a view overestimates the degree of homogeneity which existed in a rapidly expanding community which contained minority groups such as the *Udasis, Bhallas*[2] and *Minas*[3] who contested the legitimacy of the Guru-*panth*. Uncertainty over whether these groups can be considered members of, or rivals to, the Sikh *panth* continues to this day.

Guru Arjan's final contribution to the further development of the Sikh *panth* was his very death at the hands of the Mughals, which introduced a powerful narrative of martyrdom which has dominated Sikh history ever since. Subsequent Gurus and modern Sikh political and religious leaders or *sants* have invoked the example of Arjan in their attempts to defend the *panth* from its 'enemies', both internal and external. Arjan's successor, Hargobind (1595–1644), responded to his predecessor's martyrdom by arming the *panth* against the Mughals. Furthermore, Hargobind is responsible for including a temporal dimension into what had hitherto been exclusively a faith commu-nity through the construction of the *Akal Takht*, the 'throne of the immortal Lord', facing *Harimadir* in Amritsar. The dual authority of the warrior-Guru was symbolized by the two swords which Hargobind wore, *piri*, signifying spiritual authority, and *miri*, temporal authority. The addition of a temporal dimension into the *panth* paved the way for the transformation of the Nanak-*panth* into the *Khalsa panth*.

The mythology and symbolism of the *Khalsa*

After the martyrdom of the ninth Guru, Tegh Bahadur (1621–1675), his only son and successor, Gobind, sought to strengthen the bonds between members of the *panth* by imposing upon his male followers a uniform identity that would make them instantly recognizable. On *Vaisakhi* day of 1699 at Anand-pur, Guru Gobind Singh (1666–1708) initiated five volunteers, the *panj piare* (beloved or cherished five), into the new order of the *Khalsa*. The term *Khalsa*, derived from the Arabic *khalis*, literally means 'pure' but implies spiritual purity. In the Qur'an, Allah is referred to as *Ikhalis*, the 'purifier', and the term *Khalsa* similarly had religious significance for the Nanak-*panthis*, denoting purification by God. Guru Gobind sought to spiritually cleanse his com-munity by giving his five volunteers *amrit* (sweetened water) stirred with the double-edged sword introduced by Guru Hargobind, thus conferring the spir-itual and temporal authority of the Guru on to the *Khalsa*. This became known as the ceremony of the *khande ki pahul*. Those who received *amrit* this way became cleansed of their previous identities and were reborn into a 'community of the pure' as Singhs (literally 'lions').[4]

As Gurinder Singh Mann notes, the symbolism of the mythology sur-rounding the establishment of the *Khalsa* is poignant. Guru Gobind sought five Sikhs in line with Bhai Gurdas's[5] declaration that a group of five Sikhs represented the presence of *Vahiguru*. The names and origins of the five Sikhs who volunteered to give their lives to the *panth* are doubly significant, repre-senting five important Sikh virtues, and the different castes and locations which made up the *panth*. Furthermore, the sequence in which the Sikh names appear is in keeping with Sikh doctrine. According to the *Adi Granth*, the world is balanced upon the values of *Daya* (compassion) and *Dharm* (duty), which are also the names of the first two volunteers. Moreover, Sikhs are enjoined to lead a life of *Sahib* (honour), *Muhkam* (firmness) and *Himmat* (effort), which again coincidentally are the names of the next three volunteers. The towns where the volunteers came from, Lahore, Delhi, Dvarka, Jagannath Puri and Bidar, represented the major centres of the Sikh *panth*, and their caste and class backgrounds, *Khatri, Jat* and lower castes, marked the universality of Sikhism's appeal (Mann 1998: 3).

By instituting the *Khalsa*, and then undergoing the *khande ki pahul* himself, Guru Gobind acknowledged the *sovereignty* of the *Khalsa panth* and sub-mitted himself to its collective will. The *Khalsa* was not merely conceived as a spiritual fraternity of orthodox Sikhs, but as a sovereign community which could defend itself and would no longer need the tutelage of a human Guru. The spiritual and temporal dimensions of the Guru's authority were, under the doctrine of Guru-*panth*, invested in the *Khalsa panth* through the *khande ki pahul*. Thereafter, the *Khalsa* was to be held responsible for both the protection and the administration of the community, including the initiation of new followers and the collections of tithes, hitherto the responsibilities of hereditary priests or *masants*. In so doing, the institution of the *Khalsa* revolutionized the hierarchical structure of the *panth* and introduced a rigid religious and social egalitarianism that was in keeping with Guru Nanak's message but absent in contemporary Sikh practice. 'In the ranks of the *Khalsa*', according to Teja Singh, 'all were to be equal, the lowest with the highest, in race and in creed, in political rights as in religious hopes' (Teja Singh 1988: 26).

This egalitarianism was embodied in the five 'signs' or symbols of Sikh identity described by Teja Singh. For J.P.S Uberoi, the primary meaning of the five symbols lies in the ritual conjunction of two opposed forces. The unshorn hair (*kes*) is associated with the comb (*kanga*) which performs the function of constraining the hair and imparting an orderly arrangement to it. Similarly, the bangle (*kara*) imparts the same orderly control over the sword (*kirpan*) as the comb does over the hair (Uberoi 1996: 12). For Uberoi, these five symbols of Sikh religious identity were developed in opposition to prevalent cultural practices in the pre-colonial Punjab and served to construct boundaries between Sikhs and other communities, making *Kes-dhari* Sikhs an easily identifiable group in modern India and the diaspora today.

The *khande ki pahul* may similarly be read as a self-conscious attempt by Guru Gobind and subsequent Sikh religious elites to distinguish Sikhism from the other *panthic* communities of the Punjab. For Gurbhagat Singh, the *khande ki pahul* was performed to 'psychologically transform the common folk, make them *Singhs* (lions) and commit them to the new narrative that aimed at countering the symbolic violence of the two hegemonizing grand narratives'. Singh claims that in contradistinction to the Hindu concept of Brahma and the Islamic concept of Allah that articulate the 'absolute unity and totalitivity of God', Guru Gobind Singh's God is 'detotalitive' in that it has 'many different expressions, forms and temporalities' (Gurbhagat Singh 1999a: 189–190).

Another key innovation associated with the establishment of the *Khalsa* which served to construct boundaries between Sikhism and other religious traditions was Guru Gobind Singh's decision to close the Sikh canon and confer the status of Guru on the *Adi Granth*. With the dissolution of the line of human Gurus, *Khalsa* Sikhs would henceforth follow only the edicts of a written Guru: the *Guru Granth Sahib*. This closing of the Sikh canon was ostensibly based upon the belief that the core truths of the tradition had been irrevocably established, but considerable latitude existed for interpretation, as resolutions based upon interpretations of the *Guru Granth Sahib* were to guide the Sikh community through the *gurmatta*, 'will of the Guru', system. The standard version of the *Guru Granth Sahib* now available, based upon that compiled by Guru Gobind at Damdama Sahib, Talwandi Sabo, Bathinda in 1706, where he added the works of his father to the liturgy, was prepared during the reign of Maharaja Ranjit Singh. However, as Pashaura Singh has pointed out, a:

complete consensus in the Sikh community on the text of the *Adi Granth* was achieved only as a result of the Singh Sabha reforms in the late nineteenth century, which sanctified the standard Damdama version and set aside all other versions used earlier.

(Pashaura Singh 2000: 287)

In conclusion, the founding of the *Khalsa* at the end of the seventeenth century constituted a decisive break with the Nanak-*panth*, facilitating its eventual transformation into the *Khalsa panth*. Following Gurbhagat Singh, it is suggested that the primary meaning of the *Khalsa* lies in its 'rupture of Indian grand narratives' of 'Brahman-centred' Brahmanism and 'Allah-centred Islam' (Gurbhagat Singh 1999a: 190). The *Khalsa* was from its very inception 'a society for salvation and self-realization, unitarian in religion, vernacularist in culture and democratic in politics' (Uberoi 1996: 74). It was unitarian in its insistence, following Nanak, on the indivisibility of *Vahiguru*; it was vernacularist in its use of a vernacular language, Punjabi, written in *Gurmukhi* script, to record *Vahiguru*'s message as communicated by the Gurus (*gurbani*); and it was democratic in its assertion of sovereignty over the temporal and spiritual domains. The *Khalsa panth* was conceived as a sovereign body of *Kes-dhari* Sikhs with distinctive religious symbols (the five Ks), an initiation ceremony (the *khande ki pahul*) which differed from those of other *panths* in the precolonial Punjab, and a holy book (the *Guru Granth Sahib*) which underlined the credentials of the Sikhs to qualify for the status of *ahl-i kitab*, people of a book. The *Khalsa*'s claim to sovereignty was encapsulated in the salutation '*Vahiguru ji ka khalsa, Vahiguru ji ki fateh*', meaning 'The *Khalsa* belongs to *Vahiguru*, Victory to *Vahiguru* on earth', uttered after the ritual drinking of the *amrit* in the *khande ki pahul*. This declaration has two aspects to it. The first aspect is the implicit rejection of all temporal authority ('*Vahiguru ji ka khalsa*'). The *Khalsa* belongs to *Vahiguru* alone and, therefore, Sikhs are bound to follow no one else. The second aspect is that, as the *Khalsa* belongs to *Vahiguru*, it becomes the instrument for executing divine justice on earth (*Vahiguru ji ki fateh*) (Mann 1998: 19). From there, it was but a short step to proclaim '*Raj Karega Khalsa*' ('The *Khalsa* shall rule'), paving the way for the 'Sikh empire' of Maharaja Ranjit Singh.[6]

'Singh-izing the Sikhs': the *Tat Khalsa* discourse and the colonial state

It has been argued that, at the beginning of the colonial period, not only was there no cohesive or homogeneous Sikh community but there was no single definition of a Sikh. According to Richard Fox, 'a single religious community, in the sense of a shared set of traditions, cultural meanings, and social practices was absent amongst those who called themselves Sikhs in the late nineteenth-century Punjab' (Fox 1985: 108). This is borne out by the 1891 Census Report, which noted that there were 'few who maintain all the outward forms and rules of conduct of the recognised Sikh religion' (Government of India 1891). The Punjab may be seen as having been characterized by a simultaneity of religious identities, as well as by clan, caste, household and village ties. Ibbetson, the commissioner of the Census Report, had noted that in 'the border lands where the great faiths meet . . . it is often impossible to say that one prevails rather than the other, or to decide in what category the people should be classed' (Ibbetson 1883: 101). According to Harjot Oberoi, 'most Sikhs moved in and out of multiple identities, defining themselves at one moment as resident of this village, at another as part of that caste; and at yet another as belonging to a sacred tradition' (Oberoi 1994: 17). A visit to the Ganges or to the shrine of a Muslim saint was as much part of the devotional life of most Sikhs as a visit to the Golden Temple. The Sikh *panth* was a 'fuzzy', unenumerated community consisting of not only *Khalsa* Sikhs or 'Singhs' but a multiplicity of other traditions which were, in some cases, indistinguishable from Hinduism.[7] Some of these traditions, such as the *Udasis*, refused to observe the edicts of the *rahit-namas* and controlled many sites sacred to Sikhism. Furthermore, despite the egalitarian ideology professed by *Khalsa* Sikhs, many lower-caste and Untouchable Sikhs such as *Mazhabis* were denied access to major Sikh shrines.

That Sikhism today may be seen to have a hegemonic *Kes-dhari* cultural framework is, to a certain extent, a result of the Singh Sabhites' strategic and ideological elucidation of a *Tat Khalsa* discourse which negated a large terrain of Sikh belief and practice (Oberoi 1994: 305). By the turn of the century, there was, according to Oberoi, 'a growing sentiment among sections of the Sikh community that they belonged to a community distinct from the rest of the population and that members of their religion were grossly underrepresented in state institutions' (Oberoi 1994: 365). There were also, as Table 2.3 illustrates, *more* Sikhs. The recorded Sikh population almost doubled between 1881 and 1921, from 1,706,165 to 3,110,060.

Most Sikh gains in central Punjab were at the expense of those listed as 'Hindu' between 1901 and 1911 (see Table 2.4) as Singh Sabhas proliferated throughout the Punjab. Furthermore, the proportion of *Kes-dhari* Sikhs to *Sahajdhari* Sikhs rose steadily throughout the colonial period. Between 1911 and 1921, the number of Sikhs listed as 'Kesdharis' rose by over 40 per cent,

Table 2.3 Sikh population growth in the Punjab, 1881–1921

Census year	Sikh population	Variation in Sikh population (%)	Variation in total population (%)
1881	1,706,165	N/A	N/A
1891	1,849,371	+8.4	+10.1
1901	2,102,896	+13.7	+6.3
1911	2,883,729	+37.1	−2.2
1921	3,110,060	+7.8	+5.7

Source: GOI (1901, 1921: 184, 1931).

Table 2.4 Variation in Sikh and Hindu populations, 1901–1911

District/state	Variation in Sikh population (%)	Variation in Hindu population (%)
Jullunder	+40	−27
Ludhiana	+25.5	−51
Ferozpur	+14.9	−1.9
Gurdaspur	+31.9	−25
Kapurthala State	+28.9	−34.4

Source: GOI (1911, vol. 2: 438–439).

Table 2.5 Membership of selected *Kes-dhari* Sikh 'sects', 1911–1921

Sect	1911	1921	Variation (%)
Kesdharis	2,048,014	2,876,320	+40.4
Tat Khalsa	344,058	531,290	+54.4
Mazhabi	726	2,305	+217.5

Source: GOI (1921: 186).

Table 2.6 Membership of selected *Sahajdhari* Sikh 'sects', 1911–1921

Sect	1911	1921	Variation (%)
Shajdharis	450,823	228,598	−49.3
Nanakpanthis	176,036	14,179	−91.9
Udasi	591	66	−88.8

Source: GOI (1921): 186.

from 2,048,014 to 2,876,320, whilst the numbers of 'Shajdharis' fell by almost half, from 450,823 to 228,598. Significantly, the number of Sikhs included under the category of 'Tat Khalsa' rose by over 50 per cent, from 344,058 to 531,290 (see Tables 2.5 and 2.6).[8]

Oberoi's thesis that the 'enchanted universe' of the *Sanatan* tradition was replaced by a 'new' *Tat Khalsa* episteme may, however, be critiqued on the grounds that it ignores continuity with the pre-colonial past.[9] Grewal maintains that the majority of members of the Sikh *panth* were Singhs *before* the onset of colonial rule (Grewal 1999b: 247), while Pashaura Singh accuses Oberoi of tilting 'the balance of evidence artificially in favour of *Sanatan* Sikhism' (Pashaura Singh 2004: 94). This seems to be borne out by an examination of colonial Census Reports which consistently show *Sahajdhari* Sikhs as a minority within the *panth*, although this may reflect colonial perceptions of Singhs as 'true' Sikhs and *Sahajdhari* Sikhs as indistinguishable from Hindus.[10] According to the 1881 Census, there were 379,000 Sikh 'Nanakpanthis' and 839,000 Sikh 'Gobind Singhi'. The latter figure, however, included

79,000 *Hindu* 'Gobind Singhi', illustrating again the 'fuzziness' of religious boundaries in colonial Punjab (GOI 1881).

However, it is generally accepted that the Singh Sabha movement after the 1870s initiated a key turning point in modern Sikh history. This *instrumentalist* approach, which Ballantyne has labelled 'internalist' (Ballantyne 1999: 197), may be contrasted with the *constructivist* or 'externalist' approach of Richard Fox (1985, 1996) which sees a distinct Sikh identity as essentially a product of the colonial state and Orientalist scholarship. Sikhs are limited, in the 'externalist' approach, to the role of *consumers* of, rather than participants in, modernity. Such an approach reduces the Sikhs to silence, denying the contribution which Sikhs made themselves to the fashioning of their own identities. It will be argued, in contrast to the reductionist approaches of the 'internalists' and 'externalists' or 'instrumentalists' and 'constructivists', that a distinct Sikh identity arose as a result of the dialectical interaction between the Sikh tradition and the colonial state which made the construction of a Sikh modernity centred on the mythology and symbolism of the *Khalsa* possible.

British attitudes and colonial policy towards the Sikhs *did*, however, help mould and shape Sikh self-perception and facilitated the construction of religious boundaries between *Kes-dhari* Sikhs and other Punjabis, but there was no single British perception of Sikhism. The histories of the Sikhs written by Cunningham (1997 [1849]) and Macauliffe (1990 [1909]) in particular both foreshadowed and reinforced the Singh Sabha interpretation of their own history but, whilst the former regarded the Sikhs as essentially a 'nation', the latter sought to introduce Sikhism as a universal 'religion' distinct from Hinduism and Islam. From the time of Major James Browne, who produced the first British account of Sikhism in 1788, the British saw the Sikhs as a Protestant sect of Hinduism, bearing 'that kind of relation to the Hindoo religion, which the Protestant does to the Romish' (Ballantyne 1999: 199). The identification of the British with the Sikhs grew after the annexation of the Punjab in 1849 as a result of the two bloody wars waged against the Punjab's Sikh rulers. The publication of J.D. Cunningham's *History of the Sikhs* introduced Western audiences to the Sikhs for the first time and importantly introduced many Sikhs to an official colonial account of their 'own' history.

In the Preface to the Second Edition, Cunningham described the Sikhs as a 'new and peculiar *nation*' (Cunningham 1997 [1849]: xxi, italics mine) – a trope which forms the basis of contemporary Sikh demands for a separate state. Whilst Guru Nanak was credited with having 'disengaged his little society of worshippers from Hindu idolatry and Muslim superstition', it was the last Guru, Gobind, who 'bestowed upon them a distinct political existence and inspired them with the desire of being socially free and nationally independent' (Cunningham 1997 [1849]: 80). However, it was only with the emergence of the empire of Maharaja Ranjit Singh (1780–1839) that the Sikh 'nation' was born. According to Cunningham, Ranjit Singh 'laboured . . . to mould the increasing Sikh nation into a well-ordered state or commonwealth, as Gobind had developed a sect into a people, and had given application and purpose to the general institutions of Nanak' (Cunningham 1997 [1849]: 120).[11]

The origins of the second narrative, that of Sikhism as a distinct, mono-theistic and universal religion may be traced to the work of M.A. Macauliffe, who, like Cunningham, is revered as a sympathetic historian by many Sikhs today. Macauliffe sought to rehabilitate the Sikh religious tradition in Western eyes after evangelical attacks which followed in the wake of Ernest Trumpp's translation of the *Guru Granth Sahib*. Trumpp, a skilled German linguist, had been commissioned by the Secretary of State for India in 1869 to translate both the *Adi Granth* and the *Dasam Granth*. After working for eight years with limited support, he concluded that the language of the *Granth* was 'incoherent and shallow in the extreme, and couched at the same time in dark and per-plexing language, in order to cover these defects' (Trumpp 1979 [1887]: v). More damagingly, Trumpp reported to the Secretary of State that 'the Sikh Gurus taught nothing new whatever' and that there was nothing to distinguish the Sikh Gurus from 'the writings of the old Hindu Bhagats (or devotees)', which Trumpp found 'on the whole far superior to those of the Sikh Gurus as regards contents and style'.[12]

Macauliffe's stated objective was to 'endeavour to make some reparation to the Sikhs for the insults which he [Trumpp] offered to their Gurus and their religion' (Macauliffe 1990 [1909], vol.1: vii). He proposed to do this not only by translating 'faithfully' the words and hymns of the Sikh Gurus but also by pointing out the 'moral and political merits' of Sikhism, presumably for a British audience. These 'merits' included a prohibition of idolatry, hypocrisy, caste exclusiveness, infanticide, *sati*, the consumption of alcohol and tobacco, slander and 'pilgrimages to the sacred rivers and tanks of Hinduism'. The merits of Sikhism, therefore, lay in their *opposition* to Hindu religious and cultural practices and, by implication, their *affinities* with Protestant virtues and ethics. These included loyalty, gratitude, philanthropy, justice, impar-tiality, truth, honesty and 'all the moral and domestic virtues known to the holiest citizens of any country' (Macauliffe 1990 [1909], vol.1: xxiii). Macau-liffe reminded British readers that it was the Sikhs who rescued the Raj during the Mutiny of 1857 and described them as 'among the bravest, the most loyal and devoted subjects of the British Crown' (Macauliffe 1990 [1909], vol.1: xix).

Central to Macauliffe's argument was the threat posed by Hinduism to the nascent Sikh faith. Likening Brahmanical Hinduism to 'the boa constrictor of the Indian forest', Macauliffe feared that, without state support, Sikhism would disappear in the 'capacious interior' of Hinduism, as Buddhism and Islam had before it.

> When a petty enemy appears to worry it, it winds round its opponents, crushes it in its fold, and finally causes it to disappear in its capacious interior. In this way, many centuries ago Hinduism on its own ground disposed of Bud[d]hism ... in this way it has converted uneducated

Islam in India into a semi-paganism, and in this way it is disposing of the reformed and once hopeful religion of Baba Nanak.

(Macauliffe 1990 [1909], vol. 1: lvii)

Hinduism, he continued, 'has embraced Sikhism in its fold, the still compara- tively young religion is making a vigorous struggle for life, but its ultimate destruction is, it is apprehended, inevitable without state support' (Macauliffe 1990 [1909], vol.1: lvii).

Although Macauliffe did not specify what 'state support' was needed to ensure the survival of the Sikh religion, the Sikhs were by the turn of the century enmeshed in the coercive structure of the colonial state, dispropor- tionately represented in the British armed and police forces throughout the empire. By the outbreak of the First World War, Sikhs accounted for almost 40 per cent of the combat troops of the Indian army, more than the contin- gent of any other religious community. The proportion of Sikh troops in the army was over three times larger than the proportion of Sikhs in the Punjab's population and almost twenty times their representation in the Indian popu- lation (Fox 1985: 143). Sikh regiments under the command of British officers fought as far apart as Afghanistan, China and East Africa, and 97,016 Sikhs served in the British forces during the First World War. In total, over 83,000 Sikh troops, all of them 'turban wearing', laid down their lives for 'King and Empire', fighting for the British in the two world wars of the twentieth century (Cyber Sikh Museum 2003a, 2003b). British policy towards the Sikhs con- sisted of two interrelated but potentially contradictory strategies. The first aimed at securing the loyalty of the *mahants* who controlled Sikh *gurdwaras* and holy shrines. The second strategy was to recruit a cheap but dependable and, above all, obedient soldiery for the Raj by 'promoting Sikhism as a separ- ate religion and Singh as a separate social identity based on that religion' (Fox 1985: 140). In his *Handbook on Sikhs for the Use of Regimental Officers*, R.W. Falcon described the Sikh as a 'fighting man' and the army as his 'natural profession'. 'Hardy, brave and of intelligence; too slow to understand when he is beaten; obedient to discipline: attached to his officers; and careless of caste prohibitions, he is unsurpassed as a soldier in the East' (Falcon 1896: 65).

It followed that the Indian army should employ as many Sikhs and other 'martial races' as it could to ward off internal and external threats to the Raj. Unlike the case with other 'martial races', however, the boundaries between Sikhs and 'effeminate' Hindus were porous. Since loyalty was seen as a 'Sikh' and not necessarily a Punjabi virtue by officers such as Falcon, 'reversion' to Hinduism could prove costly to British designs in India. It was feared that, in the words of David Petrie, an official with the Criminal Intelligence Department, 'with the relapse into Hinduism and readoption of its supersti- tions and vicious social customs ... the Sikh loses much of his martial instincts and greatly deteriorates as a fighting soldier' (Petrie 1911: 52). Con- sequently, British officers commanding 'Sikh' regiments required all enlisted men to undergo the *khande ki pahul*.

Controlling the *gurdwaras* was another way, or so the British thought, of ensuring the loyalty of the Sikh soldiers to the Raj. In this, it is claimed that they were merely following a custom established by Ranjit Singh, but their control over Sikh shrines, including the Golden Temple, exposed a fundamental ambivalence towards the Sikhs. On the one hand Sikh collaboration with government was needed and pursued, whilst on the other hand Sikh enmity or disloyalty was feared. Consequently, the Sikhs 'had to be watched, cosseted and controlled' (Kerr 1999: 161). This was in marked contrast with the prevailing policy, informed by the development of liberal thought, of non-interference in 'native' religious affairs. However, the contradiction lay in the fact that most *mahants* were not 'Singhs' but *Sahajdhari* Sikhs, often belonging to the *Udasi* sect, and were hostile to state attempts at promoting a 'Singh' identity. Although the *mahants*, including the managers of the Golden Temple, collaborated with the British, their congregations, imbued with the Singh identity promoted by the British, attempted to reclaim their *gurdwaras*.

If the Sikhs were the mirror through which the British scholar-soldiers saw themselves in a South Asian context then the opposite is certainly true: the Singh Sabha reformers saw themselves in the reflected gaze of their British colonial masters, as the conquering 'Lions of the Punjab'. The image which the Sikh reformers internalized was indeed a 'specular' one: one without breaks in uniformity or in Lacan's words '*sans accidents*' (Gupta 1997: 101). However, as Lacan pointed out, the specular image was based on a *méconnaissance*: a 'misrecognition' or 'misconstruction' that allows the image to appear unified and homogeneous (Lacan 1977: 6). The Sikh 'Self' during the late nineteenth century was indeed far from uniform and contained many internal 'others' that needed to be purged from the *panth* in order for it to appear distinct from other religious communities in the Punjab.

The Singh Sabha movement arose as a systematic attempt to purge these impure internal 'Others' from the Sikh 'Self' by redefining Sikh identity in the light of the institutional and conceptual innovations of colonial modernity. After 1849, Sikhs and other Punjabi were confronted by unprecedented cultural challenges which made the construction of religious boundaries and re-conceptualization of ethno-religious identities imperative. These included the influence of both Christianity and the secular 'ideologies' of Liberalism and colonial difference upon 'traditional' religious beliefs and practices; the development of print capitalism, which made the imagination of new vernacular communities possible; and the introduction of a limited conception of civil society which provided the impetus towards the establishment of voluntary associations. Under siege, on the one hand, from Christian missionaries aligned with British administrators[13] and, on the other, by the semitized neo-Hinduism of the *Arya Samaj*, Sikhs endeavoured to work out *their* modernity: one which differed from that of their colonial masters and self-consciously 'Hindu' fellow Punjabis. This new Sikh modernity took time to emerge and was contested throughout by both elitist and subaltern groups within the *panth*. The task of formulating and articulating a Sikh modernity which only crystallized in the twentieth century was facilitated and at the same time made more complicated by the egalitarianism of the Sikh tradition. Unlike in the older Hindu or Islamic traditions, there existed no institutional impediments to the redefinition of Sikhism in line with *Khalsa* orthodoxy, as there was no Sikh equivalent of the *ulema* to pass definitive judgement on various interpretations of the Sikh scriptures. However, the relative lack of institutionalization meant that there existed no single Sikh religious or political elite who could lead the community after Guru Gobind Singh ended the line of human Gurus. Consequently, Sikh politics has hitherto been characterized by factionalism, often along 'caste' lines, and patterns of intra-community conflict which remain to this day.

The initial reaction to the challenge of colonial modernity came from two new sects, the *Namdharis* and the *Nirankaris*, who followed a simultaneous strategy of internal reform and external opposition to colonial rule which was to become a hallmark of the later nationalist strategy. Internally, the *Nirankaris* and *Namdharis*, also known as *Kuka* Sikhs, sought to 'purify' their tradition by purging *Sanatan* elements from daily ritual and practice. The *Kukas*, however, chose to reject colonial modernity and challenge the principal mechanism through which the colonial state sought to legitimize itself: the rule of law. In 1872, *Kuka* Sikhs led by Ram Singh attacked the Muslim principality of Malerkota and were crushed by the British.[14] Thereafter, both sects remained at the margins of the Sikh *panth*: their failure to adapt to colonial modernity serving as a useful reminder to the 'Singh' reformers who gathered in Amritsar on 1 October 1873 to form the first Singh Sabha ('assembly of Singhs').

Beneath its 'modern' façade, the Sabha remained under the control of a loyalist, landed elite with extensive ties to the British Raj.[15] However, it was the creation of a second Singh Sabha in Lahore in 1879 which paved the way for the construction of *modern* Sikh identity as understood today. The second Singh Sabha reflected the views and interests of an emerging Western educated vernacular elite, including men such as Gurmukh Singh (1849–1898), the co-sponsor of the Lahore Singh Sabha and a professor at Oriental College, Bhai Jawahir Singh Kapur (1859–1910) and Bhai Ditt Singh (1853–1901), a low-caste Sikh leader, who were keen to reconstruct Sikhism around what they saw as *Tat Khalsa* or 'true' *Khalsa* ideals. These ideals included a commitment to social equality and the elimination of *Sanatan* practices such as idol worship and other such 'superstitious' practices. Like the sympathetic colonial soldier-scholars whose work they disseminated and often funded, the *Tat Khalsa* argued that Sikhism had disintegrated since the time of the Gurus and a reassertion of 'true' values was necessary if Sikhism was to survive the challenge of Christian missionaries and the *Arya Samaj*. Consequently, 'a new moral order' or 'social imagination' (Oberoi 1994: 305–382) had to be established, institutionalized and propagated through the regional Singh Sabhas. Central to this imagination were the ten Sikh Gurus and the *Guru Granth Sahib*, which, for Oberoi, became 'the centre of the Tat Khalsa universe' (Oberoi 1994: 320).

In all, Oberoi has accounted for the establishment of 117 Singh Sabhas between 1873 and 1990, some as far away as Malaysia and Hong Kong (Oberoi 1994: 427–430). The *Tat Khalsa* reformers took the opportunities which modernization afforded them, building schools, colleges and orphanages, compiling archives and founding journals and historical societies charged with the mission of re-imagining a single Sikh past. Sikh sacred space was reconstituted at first through harnessing the powers of print capitalism. The number of printing presses increased from thirty in 1864 to over one hundred two decades later (Oberoi 1994: 275).Whilst beforehand, the transmission of Sikh cultural and religious codes was entrusted to an intermediary class of *Sanatan gianis*[16] and *bhais*[17] who interpreted the *Granth Sahib* for worshippers, the invention of the printing press enabled the new religious elite to communicate directly with the literate Sikh 'masses'. Ian Talbot points out that the number of newspapers and periodicals published in the Punjab rose from 74 to 579 between 1891 and 1941 (Talbot 1996: 15).There was, furthermore, a spectacular increase in the number of books published in the Punjab. The total number of books published increased fivefold in just five years from 1,025 in 1875 to 5,610 in 1880 (GOI 1881: 160). Although the majority of books published were written in Urdu, more books were published in Punjabi than in Hindi,[18] many of them on themes relating to Sikh identity.

Ironically, it was a tract which was first written in Hindi and then translated into Punjabi by the author which had the most impact on the subsequent development of a distinct Sikh identity. Bhai Kahan Singh Nabha's *Ham Hindu Nahin* [We Are Not Hindus] was published in 1898 in response to *Arya Samaj* claims that Sikhs were Hindus following the Punjab High Court ruling on the Dayal Singh Majithia case.[19] In it Nabha (1861–1938) made the *Tat Khalsa* case for regarding Sikhism as a separate religion from Hinduism. It was to prove one of the most influential Sikh publications of the Singh Sabha era and became 'the most comprehensive statement on the subject of Sikh identity' (Grewal 1999b: 232). In *Ham Hindu Nahin*, Nabha systematically refutes the *Arya* claims by quoting from the *Guru Granth Sahib*: the Sikhs are 'neither Hindu nor Musalman' but have their own distinct religious identity. On the question of living in 'Hindustan', Nabha gives perhaps the first exposition of the 'nationalist' position: not only do the Sikhs constitute a separate *dharm* but they also constitute a separate *qaum* (Grewal 1999b: 242). The term *qaum* translated as 'nation' denotes a *political* community. Before the publication of Nabha's work, the dominant narrative in the Sikh tradition was that the Sikhs constituted a distinct *panth*, or spiritual community. By making *panth* synonymous with *qaum*, Nabha paved the way for the politicization of Sikh identity. Thus, *Ham Hindu Nahin* may be read as 'a declaration of Sikh ethnicity' (Grewal 1999b: 250).

The stage was thus set, following the publication and widespread dissemination of Bhai Kahan Singh Nabha's book, for the *ethnicization* of this standardized Sikh identity. By the early twentieth century, the slogan '*Ham Hindu Nahin*' had been adopted by the *Tat Khalsa* reformers throughout the Punjab to denote a Sikh *ethno-religious* identity separate from Hinduism and was used during the *gurdwara* reform movement. By then, however, the *Tat Khalsa* conception of Sikhism had been institutionalized through the formation of the Chief Khalsa Diwan (CKD) and subsequently the Shiromani Gurdwara Prabandhak Committee (SGPC). A new chapter in the construction of a Sikh national identity had thus begun.

The institutionalization of a 'Sikh' identity: from the CKD to the SGPC

At the dawn of the twentieth century, no one organization could claim to speak for the Sikh *panth*. This made the representation of 'Sikh' interests, notably the protection of the external symbols of the Sikh faith, the status of Punjabi and access to government jobs, more difficult. Representatives of the Hindu and Muslim communities had already established new organizations and devised new political strategies to deal with the changing nature of colonial governmentality with its new emphasis on representative government and the rule of law. Furthermore, to the chagrin of the *Tat Khalsa* reformers, *Sanatanists* continued to control, with British support, major Sikh shrines and temples (Barrier 2004b: 198). Without a central organization to provide leadership for their community, the Sikhs ran the risk of being further marginalized in the Punjab and, to use Macauliffe's metaphor, swallowed back into the belly of the 'boa constrictor'. It was at this juncture that a new generation of leaders schooled in the Singh Sabhas, led by Sundar Singh Majithia, established the Chief Khalsa Diwan.[20]

Founded in 1902, the CKD coordinated the activities of what had hitherto been isolated Singh Sabhas and succeeded, to a certain degree, in institutionalizing the *Tat Khalsa* view of Sikhism as a separate religion with distinct rituals and a tradition devoid of Hindu influence. The CKD allowed only baptized *amritdhari* Sikhs to join its councils and offices and argued that Sikhism was centred around the *Khalsa* (Barrier 2003: 12). It sought to communicate its message in both Punjabi and English, reflecting a need to cultivate a specific Sikh *ethnic* identity rooted in the Punjabi language and also to construct a distinct narrative of Sikhism as a 'world religion' for the benefit of the colonial authorities and Western scholars. Through its two newspapers, the *Khalsa Samachar* and the English language *Khalsa Advocate*, the CKD laid claim to being the sole representative of the *panth*. 'It is only the Chief Khalsa Diwan', reported the *Khalsa Advocate*, 'through which the aspirations and grievances of the Sikh public can be formulated, religious differences settled, and public opinion directed into proper channels' (*Khalsa Advocate*, 8 March 1905, in Barrier 2003).

The CKD, with the help of scholars at Khalsa College, set out to redefine the Sikh tradition in the light of colonial modernity and the *Tat Khalsa* movement, providing Sikhs with a *narrative* of their own history which centred upon the establishment of the *Khalsa panth* by Guru Gobind, its decline after the collapse of Ranjit Singh's empire and its revival by the Singh Sabhas. The myths and symbolism of the *Khalsa* were captured in numerous publications, and the *rahit-namas* were edited, simplified and published so that they could be made accessible in Punjabi to every literate *Kes-dhari* Sikh. Furthermore, the CKD sought to mobilize the Sikh community politically. Already aware that Sikhs were a minority within the Punjab, the CKD made use of Census data to argue that Sikhism was in danger of disappearing unless it mobilized around issues of importance to the community and modernized. The Sikhs could no longer rely upon British patronage to maintain their position and needed to adapt to the new 'politics of numbers' (Barrier 1988: 159–190). Mobilization and unity were seen as the key to ensuring greater representation in the public sphere. In 1909, the CKD managed to mobilize 400 organizations throughout the world in order to win British approval for a proposal to institutionalize a distinct Sikh marriage ceremony, the *anand* (Barrier 2004b: 199).

However, the CKD operated firmly within the space created for it by the colonial state, branding as 'seditious' any attempt to infringe the law. Its 'loyalist' stance accorded with the colonial *imago* of the Singh as outlined by Richard Fox (Fox 1985). Politically close to the conservative Amritsar Singh Sabha, the CKD was regarded with considerable suspicion by more radical reformers influenced by the *Ghadar* movement[21] and seen as representing the interests of the landed gentry and, through them, the colonial state. This stance was challenged by a new generation of reformers whose Sikh identity was forged in the *Khalsa* schools of the regional Singh Sabhas. Increasingly, the CKD faced challenges to its authority from within the *panth*. When Sikh–British relations deteriorated after the *Jallianwallah Bagh* massacre of 1919[22] and then over control of *gurdwaras*, opponents of the more moderate CKD were able to rally Sikhs with the symbols and communication system made possible by the Singh Sabha movement. As Barrier points out, the interpretations of the past and emphasis on Sikh bravery and martyrdom provided much of the ideology of the Akalis as well as their heated and very effective rhetoric (Barrier 2003: 14, 2004b: 194–229).

The SGPC has, since its inception in October 1920, been central to Sikh religious nationalism. The SGPC, which may be seen as the successor of the CKD, owed its existence to the Akali agitation for *gurdwara* reform. Between 1919 and 1925 the SGPC was able to gain control over all the major Sikh shrines in the Punjab through a highly successful, organized campaign against the *mahants* and their British backers. Starting in late 1920, large numbers of reformers joined together to form separate and independent *jathas*, or groups, of Akalis under the nominal control of the Akali Dal party in an attempt to assert 'Singh' control over *gurdwaras*. What 'began as religious reformism in Punjab cities . . . ended as anticolonial revolt in Punjab villages' (Fox 1985: 87). Thousands of Sikhs were detained and hundreds killed by the colonial authorities for participating in organized *morchas*, or disciplined demonstrations, whose mass and primarily non-violent character won the support of independence leaders.[23] Indeed, the passing of the Sikh Gurdwara Act of

1925, which gave the SGPC control over the *gurdwaras* in the Punjab, may be seen as one of the first victories of organized mass resistance to colonial rule. Gandhi certainly regarded the non-violent character of the Akali movement as a victory for the brand of Indian nationalism he espoused. After the British had been forced to hand over the keys of the Golden Temple to the SGPC, Gandhi sent the following telegram to the SGPC leader, Baba Kharak Singh (1868–1963): 'First battle for freedom won. Congratulations' (Mohinder Singh 1997: 226). Although the reformers had begun to speak the language of 'Indian' nationalism, their understanding of nationalism was rooted in the experiences and concerns of *their* 'community' – one which the Singh Sabha movement and the CKD helped to define. The Akalis were fighting against the colonial authorities for control over *their* shrines on behalf of *their* qaum. A tactical alliance with the Indian National Congress, which was similarly engaged in a 'freedom struggle' against British rule, was therefore necessary. For Congress, the Akali movement presented an opportunity to further its own programme of non-cooperation launched by Gandhi and to strengthen its position in the Punjab (Mohinder Singh 1997: 230). Akali participation in *the* 'freedom struggle', however, was always conditional, despite the sacrifices which Sikhs were to make in the fight for India's freedom. As long as the prevailing image of India remained that of Mahatma Gandhi, a loose, consociational arrangement of different *qaums*, each with their own interests and institutions, then the Akalis were prepared to make sacrifices for 'India'. Once India had been defined as a *secular*, sovereign socialist republic in the Constitution of the new nation, however, the relationship between the Akalis and the nation-state proved to be more problematic.

The Sikh Gurdwaras Act institutionalized the role of the SGPC, set up to manage the *gurdwaras*, and transformed its political wing, the Shiromani Akali Dal (SAD) into a political party representing Sikh interests. The SGPC is an elected, representative organization open to all Sikhs, and except for short intervals has remained under the control of the SAD or one of its factions. To this day the SGPC continues to be the primary institutional expression of Sikh identity. The importance of the SGPC, which reserves the right to legislate on all issues concerning the *panth*, cannot be overestimated. It is perhaps best exemplified by Attar Singh's essentialist assertion that:

> in the formation of the SGPC, the disinherited Sikh mind found a symbol of its corporate existence to enshrine the memories of its past glory, a substitute for the theo-political personality negated by the end of the Sikh supremacy in 1849.
>
> (A. Singh 1988: 228)

The SGPC enshrined the *Tat Khalsa* narrative of Sikh identity in the Sikh *Rahit Maryada*, which purports to provide a code of conduct for all Sikhs. In October 1931 a detailed draft was prepared by a subcommittee of the SGPC at the *Akal Takht*. The draft, which was prepared by prominent *Tat Khalsa* intellectuals such as Professor Teja Singh of Khalsa College (1894–1958) and Bhai Vir Singh (1872–1957), was finally approved by the SGPC in 1936 and published after partition in 1950. Over 300,000 copies in Punjabi and English have been printed subsequently (Barrier 2004b: 204). The *Rahit Maryada* begins by defining a Sikh as:

> Any human being who faithfully believes in
> i   One Immortal Being,
> ii   Ten Gurus, from Guru Nanak Sahib to Guru Gobind Singh Sahib,
> iii The Guru Granth Sahib,
> iv   The utterances and teachings of the ten Gurus and
> v   the *baptism* bequeathed by the tenth Guru,
> and *who does not owe allegiance to any other religion*, is a Sikh.
>
> (SGPC 1994: 1, emphasis mine)

Although the SGPC's definition of a Sikh was wide enough to include *Sahajdhari* and other non-*Khalsa* Sikhs, it firmly drew the boundaries between Sikhism and other religions. Henceforth, according to the SGPC, it was not possible to be *both* a Sikh and a Hindu: a choice had to be made. *Udasis*, Nanak-*panthis* and other *Sanatanists* had to conform to the *Rahit Maryada* if they wished to be considered 'proper' Sikhs and participate in SGPC elections. This entailed undergoing baptism and becoming *amritdhari* and joining the *Khalsa panth*. Once the religious boundaries between Sikhs and others had been established, and multiple religious identities outlawed in the *panth*, it was only a short step to making the case, as Kahn Singh Nabha had done, for regarding the Punjabi-speaking, *Kes-dhari* Sikhs as an 'ethnic' group, deserving of the same protection and considerations as the Muslim minority in India.

The feeling of 'communal' consciousness was reinforced by Article II of the *Rahit*, which affirmed that a Sikh's life has two aspects: 'individual or personal and corporate or Panthic' (SGPC 1994: 1). Whilst the personal life of a Sikh was devoted to meditation on *nam* (the 'Divine Substance') and to following the Gurus' teachings, the corporate life of a Sikh entailed a commitment to the *panth*. The *panth* was viewed as a single, corporate entity which included all Sikhs. Significantly, like the Indian nation which Nehru was in the process of 'discovering', the *panth* was conceived of as an essentially democratic and egalitarian polity, with the SGPC acting as its parliament, its constituent assembly. So hegemonic a role has the SGPC exercised in the Sikh community that the 'secular' Indian National Congress (INC) and even the Communists (CPI/CPI (M)) have felt obliged to participate in Committee elections, which have been held every five years since 1926 (except for a break of fourteen years between 1965 and 1979).

Conclusion

In conclusion, the colonial period, as it has come to be known, saw a redefinition and reinterpretation of what it meant to be Sikh. Whereas, at the onset of colonial rule, multiple religious identities in the Punjab were possible, there existed by the end of the nineteenth century a more homogeneous, *modern* conception of Sikh identity, as *internal* religious boundaries between *Kes-dhari* and *Sahajdhari* Sikhs and *external* boundaries between Sikhs and other religious communities, in particular the Hindu community, had become progressively less 'fuzzy' and more clearly demarcated. The policies of the colonial state, and the writings of sympathetic colonial soldier-scholars such as J.D. Cunningham and M.A. Macauliffe, certainly contributed to the construction of religious boundaries through the promotion of a standardized 'Singh' identity, particularly in the Indian army, where the Sikhs were regarded as a 'martial race'. However, the state's preference for the 'loyalist' stance of the Amritsar Singh Sabha and its desire to maintain control of their *gurdwaras* by appointing *mahants* operating out of the *Sanatan* tradition alienated many 'Singhs' and was to lead to confrontation in the twentieth century.

The key role in the process of 'Singh-izing' the Sikhs was played by the Lahore faction of the Singh Sabha movement, which articulated a *Tat Khalsa* discourse centred upon the Guru-*panth* and *Guru Granth*. The *Tat Khalsa* reformers took advantage of the social and cultural forces unleashed by colonial modernity to establish a highly systematized discourse of what it meant to be a Sikh. Henceforth, a Sikh was 'one who fully subscribed to the Five Ks, visited only what were defined exclusively as Sikh shrines, considered Punjabi the sacred language of the Sikhs, conducted his *rites de passage* according to the prescribed rituals, and did not consume prohibited foods' (Oberoi 1994: 25). Consequently, for the *Tat Khalsa* reformers, only *Kes-dhari* Singhs were to be regarded as 'true' Sikhs. The Sikh *panth* was thus equated with the *Khalsa panth*, and non-*Kes-dhari* Sikhs as well as those *Kes-dhari* 'sects' such as the *Namdharis* and *Nirankaris* which refused to conform to *Tat Khalsa* orthodoxy were progressively marginalized from the Sikh 'mainstream'.

Seen in this light, the Sikh Gurdwara Act of 1925 may be seen as a victory not only of the reformers over the colonial state, but of the *Tat Khalsa* approach over a more pluralistic, and less egalitarian, understanding of Sikh religious identity. For Rajiv Kapur, 'the act marked the turning point in the movement towards the reformulation of Sikh identity and the development of a distinct Sikh communal consciousness' (Kapur 1986: 191). A Sikh came to be seen not only as someone who believed in the ten Gurus and the *Guru Granth Sahib* but also importantly as someone who had no *other* religious identity. Although the Sikh Gurdwara Act has undergone thirty amendments, the basic principles and institutions established by it have remained the same.

3 The territorialization of the *qaum*

Sikh 'national' identity in independent India

[T]he only chance of survival of the Sikhs as a separate community is to create a state in which they form a compact group, where the teaching of Gurmukhi is compulsory, and where there is an atmosphere of respect for the traditions of their Khalsa forefathers.

(Khuswant Singh 1966: 305)

At the beginning of what Harjot Oberoi terms the 'nation-state phase' of Sikh history (Oberoi 1987), the Sikhs possessed a coherent, if not homogeneous, ethno-religious identity based on the myths and symbols of the *Khalsa* as first defined by the *Tat Khalsa* faction of the Singh Sabha movement and enshrined in the SGPC's definition of a Sikh. The Sikhs also possessed their own 'political system'[1] (Wallace 1981), centred on the SGPC, an elected organization open to all Sikhs empowered by the Sikh Gurdwara Act to supervise the running of *gurdwaras* in the Punjab and the SAD, whose role it was to define, articulate and safeguard 'Sikh' interests. It could be argued therefore that the Sikhs corresponded to what A.D. Smith has termed a politicized *ethnie* or nation (A.D. Smith 1999). Unlike any other *ethnie*, however, the Sikh *qaum* lacked a territorial base, a Sikh 'homeland', and a language they could exclusively call their own. Punjabi was the common language of all who lived in the 'land of the five rivers' in which the Sikhs were in a minority. By the end of the Nehruvian period of modern Indian political history, however, the Sikhs had both acquired a homeland within independent India and successfully claimed Punjabi written in *Gurmukhi* script as their own sacred language.

The Sikh 'political system' coexisted with, and potentially threatened, the state and central political systems of the Punjab and India. The Nehruvian 'idea of India' (Khilnani 1997) involved both a continuation and a rejection of colonial modernity.[2] By articulating India's demand for *swaraj* (self-rule) using a conceptual vocabulary derived from the legitimizing ideology of colonialism, Nehru committed India to modernity, but it would be a *different* modernity (Prakash 1999) from that of the West, or rather a different modernity from that which the colonizers had hitherto imposed upon the colonized through the colonial state. The main administrative functions of the state, the collection of revenue and the maintenance of law and order, were to be kept, but its role was to be transformed. India was, henceforth, to be a 'sovereign, socialist, secular democratic republic' committed to securing for its citizens social, economic and political justice; liberty of thought, expression, belief, faith and worship; and equality of status and opportunity (GOI 1949a).

The Nehruvian secular settlement

Nehru sought to effect the democratic transformation of Indian society that colonial rule had failed, or rather been unwilling, to accomplish. The state was to become the major instrument with which to accomplish the 'delayed nationalisation of society' (Balibar 1991: 92). Nehru's vision of India entailed a commitment to a modern, secular society where the state would seek to keep 'communal passions' in check (Nehru 2003 [1945]). Ashis Nandy has claimed that the Nehruvian elite sought to implement 'the same civilising mission that the colonial state had once taken upon itself vis-à-vis the ancient faiths of the subcontinent' (Nandy 1998b: 323). Vital differences, however, existed between colonial and elite-nationalist rule. The British colonial authorities had previously recognized and institutionalized religious and cultural differences between Hindus and Muslims in the subcontinent through the principle of separate electorates and quotas on recruitment to administrative positions. The Nehruvian state abolished these in favour of a 'first-past-the-post system', introduced universal adult suffrage and enshrined the principle of equal rights irrespective of religion in the Indian Constitution.[3] Furthermore, although the Constitution of India was to be federal, states would not be created or reorganized on the basis of religion. This was seen by the Nehruvian leadership as an unnecessary concession to 'communal' forces which could undermine the unity and integrity of the Indian nation. For, as Sudipta Kaviraj has pointed out, admitting 'that those whose mental world was often communal could also be nationalists' disturbed the harmony of the official universe of Indian state-nationalism (Kaviraj 1992: 5).

However, the Indian state was never secular in a Western sense. Secularism in the West developed in the context of the sixteenth-century inter-sectarian wars in early modern Europe. As worked out from the time of the Peace of Westphalia onwards, secularism involves three distinct but interrelated relations concerning state, religion and the individual. The first relation concerns individuals and their religion, from which the state is excluded. This is guaranteed by constitutional rights which safeguard the individual freedom of worship and expression. The second relation concerns that between individuals and the state, from which religion is excluded. Citizens in secular societies are granted equal rights irrespective of religious affiliation. Finally, secularism entails the mutual exclusion of state and society, so that the state does not interfere in the spiritual and religion does not encroach on the temporal domain (D.E. Smith 1963). Secularism in the Western sense refers, therefore, to the strict separation of religion and state in order to guarantee individual citizens equal rights to religious freedom.

The Indian variant of secularism, *Sarva Dharma Sambhava* (Let all religions flourish), does not attempt to banish religion from the public sphere but sees it as an integral part of India's democracy. Although the post-colonial Indian state abolished separate electorates, it continued to uphold the colonial distinction between majority and minority religious communities, most particularly in the realm of personal and civil law. At the time of the framing of the Constitution of India, Hinduism was seen as the religion of the majority, and a Committee on the Rights of Minorities was established to identify the cultural and political rights of religious minorities. According to one of its more recent defenders, secularism in India was neither intended to exclude religious practice or institutions from the domain of politics nor to guarantee state non-interference in religious affairs, but merely to entail equal respect or consideration of all religions (Bhargava 1998b). Equal respect, however, does not *necessarily* imply equal treatment. Indeed, it has been argued that, in order to promote equal respect for all religions, the state has, in some cases, been forced to treat different religious communities differently[4] (Bhargava 1998b: 531). This contextual interpretation of secularism, which Bhargava terms 'principled distance', allows the state to intervene or refrain from intervening in the religious affairs of a community depending on whether the proposed intervention would promote religious liberty and equality of citizenship. Hence, in Bhargava's view, the Indian state was justified in introducing temple rights to Dalits as, by allowing higher-caste Hindus to continue to refuse Dalits entry into Hindu temples, the state was denying Dalits their constitutional right to freedom of worship.

However, the state's attempts to regulate Hinduism by granting Dalits entry into Hindu places of worship, making polygamy and child marriage illegal and introducing the right to divorce are clear examples of state interference in the private sphere of religious affairs. The fact that a Hindu Code Act established a uniform civil code for all 'Hindus' in the country (including Sikhs), while leaving Muslims with their own personal law, furthermore, compromises the state's claim to be secular. On the one hand, state intervention in 'Hindu' and not Muslim religious affairs gave rise to charges of 'minorityism' from the RSS representing the interests of those Hindu upper castes eager to preserve their rights and privileges. The Indian state is regarded by these groups as 'pseudo-secular' in that its secular character obscures the fact that it actively promotes the interests of atheists and religious minorities. On the other hand, the state's interest in the religious affairs of one community and not the other upholds the colonial distinction between majority and minority religious communities, paving the way for the equation of 'Hindu' with 'Indian' in the popular imagination. The adoption, furthermore, of Hindi as the official 'national' language and the implementation of bans on cow slaughter in most states suggest that a clear distinction between Congress 'secularism' and Hindu majoritarianism cannot always be made (Embree 1990; Upadhyaya 1992; Gurharpal Singh 2000).

The Shiromani Akali Dal (SAD) and the movement for the Punjabi *Suba*

For many Sikhs, including the Akali leadership, the Nehruvian secular settlement as encapsulated in the Constitution was problematic on two grounds. First, the inclusion of Sikhs under the category of 'Hindu' under Article 25 (2b) of the Indian Constitution for the purposes of the Hindu Code Act ignores the distinctiveness of Sikh religious and political identity. This was compounded by the Hindu Marriage Act of 1955, which again included Sikhs under the category of Hindu. This seemingly negated the achievement of the CKD and Singh Sabhites in legalizing the *anand* ceremony in 1909, which was subsequently included in the *Rahit Maryada* (SGPC 1994: 26–29). Second, by refusing to reorganize state boundaries on the basis of religious identities, Nehru and the nationalist movement had reneged on their alleged 'promise' to the pre-independence Sikh leadership of the SAD. In 1929, in the face of Akali opposition to the Nehru report, Congress had passed a resolution assuring 'the Sikhs, Muslims and other minorities that no solution thereof in any future constitution will be acceptable to the Congress that does not give full satisfaction to the parties concerned' (Mohinder Singh 1997: 235). In return for remaining within India, the Sikhs were promised by Nehru that they too could 'experience the glow of freedom'.[5]

Although what this promise entailed was never specified, the Sikh leadership took this to mean a 'homeland' within independent, federal India once the Sikh community had 'regrouped' (Brass 2003) in an East Punjab 'ethnically cleansed' of Muslims.[6] The demand for the creation of a separate Sikh homeland was not new to Sikh politics. The belief that Sikhism could not survive without a state of its own may be traced back to the demand, first voiced by the CKD, for a one-third share in the Punjabi legislature, a share of political power not commensurate with its numerical strength. This was followed by a demand by the Akali leadership for an *Azad Punjab* in 1942: the SAD advocated a redrawing of the boundaries of the Punjab to detach the Muslim majority districts and create a new province in which most of the Sikh population would be included and no single religious community would have a majority (Nayar 1966: 84). Finally, in March 1946, the Executive Committee of the Akali Dal passed a resolution demanding 'the creation of a Sikh state which would include a substantial majority of the Sikh population and their sacred shrines and historical gurdwaras with the provision for the transfer and exchange of population and property' (SGPC 1946).

However, Sikhs remained in a minority in the Indian state of Punjab. Sikhs accounted for only 30 per cent of the population in their 'homeland' (Narang 1997: 246). Furthermore, Hindi – the 'national' language of the

Hindu majority – and not Punjabi, the 'spoken' language of both communities, was acknowledged as the language of the state. Since the reorganization of states on the basis of religious identity was unacceptable to India's post-colonial leadership, SAD strategy sought to 'camouflage' their designs by arguing in favour of the reorganization of the Punjab on the basis of language in order to create a Punjabi-speaking state. According to Baldev Raj Nayar, the 'real objective' of the demand for the redemarcation of the boundaries of the state of Punjab was 'the creation of a state in which the Sikhs as a religious community would become the dominant political power as a result of changing the population proportions in favour of that community' (Nayar 1966: 150). This conclusion is borne out by the strategies and symbolism employed by the Akali Dal leadership under Master Tara Singh (1885–1967) during the 1950s and early 1960s.

The stated objective of the SAD in post-colonial India, according to its 1961 Constitution, was to 'work for the protection of Sikh rights and ensuring the Sikhs' continued existence as an independent entity' (SAD 1961: 1). To this end, the SAD, which has consistently controlled the SGPC by democratic means since its very inception, has pursued a variety of different political strategies within independent India. The first strategy involved the use of methods which were within the framework of the existing Constitution. These included fielding candidates for elections to the state legislature, petitioning the government, and the holding of open meetings in which the grievances of the Sikh community were aired. However, the SAD was never able to capture a majority of the popular vote in 'Punjabi-speaking', i.e. Sikh majority, areas, and its demands, most notably over separate electorates for Sikhs, the inclusion of Sikh scheduled castes into scheduled caste reservations and, most notably, the creation of a Punjabi-speaking state, were dismissed by the centre. Furthermore, once the SAD had succeeded in capturing state power in PEPSU, which comprised the former Sikh princely states to the east of the state of Punjab, as part of a United Front coalition, the Akali-led government was dismissed by the imposition of President's Rule (Gurharpal Singh 2000: 103).

The second strategy in the immediate post-independence period consisted of 'infiltrating' the INC. Since the INC dominated Indian politics, it made sense for the SAD to join the Congress 'one-party dominance' system (Kothari 1964) in order to apply pressure on the state to respond to Sikh demands from within. Throughout the 1950s and 1960s the INC was the only party with a national organization, built of a network of political affiliations downwards, and capable of assimilating divergent interests upwards to the centre. The system consisted of a 'party of consensus' and a 'party of pressure'. The existence of an inbuilt corrective through factionalism within the ruling party and the latent threat from outside the margin of pressure posed by oppositional parties seemingly guaranteed state responsiveness to societal demands. Thus, in 1948 and 1956, the SAD joined the Congress Party and became part of the state government. From 1956 to 1964, Akali 'infiltration' of Congress was actively encouraged by the Punjab chief minister, Partap Singh Kairon, who argued that post-partition Sikh interests could only be guaranteed within Congress (Gurharpal Singh 2000: 107). Infiltration, however, did *not* lead to the realization of Akali objectives at state level; neither was the INC able to make inroads in the Sikh 'political system'.

The final strategy, termed the 'agitational strategy' by Nayar (Nayar 1966: 173), involved the launching of a series of mainly non-violent but confrontational agitations called *morchas*, similar to the ones which the Akalis launched against the British during the 'Third Sikh War'. *Morchas* are usually rallies held inside the vicinity of a *gurdwara* and become confrontational once the *jathas* move outside to deliberately court arrest. In 1955 and 1960–1961, the SAD launched two such *morchas* in the hope of securing a Punjabi *Suba*, a Punjabi-speaking state, leading to the arrest of 12,000 and between 26,000 and 57,000 Akalis respectively (Nayar 1966: 173–174). The political use of religious symbolism by the Akali leadership was a significant characteristic of the agitation for the *Suba* and has been an important factor in giving the Sikh nation what Walker Connor refers to as its 'psychological bond' (Connor 1994). Master Tara Singh, asserting the 'right of self-determination for the Panth in matters religious, social and political' (Nayar 1966: 153), led numerous *morchas* and twice threatened self-immolation in pursuit of the goal of the Punjabi *Suba*. In the post-independence nationalist discourse, the SAD was equated with the *panth*, and Congress candidates were regularly branded 'traitors' even when *Kes-dhari* Sikhs. The conscious or unconscious use of evocative symbols stressing the Sikh tradition of martyrdom and militancy such as the adoption of Guru Hargobind's two swords, *miri* and *piri*, drew attention to the inseparability of the religious and political authority of the SGPC–SAD nexus. *Morchas* have been initiated and maintained from within the Golden Temple, where the holding of pledges before the *Akal Takht* has become a permanent feature of most Akali movements (P.S. Verma 1987: 258) and a *dharam yudh*, a 'battle for righteousness' or religious war, was even declared.

Initially, the SAD sought to protect Sikh rights within independent India through constitutional means. The Akali policy was first to demand constitutional safeguards and then to campaign for Punjabi in *Gurmukhi* script as a symbol of their cultural identity. They sought to do this by 'infiltrating' the Congress Party through a merger in 1948. By April 1949, however, the slogan of a 'Punjabi *Suba*', which had been first voiced by Master Tara Singh, was adopted at an Akali convention (Grewal 1994: 182). The Constituent Assembly rejected outright the Akali demands for a separate electorate and a reservation of seats in the legislature for Sikhs as a 'communal', but the Congress state leadership was more willing to consider the SAD demand that Punjabi in *Gurmukhi* script be recognized as the official language of the Punjab. A compromise formula was put forth by the chief minister of the Punjab, Bhim Sen Sachar. The 'Sachar formula', as it came to be known, proposed to divide the state into a Punjabi-speaking and a Hindi-speaking zone. In the Punjabi zone, the medium of instruction was to be Punjabi written in *Gurmukhi* script and, in the Hindi zone, Hindi in *Devangari* script. In order to function as a state, however, compulsory learning of both languages in each zone was necessary.

The Sachar formula proved unacceptable to those Punjabi Hindu leaders close to the RSS within the INC, and Sachar was replaced by Gopi Chand Bhargava, with the support of the Akali Congressmen, led by Giani Kartar Singh. The dismissal of Sachar and rejection of Akali demands led Master Tara Singh to assert the 'right of self-determination' on behalf of the Sikhs. The Sikhs, Master Tara Singh reasoned, 'have a different culture from the Hindus' in as much as the 'language of the Sikhs was different . . . so too their traditions and histories' and 'social order' (Tara Singh, quoted in Narang 1997: 251). He subsequently ordered all Akalis to leave the INC. Hindu organizations and press led by Congressmen such as Lala Jagjat Narain and Barbi Dass, and the Bharatiya Jan Sangh leader, Dr Shyama Prasad Mukherjee, reacted by urging their fellow Hindus to return Hindi instead of Punjabi as their mother tongue in the 1951 Census. Since Punjabi was being claimed by the Sikh leadership exclusively as a 'Sikh' language, they reasoned that the creation of a Punjabi *Suba* would lead to the creation of a Sikh homeland in which Hindus would be discriminated against. However, their slogan of 'Hindi, Hindu, Hindustan' evoked memories of the *Arya Samaj* campaigns to 'reconvert' the Sikhs in the nineteenth century and further 'communalized' the issue of linguistic reorganization. According to Brass, the repudiation of Punjabi by Punjabi Hindus was 'an overt and deliberate political act designed to undercut the linguistic basis of the Punjabi *Suba* demand' (Brass 1974: 327). It was one which enabled the SAD to claim Punjabi as exclusively a 'Sikh' language.

When the SAD held it a 'question of life and death for the Sikhs' that a Punjabi *Suba* be created in its election manifesto of 1952, it equated the survival of the Sikh religion with the linguistic reorganization of the state. The clearest theoretical exposition of the Akali demand for a Punjabi *Suba* was put forward by Gurnam Singh in 1960. In *A Unilingual Punjabi State and Sikh Unrest*, Gurnam Singh, who subsequently became leader of the SAD in the Punjab legislature, asserted the indivisibility of the Sikh *panth* and their desire for a homeland within India. For Gurnam Singh, 'there is no ultimate dichotomy in the true Sikh doctrine between this world and the next, the secular and the religious, the political and the spiritual' (Gurnam Singh 1960: 12–13). Consequently, the Sikhs 'must be approached and dealt with at state level as a collective group and entity' (Gurnam Singh 1960: 11). This entailed not 'atomising' the Sikh *panth* into 'individual citizens' (Gurnam Singh 1960: 17), which was precisely the objective of the Nehruvian leadership. What the Akali leadership was arguing for, in other words, was that a 'state' was needed where the 'Sikh' subject could be treated as part of a collective entity, the *Khalsa panth*, and not as individual subjects of a liberal-democratic state. The Akali demand, therefore, was for a state within a state: a 'Sikh' homeland, including a substantial Punjabi-speaking Hindu minority, within Hindu-dominated India.

The use of a religious vocabulary to articulate an ostensibly secular demand made it easier for the Nehruvian leadership to stigmatize the Punjabi *Suba* as 'communal'. By defining the SAD's demands as 'communal', the INC at national and state level 'succeeded in constructing a discourse of de-legitimization which elided the logic of hegemony implicit in the "principled" opposition to the linguistic re-organization of the Punjab' (Gurharpal Singh 2000: 107). Since Punjabi Hindus had, for ideological reasons, declared Hindi to be the chosen official language in the 1951 and 1961 Censuses, the Nehruvian leadership consistently refused to cede the *Suba*. The States Reorganisation Commission rejected it on the grounds that it lacked the general support of the people inhabiting the region. Furthermore, they pointed out, much to the annoyance of the Sikhs, that Punjabi was not sufficiently grammatically different from Hindi to constitute a separate language (H. Deol 2000: 95). The implications were clear: if the Commission did not recognize Punjabi as sufficiently distinct from Hindi, then it followed that they did not consider the Sikh *ethnie* as distinct from the Hindu majority. This served the interests of the Hindu elite who continued to dominate Punjab politics in the Nehruvian era.

Finally, in 1966 Nehru's daughter, Indira Gandhi, relented in an attempt to further divide the Akali Dal between the faction led by the 'communal' Tara Singh, with his base amongst the urban *Khatri* refugees from West Punjab, and that led by Sant Fateh Singh, a more 'secular' leader representing the interests of the predominantly *Jat* farmers of East Punjab. Sant Fateh Singh had succeeded Master Tara Singh as 'dictator' of the 1960–1961 *morcha* upon the latter's imprisonment. His emphasis upon language rather than Sikh identity earned him the support of other political groups such as the Communists and Socialists and lessened the animosity of the Punjabi Hindus. After the 1962 elections in which the SAD again failed to capture a majority of votes in the Punjabi-speaking region of Punjab, winning just nineteen seats to the INC's forty-nine (Election Commission 1963), the Akali Dal split between the 'Master' and 'Sant' factions with the latter emerging dominant. Sant Fateh Singh interpreted the election defeat and the resulting split not as a defeat for the Punjabi *Suba* but as a rejection of the means by which Master Tara Singh sought to secure that end. By making the case for the Punjabi *Suba* exclusively on linguistic grounds, Sant Fateh Singh managed to win over the Hindu Congress and Jana Sangh elites in Haryana and Himachal Pradesh who were eager to establish states of their own. However, it took the death of Nehru in 1964 and then of his successor, Lal Bahadur Shastri, in 1966, as well as Sikh sacrifices in the Indo-Chinese and Indo-Pakistan wars, to win the support of the INC leadership. Unsure of support from her own party, which at the time was dominated by factions and powerful state bosses, Prime Minister Indira Gandhi sought support from outside in order to consolidate her position and win the forthcoming general election. By requesting the

Congress president to summon a meeting of the party's committee to discuss the Punjab issue, Indira Gandhi effectively put pressure on her own party to accept the Punjabi *Suba*. Following the acceptance of the Working Committee resolution to create a Punjabi-speaking state by first the government and then Parliament, Punjab was divided into Punjabi-speaking (Punjab) and Hindi-speaking states (Haryana and Himachal Pradesh) on 1 November 1966. The new Punjabi-speaking state consisted of 41 per cent of the area and 55 per cent of the population of the old Punjab, with the Sikhs in a majority (Narang 1997: 263). Although the Akalis got their Sikh-majority state, this was to prove the first of many fateful interventions by the central government leadership under Indira Gandhi in the 'Sikh political system' – one which arguably led to the tragedy of 1984.

In conclusion, the importance attached to the creation of a Punjabi-speaking state by the SAD, one in which Sikhs would constitute a majority, and the declaration of a religious war, *dharam yudh*, to achieve this goal, testifies to the fundamentally *nationalist* nature of the Akali demand. The adoption of Punjabi as the language of the *panth* by the Sikh leadership arguably left the non-Sikh majority with little option but to record their language preference, Hindi, rather than the language spoken at home, Punjabi, in the 1951 and 1961 Censuses, although this view ignores the role played by Punjabi Hindu elites in the RSS and INC in 'communalizing' the demand for a Punjabi-speaking state (Nayar 1966; Brass 1974). This further strengthened the religious boundaries between Sikhs and Hindus which had been constructed during the colonial period by the *Tat Khalsa* reformers and institutionalized by the establishment of a Sikh 'political system' within independent India. Indeed, the protracted struggle for the Punjabi *Suba* 'cemented territoriality into Sikh identity' (Oberoi 1987: 39–40) as the Punjabi language, and through it the Punjab, was claimed by the SAD exclusively on behalf of the Sikh 'nation'.

The 'violence' of the Green Revolution and Sikh 'kulak' nationalism

The concession of the Punjabi *Suba* created a de facto Sikh majority state in liberal-democratic Hindu-dominated India, but this was far from the Sikh 'homeland' envisaged by Akali religio-political elites, particularly since many Punjabi-speaking areas were not included within the borders of the new state, and Chandigarh, the state capital, was to be administered as a Union territory and shared with Haryana. Although the death of Master Tara Singh soon after the reorganization of the Punjab deprived the Akali movement of its most vociferous advocate for a Sikh homeland, a new generation of leaders rose up from within the ranks of the SGPC to challenge the 'secular' leadership of Sant Fateh Singh's faction of the Akali Dal. Following Lacan, it can be argued that the vision which these elites, and those outside of the 'Sikh political system', expounded upon was a 'specular' *imago*, that of a unified Sikh *qaum*. This contrasted with the *fragmented* nature of the Sikh 'body' divided into various factions, castes and classes.[7] The fragmentation of the Sikh *panth* was accelerated by the 'violence of the Green Revolution' (Shiva 1997), which may be seen as a forerunner of contemporary economic globalization in India. The Green Revolution may be considered 'violent' in the unevenness and scope of its transformation of Punjabi society. As with contemporary globalization in India, it disproportionately benefited the higher castes and classes, particularly the richer *Jat* farmers, who dominated regional politics, whilst leading to the creation of a class of landless labourers. This has led instrumentalists and other modernists to equate Sikh 'nationalism' with the interests of the *Jat* 'kulak' class (Jeffrey 1986; Narang 1986; Purewal 2000). Certainly, the transformation of the SAD into a party representing the economic interests of wealthy *Jat* farmers was striking. In 1960, it is estimated that the *Khatris*, the urban petty bourgeoisie, controlled over half of the key positions within the SGPC but by the end of the decade their numbers had dwindled to a negligible level (Purewal 2000: 102). It will be argued, however, that Sikh nationalism arose in the 1970s and early 1980s as a *reaction* to the increasing fragmentation of the *panth* and, in view of the tragic consequences which its development and subsequent clash with the centre under Indira Gandhi had for the Punjab, it cannot be reduced to the interests of any one elite or class.

In the post-independence period, the agrarian structure in the Punjab has undergone far-reaching changes primarily as a result of land reforms implemented soon after independence and rapid changes in the technology of production in agriculture after the creation of a Sikh-majority Punjab in the late 1960s. However, unequal distribution of land, partly as a result of the failure of the Land Ceiling Acts, led to the emergence of the big and middle farmers amongst the *Jats*. This process was cemented by the Green Revolution. The Green Revolution refers to the introduction of high-yield variety (HYV) grain and rice developed in the US with the support of the Ford Foundation. The main aim behind the export of HYVs, first to Mexico in the 1940s and subsequently to South-East and South Asia, was to stave off the threat of 'red' revolution by increasing agricultural productivity and, therefore, starving radical movements of support. In India, a hostile, 'socialist' democracy, the aim was to enable agri-business multinationals (MNCs) to penetrate the protectionist Indian market without having to bribe a government official to obtain a 'licence'. From the Indian point of view, it was hoped that increased agricultural productivity would eventually lead to self-sufficiency in food and that this would lessen India's dependence on external (and particularly US) food aid. However, in order to lessen external dependence, the government considered it necessary to increase its own dependence on the rich farmers of western Uttar Pradesh, Haryana and the Punjab. The farmers of these three states received a disproportionate amount of state investment in agriculture, with the Punjab allocated the largest share.[8]

In terms of meeting its main stated aim (increasing agricultural productivity), the Green Revolution exceeded expectations when it was implemented in the Punjab. India indeed became self-sufficient in food grain as production in the Punjab increased from 2 million to 20 million tonnes in 1990–1991. Green Revolution Punjab literally fed the rest of India as the 'bread basket' of the nation, contributing 60–70 per cent of total wheat and 50–55 per cent of total rice production (Purewal 2000: 55–56). The agricultural surpluses generated by the Green Revolution did provide an assured market to consumer goods, but the strategy did not provide channels for profitable investment of agricultural surpluses in industry and trade. Government investment in the industrial sector, in contrast with the agricultural sector, remained low throughout the post-Green Revolution period. In the sixth five-year plan, only 0.04 per cent of the central government total budget for heavy industry was invested in the Punjab (Purewal 2000: 65). Consequently, the main industry remained agriculture. In 1981, shortly before Sikh militancy became a 'problem' for the Indian state, agriculture and livestock contributed 58.12 per cent of state income at 1970–1971 prices, employing 59.1 per cent of the state's total workforce (Gill and Singhal 1984: 604).

The unevenness of capitalist development in the agricultural sector polarized Punjabi society. The ratio of landless workers in the total agricultural workforce rose from 17.3 per cent in 1961 to 32.1 per cent in 1971 and more than 40 per cent in 1980. The same year it was estimated that 10 per cent of rural households controlled 75 per cent of all agricultural wealth whilst the poorest 70 per cent possessed less than 7 per cent (Purewal 2000: 62–63). This has led many to conclude that the distribution of operated land has shifted in favour of richer farmers since the introduction of the new technology (Shiva 1997: 177). Rising unemployment, growing disparities of wealth and income leading to unequal conditions for taking advantage of opportunities, and poverty gave rise to social anger which found religious expression (H. Deol 2000). The Green Revolution ushered in a mass society by dislocating, atomizing and destroying traditional village Punjab (Jeffrey 1986: 28–32). The old institutional framework of Punjab politics based on limited participation of *Jat* and *Khatri* elites was unable to meet the demands of the new social order. Consequently, in this atmosphere of insecurity and fear it has been easier for 'communal' ideologies to flourish. For Jeffrey, 'it is not surprising that in this pool of disenchantment some people began to clutch at the straw of religious revivalism' (Jeffrey 1985: 27). Similarly, for Vandana Shiva, the

> religious resurgence of the Sikhs that took place in the early 1980s was an expression of a search for identity in an ethical and cultural vacuum that has been created by destroying all value except that which serves the market place.
>
> (Shiva 1997: 191)

Shiva sees the Green Revolution as bringing about a *cultural* revolution in the

Punjab, one that replaced 'the traditional peasant values of cooperation with competition, of prudent living with conspicuous consumption, of soil and crop husbandry with the calculus of subsidies, profits and remunerative prices' (Shiva 1997: 184–185).

Sikh religious nationalism during the late 1970s and 1980s may be seen as a response to the erosion of cultural values that proceeds from rapid modernization but it was a response reluctantly supported during the 1980s by a self-serving 'secular' elite who were to abandon separatist politics in the 1990s when it became apparent that power sharing in the centre as part of a National Democratic Alliance in the late 1990s was a possibility. This elite did not consist of, or attempt to serve the interests of, the Sikh *Jats* as a whole, but merely an 'economically and socially influential section . . . keen to nurse their own vested interests and to perpetuate the arrangements which helped them become rich' (Narang 1986: 90). Once the Congress-controlled state government, directly imposed by the centre on the Punjab through President's Rule, had successfully crushed Sikh militancy, the Badal faction of the SAD was able to distance itself from the demand for *Khalistan*, the name given to an independent Sikh homeland, by successfully reinventing itself as a regional movement representing the interests of the farmers of the Punjab. As part of a coalition with the BJP, it was able to win the 1997 Punjab Legislative Assembly elections, winning 75 out of a total of 117 seats and capturing 37.6 per cent of the popular vote (Gurharpal Singh 1998: 237).

Although the impetus towards the articulation of Sikh religious nationalism did not come from within the Sikh 'political system' but from outside, the territorialization of Akali demands in the movement for the creation of a Punjabi-speaking state and the use of separatist vocabulary to articulate those demands may be seen to have created space for both the advocacy of *Khalistan* and the rise of Jarnail Singh Bhindranwale.

Imagining *Khalistan*

The demand for *Khalistan*, the Sikh 'land of the pure', was ostensibly articulated before 1984 by Sikhs living outside the Punjab, in the diaspora (Tatla 1999). However, the term *Khalistan* was first coined by Dr V.S. Bhatti to denote an independent Sikh state in March 1940. Dr Bhatti made the case for a separate Sikh state in a pamphlet entitled 'Khalistan' in response to the Muslim League's Lahore Resolution. Whilst Master Tara Singh declared that the Akalis would fight any future Pakistan 'tooth and nail' (Tan Tai Yong 1994: 169), Dr Bhatti based his demand for a separate Sikh state on the presumption that Pakistan was bound to be established sooner or later and that, as a potentially theocratic Islamic state, Pakistan was likely to be hostile to Sikhism. The *Khalistan* proposed by Bhatti was meant to include three main areas: the central districts of Punjab province then directly administered by the British, including Ludhiana, Jullunder, Ambala, Ferozpur, Amritsar and Lahore; the 'princely states' of the Cis-Sutlej, including Patiala, Nabha,

Faridkot and Malerkolta; and the 'Shimla Group' of states. *Khalistan* was imagined as a theocratic state, a mirror-image of 'Muslim' Pakistan, led by the Maharaja of Patiala with the aid of a cabinet consisting of representative federating units (Riar 1996: 233) The *Khalistan* demand proposed by Bhatti appealed to those Sikhs outside of the Sikh 'political system', most notably ex-Ghadarites such as Baba Gurdit Singh, who flirted with the INC but was firmly opposed by SAD president Master Tara Singh, who sought a Sikh homeland within independent India.

For *Khalistan*'s more recent exponents, particularly those in the diaspora, fear of remaining a permanent minority in 'Hindustan' has replaced the creation of Pakistan to the west as its main legitimizing principle. 'Hindu' India becomes the 'threatening Other' (Jaffrelot 1996) which permits *Khalistan* to be imagined. Even Inderjit Singh, editor of the moderate English-language periodical the *Sikh Messenger*, has stressed that India has never been a secular state but a Hindu one oppressing minorities (Ahmed 1988: 39–40). The late Dr Jagjit Singh Chauhan (1927–2007), a former minister in the first Akali-led Punjab government[9] and president of the Khalistan Council, based his vision on the fear that, as long as Sikhs live in India, the 'Hindu' caste system will impinge upon Sikh society. In a half-page advertisement which appeared in the *New York Times* on 12 October 1971, Chauhan famously outlined the case for *Khalistan*:

> The world has been oblivious to the fate of 12 million Sikhs living under political domination in India and in constant fear of *genocide*. Another 6 million of us live abroad in alienation and exile waiting for the day of deliverance. But all of us, wherever we are, have struggled hard and in silence all these years for our political and cultural redemption. We are going to wait no more. Today we are launching a final crusade till victory is achieved.

The Sikhs, according to Chauhan, were a 'religious, ethnic, and cultural entity, distinct from the Hindus that rule India'. A 'nation in our own right', Sikhs have 'endured persecution and endless suffering at the hands of an intolerant, mercenary majority that rules India – the Hindus' (*New York Times*, 12 October 1971).

Chauhan imagined *Khalistan*, far from being a theocratic state, to be an independent Punjab, open to both Sikhs and Hindus, based on the 'traditional' Sikh values of tolerance and coexistence best exemplified by the reign of Maharaja Ranjit Singh, in contrast to 'Hindustan', a state based on the 'tyranny' of the Hindu majority.[10] In Chauhan's view, it is India that is 'communal' and *Khalistan* a 'secular' demand, an opinion shared by Surjan Singh. In his *Case for the Republic of Khalistan* (1982) published by the Babbar Khalsa in Vancouver, BC, Surjan Singh considers the Sikhs to have twice been 'betrayed' by India's Hindu rulers. First in 1947, the Sikhs were 'duped' in consenting to the Radcliffe boundary award by the 'vows and promises of the Hindu Trilogy, Gandhi, Nehru and Patel, who could hardly wait to see power transferred to them though it involved the vivisection of the Punjab – the vital homeland of the Sikhs'. The second time was in 1966 when the reorganization of the boundaries of the Punjab by the Indian government ensured that 'vital industry that was formerly located in the Punjab went out of it'. Consequently, 'independence' meant freedom only for 'the majority community of Hindus who were now the rulers of India'. The Sikhs remained 'without independence' (Surjan Singh 1982: 7). *Khalistan*, however, 'will not be a theocracy' since 'Sikhs will form a little more than half of the population of the Sikh state' consisting of the 'Sikh majority areas in north western India' (Surjan Singh 1982: 8–12).

The 'communalization' of the Punjab and state terrorism

The view that India was essentially a Hindu polity was reinforced by the 'communalization' of Indian politics under Indira Gandhi (Gupta 1985). Mrs Gandhi 'communalized' Punjabi politics in two main respects: through appeals to a pan-Indian Hindu community at national level, and through direct intervention in the Sikh 'political system' at state level. At national level, Indira Gandhi, in her battle to assert her authority over the party organization headed by state bosses, embarked on a populist transformation of Congress which increasingly became insensitive to regional problems as she 'ruthlessly' centralized power (Brass 1991: 210). The 1969 INC split was accompanied by a growing tendency towards bypassing the regular consultative political processes and its replacement by a bureaucratic and administrative manner of decision making. This effectively withdrew, as Sudipta Kaviraj has pointed out, the most significant decisions about the state from the public political process (Kaviraj 1986). There followed a series of plebiscitary elections fought on slogans, most notably on the Bangladesh war and the eradication of poverty (*'garibi hatao'*). The progressive marginalization of the opposition and centralization of authority culminated in the declaration of a state of emergency and the suspension of parliamentary democracy in June 1975. Indeed, it was during the Emergency, when Sikh grievances were deprived of legitimate channels, that Indira Gandhi started to directly intervene in the Sikh 'political system'.

The Anandpur Sahib Resolution (ASR), a document written and largely forgotten in 1973, yet resurrected amid controversy a decade latter, afforded Indira Gandhi the opportunity to depict the SAD as a 'separatist' organization and to present herself as India's saviour, in the same way in which Nehru had branded the demand for a Punjabi *Suba* as 'communal' and had, in turn, embodied the secular principles upon which India was founded.[11] Although the demands of the ASR were primarily secular, the language used to articulate those demands enabled Indira Gandhi and the Punjab Congress Party to interpret it as a religiously inspired secessionist document. The resolution stated that the SAD 'was the very embodiment of the hopes and aspirations of the Sikh *nation*[12] and as such is fully entitled to its representation' (SAD 1973: 1, emphasis mine). A Sikh 'nation' was, thus, assumed to already be in existence whose interests were to be exclusively represented by the SAD.[13] In the ASR, the SAD resolved to achieve the following aims:

1   The propagation of Sikhism and its code of conduct, with a condemnation of atheism.
2   To preserve and keep alive the concept of the distinct and independent entity of the Panth and the creation of an environment *where Sikh sentiment can find full expression, satisfaction and growth.*
3   The eradication of poverty and starvation, by increased production and more equitable distribution of wealth and the establishment of a just social order without any exploitation.
4   The removal of illiteracy, untouchability and casteism as laid down in the Sikh scriptures.
5   To strive for the removal of diseases and ill-health, denouncement of the use of intoxicants and enlargement of facilities for physical well being to prepare the nation for national defence.

                                              (SAD 1973: 1–2, emphasis mine)

These aims bound the SAD not only to the defence and 'propagation' of 'Sikhism' as defined by the *Tat Khalsa* and institutionalized in the SGPC, but also to the creation of an 'environment where Sikh sentiment can find full expression' (SAD 1973). The ambiguity of the last statement allowed Indira Gandhi to brand the ASR secessionist, despite its commitment to 'have the Constitution of India recast in real *federal* principles' (SAD 1973, emphasis mine). It was argued that only in an independent Sikh state would Sikh sentiment find 'full expression, satisfaction and growth'. This view was compounded by the stated political goal of the SAD which was to 'seek . . . the creation of a congenial environment and a political set up' whereby the '*pre-eminence of the Khalsa*' could be established (SAD 1973: 3, emphasis in the original). In order to achieve this goal, the SAD demanded to have 'all those Punjabi-speaking areas, deliberately kept out of the Punjab . . . merged with the Punjab to constitute a single administrative unit where the interests of *Sikhs and Sikhism* are specifically protected' (SAD 1973: 4, emphasis mine). Furthermore:

> In this new Punjab and in other States, the Centre's interference would be restricted to defence, Foreign Relations, currency and general communication; all other departments would be in the jurisdiction of Punjab and other states, which would be fully entitled to frame their own laws on these subjects for administration.

                                                        (SAD 1973: 4)

Seen in this light, the ASR was nothing less than a restatement of the original Akali demand first raised before partition for a Sikh 'homeland' within India. The SAD acknowledged in Resolution no. 1 of the ASR as adopted in its 1978 conference that 'India is a federal and republican geographical entity of different languages, religions and cultures' and that consequently the above measures were needed in order to 'safeguard the fundamental rights of the religious and linguistic minorities' (SAD 1978: 2). A considerable amount of continuity, therefore, has characterized SAD demands since 1947, and it has been the centre's unwillingness to consider them which ultimately led to the tragedy of 1984. Between 1982 and 1984 the SAD under the leadership of Sant Harchand Singh Longowal led a *dharam yudh* against the Congress state government in an attempt to force them to endorse the ASR. Over 30,000 Akalis were arrested in the first two and a half months as Akali *jathas* marched out of *Darbar Sahib* every day, thus violating an order banning the assembly of more than five persons (H. Deol 2000: 105). The *dharam yudh* consisted of a series of organized *morchas* which sought to bring the Punjab to a standstill by blocking canals (*nahar-roko*), roads (*rasta-roko*) and the railways (*kam-roko*). Such activities were reminiscent of the *morchas* led by Master Tara Singh and Sant Fateh Singh in support of the Punjabi *Suba* and succeeded in mobilizing a Sikh community polarized by the Green Revolution.

Mrs Gandhi sought to meet the 'threat' to India's territorial integrity posed by the SAD by further encouraging its separatist tendencies in an attempt to split the movement and subsequently crush it. She sought to do so by supporting the fundamentalist challenge to the SAD posed by Jarnail Singh Bhindranwale and his Dal Khalsa party in the 1979 SGPC elections (Tully and Jacob 1985; Brass 1991). Initially, her alliance with Bhindranwale was fruitful, as the Akali administration lost control of the state government in the 1980 elections. However, Bhindranwale proved to be a 'Lion of the Punjab' that Mrs Gandhi couldn't tame and his actions, or rather the terrorist activities which his militancy helped inspire, soon proved to be an embarrassment to the centre by alienating their 'natural' constituency of Punjabi Hindus. The 'arrest' of Bhindranwale for the murder in September 1981 of Lala Jagat Narain, a prominent Punjabi Hindu newspaper proprietor active in both the RSS and the INC, succeeded only in driving Bhindranwale into the arms of the Akalis as the *dharam yudh* threatened to become violent. After the murder of Hindu passengers travelling on a bus to New Delhi by armed Sikh militants, seemingly in retaliation for the widespread harassment of Sikhs by the security forces, the centre imposed President's Rule in October 1983. The imposition of President's Rule marked the beginning of a resort to what Gurharpal Singh has termed 'violent control' which exposed the limitations of Mrs Gandhi's variation of her father's strategy of 'hegemonic control'.[14] After the Akalis had threatened to launch a new campaign of mass non-cooperation that included boycotting the payment of water rates and land revenue to the state government, Mrs Gandhi ordered Indian troops to storm the Golden Temple complex in June 1984 in order to finally remove the threat posed by Sikh separatism as embodied by Bhindranwale. This act of state terror reminiscent of the *Jallianwallah Bagh* massacre precipitated the 'militarization' of the Sikh *qaum* and the growth of an armed movement in the mid-1980s dedicated to the establishment of a separate Sikh state.

The militarization of the *qaum*

Although the eruption of violence was in large part a reaction to the actions of the centre, Sikh armed militancy, although not sanctioned by the SAD, pre-dated the storming of the Golden Temple. Pramod Kumar noted that in the 1980s terrorism in the Punjab had produced the highest rate of killing as compared to any other terrorist movement in the world (Kumar 1995). Historically, violence as a mode of political discourse in Punjab has been considered legitimate. The establishment of the *Khalsa* and the injunction to wear the *kirpan* legitimized the use of violence as a means of collective self-defence and, as Fox amongst others has argued, the British used religion-based martial skills as the organizing principle of fighting units. This served to reinforce the concept of martial militancy which was used effectively against the British in the period 1913–1918 by the Ghadarites and the Babbar Akalis.[15] The legitimization of the use of violence in defence of the *panth* is made possible only by the 'myths and memories' (A.D. Smith 1999) of martyrdom and sacrifice within the Sikh tradition which is embodied in the *Khalsa*. In the early part of the twentieth century, the non-violence and self-sacrifice of the Akali *jathas* during the *gurdwara* reform agitation, despite deaths at the hands of the British, won the Akalis the praise and support of the 'leader' of non-violent resistance against colonial rule, Mahatma Gandhi.[16] After independence, both Master Tara Singh and his successor, Sant Fateh Singh, fasted for the establishment of a Punjabi-speaking state and threatened self-immolation if their demands were not met. This tactic was also used after the concession of the Punjabi *Suba* by Darshan Singh Pheruman, an opponent of the moderate Akali leadership, and resulted in his death (Gurharpal Singh 2000: 109).

The movement for Khalistan gained important impetus from the 'martyrdom' of Jarnail Singh Bhindranwale (1947–1984) at the hands of the Indian state. Bhindranwale was heir to a tradition which pre-dates the founding of the *Khalsa* by Guru Gobind Singh back to Guru Arjan. As head of the *Damdami Taksal*, an influential seminary noted for its 'orthodox' *amritdhari* teachings, Bhindranwale carried a silver arrow around with him, a symbol of the tenth Guru, and spoke to the disenfranchised, alienated youth of post-Green Revolution Punjab in a language rooted entirely in a religious vocabulary steeped in the symbolism and mythology of the *Khalsa*. For Bhindranwale, the only true Sikh was an *amritdhari* willing to martyr himself for the *Khalsa panth* by fighting against its 'enemies'. The latter included 'heretical' Sikh sects such as the *Nirankaris*, Punjabi Hindus and the 'pseudo-secular' Indian state. Martyrdom, however, had to be courted by inflicting acts of violence upon the *panth*'s enemies in order to draw them out into the open. Thus, Bhindranwale, who personally identified himself with Baba Deep Singh, a victim of Mughal religious intolerance, courted martyrdom and found it in Operation Blue Star. Baba Deep Singh, according to *Tat Khalsa* 'legend', lost his head in a battle with the Ahmed Shah Abdali's Afghans but is said to have carried it in his hands to lay it down in the Golden Temple complex. Bhindranwale, who had the chance to escape the equally symbolic and violent assault upon the *Akal Takht* some two and a half centuries later by a back route, chose to stand his ground and died fighting. He is alleged to have said, 'Baba Deep Singh had to struggle for several miles to lay his head in this place, while I am privileged to be able to give mine right here' (Mahmood 1997: 23).

Although Bhindranwale did not come out in favour of *Khalistan*, his demonization of, and the violence his followers inflicted upon, *Nirankaris*, other *Sahajdhari* Sikhs and Punjabi Hindus lent support to the separatist cause. This demonization of 'threatening Others' was in keeping with the strategies and symbolism which the *Tat Khalsa* reformers had employed to create a unified, homogeneous Sikh Self. Indeed, Bhindranwale's reading of Sikh history as essentially conflictual and violent corresponds to the 'myth of the Khalsa' which McLeod outlines as the dominant interpretation of history taught in *Khalsa* schools (McLeod 1992: 244–362). What was different about Bhindranwale and the younger generation of Sikh terrorists he inspired was the means by which they chose to affirm their separateness. In the thirteen radio cassettes and the three videotapes containing his speeches, the recurring theme is that India is not a secular but a Hindu state. Sikhs are advised to acquire firearms with a view to defending themselves effectively. About *Khalistan* he remarks: 'We are neither for nor against Khalistan . . . We want to live in India as equal citizens, but if that is not possible then we have nothing against the government giving us our own state' (Bhindranwale, quoted in Ahmed 1988: 35–36). His lasting legacy to the militants such as the Khalistan Liberation Force (KLF), Khalistan Commando Force (KCF),[17] Bhindranwale Tigers (BT) and Babbar Khalsa International (BKI) that succeeded him was to 'break the state's monopoly on morally sanctioned killing' (Juergensmeyer 1992: 384). Akali leaders had never before officially sanctioned acts of violence in defence of the Sikh *qaum*, but their sacralization of secular demands and the stress placed on the *Khalsa*'s violent past and militant tradition helped provide Bhindranwale with the justification he needed to declare war on the 'enemies of the *panth*'.

Violence is, as Juergensmeyer points out, enormously empowering. The breaking of the state's monopoly of morally sanctioned violence by a younger, alienated generation of militants may be seen as a daring claim of political independence. For, through their actions, they acquired a status of authority rivalling that of the state, even going so far as to set up courts and government offices (Pettigrew 1995; Gupta 1997). Anyone who challenged their authority by recognizing that of the State was seen as a 'traitor to the *panth*' and punished accordingly. Thus, Sant Harchand Singh Longowal, who as leader of the largest Akali faction spent a lifetime seeking to further the interests of the *panth*, was murdered for signing an accord with the Indian prime minister, Rajiv Gandhi, even though important Akali demands seemed to have been conceded (but subsequently not implemented).[18] Although elections were held in 1985 as part of the Rajiv–Longowal pact which returned an Akali administration to power, with Barnala Singh becoming chief minister, they were boycotted by the United Akali Dal party, headed by Baba Joginder Singh, father of Bhindranwale. Thereafter, the SAD further split as twenty-seven MLAs led by Parkash Singh Badal left and subsequently merged with the UAD, leaving the Barnala Singh ministry dependent upon Congress support (Gurharpal Singh 2000: 132). The SAD, furthermore, lost control of the Sikh 'political system' as militant organizations such as the UAD, All-India Sikh Students' Federation (AISSF), Damdam Taksal (DT) and Panthic Committee gained control over the Golden Temple complex with the support of the armed paramilitary groups. From the *Darbar Sahib*, a *Sarbat Khalsa*, an assembly of the *Khalsa* as first instituted by Guru Gobind Singh, declared the independence of *Khalistan* on 29 April 1986. The centre reacted by returning to a strategy of 'violent control' which further undermined the 'moderate' Akali leadership whilst unleashing a wave of state terror throughout the Punjab.[19] In June 1987 it dismissed Barnala Singh's ministry and reimposed President's Rule. Consequently, the Akali leadership, out of state power and marginalized within the Sikh 'political system', 'gradually edged, often unwillingly at the prompting of armed militants, from claims of regional autonomy under the ASR (1985–1989) to Sikh self-determination (1990–1991)' (Gurharpal Singh 1992: 991). A Sikh *nation* had thus been born: one in search of statehood.

Conclusion

> [I]n each of us, in varying proportions, there is part of yesterday's man who inevitably predominates in us, since the present amounts to little compared with the long past in the course of which we were formed and from which we result. Yet we do not sense this man of the past, because he is inveterate in us; he makes up the unconscious part of ourselves.
>
> (Durkheim, quoted in Bourdieu 1977: 79)

In conclusion, it seems that the contemporary Sikh tradition upon which Sikh religio-political elites base their claims to nationhood is a result of relatively recent mobilization. We have seen how Sikh religious and political elites in the twentieth century imbued with a *Tat Khalsa* identity contributed to the construction of a Sikh national identity by *imagining* the Sikhs as an *ethnie* possessing a separate religion, history, institutions, territory and martial traditions. A distinct Sikh identity arose as a result of the dialectical interaction between the Sikh tradition and the colonial state which made the construction of a Sikh modernity centred on the mythology and symbolism of the *Khalsa* possible. Internal and external religious boundaries between Sikhs and Hindus and *Kes-dhari* and *Sahajdhari* Sikhs respectively were institutionalized first by the colonial state's project of classification and enumeration as best exemplified by the Census and subsequently by the establishment of the SGPC. The SGPC together with the various factions of the Akali Dal constitute a Sikh 'political system' which has succeeded in keeping the idea of a distinct Sikh *qaum* alive in independent, secular India through campaigns for a linguistically defined Sikh 'homeland'. The use of ethno-religious symbols to articulate that demand and its subsequent 'communal-ization' by the Indian government under Indira Gandhi created space for a *nationalist* challenge to both the Sikh 'political system' and the Indian state by armed militants seeking to create an independent Sikh state: *Khalistan*.

The legitimacy which the central institutions of the Sikh 'political system' – tarnished as they are by factionalism, allegations of corruption (in the case of the Badal faction of the Akali Dal) and past support for armed militancy (former SGPC president Gurcharan Singh Tohra) – continue to enjoy amongst the Sikhs of the Punjab lies in the Sikh religio-political establishment's successful appropriation of the mythology and symbolism of the *Khalsa*. These 'myths and memories' of the *Khalsa*, with its narratives of martyrdom and self-sacrifice, continue to resonate with *Kes-dhari* Sikhs everywhere because they are *embodied* in the 'Five Ks'. In this sense, it is impossible for a male *Kes-dhari* Sikh to escape from the 'myth of the *Khalsa*' with its violent history, as it is inscribed in his very appearance. The body thus functions as *memory*, reminding the Sikh that he is a member of a 'sovereign' religio-political *qaum*, the *Khalsa panth*, 'that his father is Guru Gobind Singh and his mother is Mata Sahib Kaur, that he was born in Kesgarh and lives in Anandpur'. That is why the Sikh body has become the battleground in the conflict between the *Khalsa panth* and the secular state, particularly in the liberal-democratic West, as we shall see in Chapters 5 to 7. For, as Bourdieu points out:

> If all societies . . . that seek to produce a new man through a process of 'deculturation' and 'reculturation' set such store on the seemingly most insignificant details of *dress, bearing*, physical and verbal *manners*, the reason is that, treating the body as memory, they entrust to it in abbreviated and practical, i.e. mnemonic, form the fundamental principles of the arbitrary content of culture. The principles em-bodied in this way are placed beyond the grasp of consciousness, and hence cannot be touched by voluntary, deliberate transformation.
>
> (Bourdieu 1977: 94, emphasis in the original)

It is the very 'em-bodiment' of *Khalsa* identity through the 'Five Ks', involving the *remembering* of the 'forgotten' Sikh tradition of martyrdom and sacrifice, that may explain the appearance of *continuity* within the Sikh

4 From *Khalistan* to *Punjabiat*

Globalization, *Hindutva* and the decline of Sikh militancy

[W]ith a Sikh Prime Minister and a Sikh army chief of staff, the shadow of 1984 can now truly be forgotten.

(K. Singh 2006)

This chapter will account for the demise of Sikh separatism in India in the Punjab in the aftermath of Operation Blue Star. It will be argued that, although the movement was initially crushed by a reassertion of state and central government power using a strategy of 'violent control' as Gurharpal Singh suggests (Singh 2000), the demise of Congress hegemony afforded Sikh elites an opportunity to articulate Sikh demands to the Indian political system from *within* the democratic system. The economic reforms which Dr Manmohan Singh initiated as finance minister in Narasimha Rao's government in particular facilitated a structural transformation in Indian politics, economics and society resulting in both regional and Hindu 'nationalist' challenges to the Congress 'system' (Kothari 1964).

The Congress 'one-party dominance' system had, in any case, started to rot from within. This process, as the previous chapter made clear, accelerated under Indira Gandhi's ruthless centralization of power as the state became increasingly repressive and, after 1980, chauvinistic (Gupta 1985, 1997; Kaviraj 1986; Brass 1991, 1994 [1990]; Kothari 1998). The assassination of the prime minister by her Sikh bodyguards led to the further communalization of Indian politics by allowing the INC, in the immediate aftermath of her death, to juxtapose a Hindu/Indian 'Self' against a Sikh 'Other', with tragic consequences for the Sikhs of Delhi (see Chapter 5). This facilitated the re-emergence, consolidation and articulation by the Rashtriya Swayamsevak Sangh (RSS) of a Hindu 'nationalist' ideology which, although long suppressed by the Nehruvian state, informed the way in which the state dealt with ethno-religious minorities in practice. For the RSS and its political wing, the Bharatiya Janata Party (BJP), however, Muslims replaced Sikhs as the 'Other' against which the Hindu 'Self' defined itself. This has precipitated the emergence of an SAD (Badal)–BJP alliance in the Punjab which has successfully contested state elections by emphasizing a *regional* rather than a religious/national identity, thus easing communal tensions. The scars of 1984, however, have not completely healed, and the SAD (Badal) has faced challenges to its legitimacy from *within* the Sikh religio-political system.

Paradoxically, the very failure of the BJP to 'rebrand' India as a homogeneous Hindu nation-state based on 'One Nation, One People and One Culture' (BJP 2004) has given the INC an opportunity to heal those scars at both a regional and a national level. At a regional level, the INC has also embraced a regionalist discourse under Captain Amarinder Singh. In particular, Amarinder Singh's decision, as chief minister, to unilaterally abrogate the 1981 river waters treaty with neighbouring states as chief minister removed a key Akali grievance against the centre. Furthermore, the appointment of Dr Manmohan Singh as prime minister, by the INC president – and Rajiv Gandhi's widow – Sonia Gandhi, has convinced many Sikhs formerly sympathetic to the militant cause to move away, at least temporarily, from *Khalistan* and to focus on Punjab.

Economic liberalization in India

Although economic globalization in South Asia precedes the contemporary phase of liberalization, the introduction of wide-ranging economic liberalization measures in South Asia coincided with the end of the Cold War. No longer able to count on the continued economic support of the Soviet Union and the markets of Eastern Bloc countries, India under the then finance minister, Dr Manmohan Singh, arguably had no alternative but to seek an IMF stand-by loan when confronted by an acute balance of payments crisis in August 1991. The Indian economy had hitherto followed a policy of import substitution and state socialism since independence which was seen as necessary in order to remedy the legacies of colonial rule: backwardness and poverty. On the eve of independence, India's first prime minister, Jawaharlal Nehru, made a 'tryst with destiny' which included a commitment to 'the ending of poverty and ignorance and disease and the inequality of opportunity'. In his speech to the Constituent Assembly, he argued that:

> Freedom and power bring responsibility. The responsibility rests upon this Assembly, a sovereign body representing the sovereign people of India. Before the birth of freedom, we have endured all the pains of labour and our hearts are heavy with the memory of this sorrow. Some of those pains continue even now. Nevertheless, the past is over and it is the future that beckons to us now. That future is not one of ease or resting but of incessant striving so that we might fulfil the pledges we have so often taken and the One we shall take today. The service of India means the service of the millions who suffer. It means the ending of poverty and ignorance and disease and inequality of opportunity. The ambition of the greatest man of our generation has been to wipe every tear from every

eye. That may be beyond us but as long as there are tears and suffering, so long our work will not be over.

(Nehru 1947)

India, in Nehru's words, must 'break with the dead wood of the past and not allow it to dominate the present' (Nehru 2003 [1945]: 509). Science offered a way forward since it 'opened up innumerable avenues for the growth of knowledge and added to the power of man to such an extent that for the first time it was possible to conceive that man could triumph over and shape his physical environment' (Nehru 2003 [1945]: 511). In achieving mastery over nature with the application of modern scientific techniques to the economy, Indians would cast off their narrow outlooks and act as a people. The appalling poverty and rural misery that India was faced with at present were attributed to colonial *policies* not with the instruments of governmentality they had introduced. Nehru argued against Gandhi, that there was nothing quintessentially *Western* about modernity; modernity was universal. The state, although an instrument of oppression and exploitation under colonial rule, would behave differently once independence had been achieved. It would become a vehicle for national liberation and rejuvenation, bringing tangible, material rewards for the 'sons of the soil'. However, by tying the legitimacy of the new national state to its ability to meet the needs of its citizens, Nehru created opportunities for challenges, by 'communal' organizations, to the state's authority in times of economic decline or hardship.

Planning was central to the achievement of this task. The establishment of the Planning Commission in 1950 enabled the state to direct India's economy through a series of five-year plans. As a result of state intervention in the economy, India was able to record high rates of growth in the early years of independence. The 1950s and 1960s saw rates of industrial growth of around 7 per cent per annum (Corbridge and Harriss 2000: 60). However, although economic development and the alleviation of poverty were stated government goals, India was unable to match the success of its neighbours in East Asian states in the years that followed. Between 1970 and 1982, India recorded a growth rate of just 4.3 per cent per annum (Corbridge and Harriss 2000: 78).

Neo-liberals have long contrasted the success of the export-led strategies of the East Asian 'tiger economies' with the import substitution strategies adopted by states in Latin America and India. According to one of the architects of India's present policy of economic liberalization, Jagdish Bhagwati:

> the energy, talents, and worldly ambitions of India's many millions . . . need merely an appropriate policy framework to produce the economic magic that Jawaharlal Nehru wished for his compatriots but which, like many well-meaning intellectuals of his time, he mistakenly sought in now discredited economic doctrines.

(Bhagwati 1993: 98)

However, India fared poorly not only in comparison to the 'tiger economies' but also to the People's Republic of China (PRC) and other socialist societies. Sen and Drèze make the point that India has been left behind by societies that have pursued a variety of different economic policies, from market-oriented capitalism to communist-led socialism (Sen and Drèze 1999: 2). Despite no major famine occurring in India since independence (Sen and Drèze 1999: 181), rural and urban poverty remained endemic, with almost half the population living below the poverty line in 1960–1961 (Corbridge and Harriss 2000: 62).

In contrast to the conventional neo-liberal wisdom, India's failure to realize Nehru's 'tryst with destiny' was not primarily economic but political, lying in the failure of the Nehruvian leadership to 'institutionalize their ideological preferences' (Kothari 1998). The state elite, led by Nehru, that had inherited power from the British enjoyed an unprecedented degree of legitimacy, having led India to independence during the freedom struggle and presided over the adoption of a Constitution which proclaimed India's commitment to a *democratic* socialist path. However, the Nehruvian leadership of the Congress Party entered into alliances to achieve its developmental goals with regional power-brokers who managed to blunt the radical thrust of the policies of the central government. This resulted in the institutionalization of a system which led to the 'growing marginalization of millions of people, increasing inequity . . . and growing discontent over time' (Kothari 1998: 28) which benefited the classes which dominated India's post-colonial political economy. Following Bardhan, these can be identified as the industrial capitalist class or *bourgeoisie*, the rich farmers or kulaks and the public sector professionals or bureaucrats (Bardhan 1984: 54). These classes were drawn from different sections of India's diverse population and by no means had developed a common ideological framework by the time of independence. Indeed, the conflict of interests between the urban and industrial classes on the one hand and the kulak[1] class on the other has become more acute in recent years and has continued to frustrate the government's attempts to reform the economy. For Corbridge and Harriss, the economic dominance of this numerically small class of rich peasants, which controls a large share of the land, is bound up with the 'reproduction of the pervasive poverty which is overwhelmingly characteristic of India' (Corbridge and Harriss 2000: 83).

The onset of economic liberalization, however, has disproportionately benefited the dominant classes, giving rise to even greater inequality between an expanding high-income, predominantly Hindu middle class and the urban and rural poor. The implementation of structurally adjusted policies (SAPs) has led to the deregulation of the economy and privatization; reduced public expenditure; devaluation; and an increase in foreign direct investment. Since 1991 numerous measures have been adopted to remove restrictions on the role of private enterprise in India, and export-led growth has become a major thrust of India's strategy. As a result of these economic reforms, India's manufacturing industries have witnessed dramatic growth of between 6 and 10 per cent per annum,[2] leading to the accumulation of huge foreign exchange resources, estimated at $131,934 million (EIU 2006: 5). The dismantling of the infamous 'licensing and permit Raj', whereby every company seeking to invest in India needed to obtain a permit from the government, led to an increase in foreign direct investment as important fields which were earlier closed to foreign investors, like mining, oil exploration, transport and telecommunications, were opened. Of particular importance has been India's entry into the field of Information Technology as a major source of cheap, skilled software engineers.

However, the globalization process in India has so far focused on integrating markets without improving the condition of the rural and urban poor. Indeed, for most South Asians the outcomes of globalization have been higher prices, fewer employment opportunities, increased disparities in income and a higher incidence of poverty (Mahbub Ul Haq Human Development Centre 2002: 17). Existing low levels of expenditure on health, poverty alleviation programmes and education either have been maintained or are declining, whilst military spending after 9/11 shows no sign of decreasing. The *Human Development in South Asia 2001* report estimated that about *half a billion* people have experienced a decline in their incomes in South Asia during the globalization phase (Mahbub Ul Haq Human Development Centre 2002: 2). Although the authors of the report did claim that eventually everyone would gain from economic liberalization, the benefits of economic growth have hitherto been disproportionately enjoyed by the educated urban population, India's new 'middle class', who have the social, economic, cultural and political capital to take advantage of the greater mobility of capital and labour (Fernandes 2006). The poor, meanwhile, have borne the heaviest burden of the costs of structural adjustment: 34.7 per cent of India's population live on less than $1 a day, 24 per cent are undernourished and 39 per cent are unable to read or write (see Table 4.1).

It would seem, therefore, that greater economic integration has yet to translate into a sustained reduction in absolute poverty, as Indian Prime Minister Dr Manmohan Singh recognized in his speech marking the fifty-ninth anniversary of India's independence:

> India is certainly on the march. Yet, we have miles to go before we can truly say that we have made our tryst with destiny. Sixty years ago,

Table 4.1 Indian development indicators, 2000–2005

	HDI rank (2005)	Population living below $1 (%) (2003)	Under-nourished people (% of total population) (2001)	Adult literacy rate (%) (2003)	GDP per capita (US$ at PPP) (2003)
India	127	34.7	24	61	2,892

Adapted from UNDP (2003: 199, 2005: 219–253); EIU (2002: 18, 2005: 25, 2006: 5).

Panditji told us that the two challenges before a free India was to end the ancient scourge of poverty, ignorance and disease and end the inequality of opportunity. India has marched a great distance forward in these sixty years, but the challenge of banishing poverty remains with us. We have yet to banish hunger from our land. We have yet to eradicate illiteracy. We have yet to ensure that every Indian enjoys good health.

(Manmohan Singh 2006)

Once *the* critical, if not primary, goal of economic development, the eradication of poverty – despite lip-service from Manmohan Singh – now appears a distant aspiration and has effectively been *privatized*. The burden of poverty alleviation has fallen disproportionately on civil society, with non-governmental organizations (NGOs) becoming the principal dispensers of welfare in South Asia (Pasha 1996: 637–638). Although the triumph of the INC in the 2004 elections has been widely interpreted as representing a victory for the Nehruvian principles upon which India was founded in 1947, there has been no radical rethinking of India's commitment to economic liberalization, which has led to impressive rates of economic growth, but also greater human insecurity, which has also been felt in the once prosperous rural Punjab. Neither have the INC and its allies been able to provide an ideological riposte to the BJP's attempt to rebrand India as a predominately *Hindu* polity.

Rebranding India: the challenge of Hindu nationalism

According to the hegemonic neo-liberal or hyperglobalist variant of globalization theory, economic globalization, or the expansion of capitalism, inevitably leads to the dissemination of liberal ideas about rights and radically alters the relationship between the individual and community. This in turn leads to greater *secularization* and *democratization*: the separation of the religious and the political spheres and the strengthening of liberal-democratic structures (Held *et al.* 1999; Scholte 2005). In India, however, the onset of economic globalization has transformed the political landscape, resulting in an ethno-religious revival which has challenged the secular foundations of the Indian state, first in the Punjab with the onset of the Green Revolution in the 1970s (see Chapter 3) and then, in the 1990s, in India as a whole.

In India, globalization has contributed to the emergence of a Hindu cultural nationalism as advocated by the BJP. Hindu nationalism may be seen as a middle-class, high-caste project of 'cultural homogenization' (Appadurai 1996) that seeks to create a unified, homogeneous Hindu political identity by subsuming regional differences and caste hierarchies under the general category of 'Hindu'. Hindu nationalists maintain that, in a modern, democratic polity, the culture of the majority should prevail in the public domain. Hinduism, for Hindu nationalists, because of its innate tolerance for diversity, permits minority cultures to flourish and is constitutive of an Indian national culture. Hence the BJP's election manifesto refers to India's 'unique cultural and social diversity' which it believes has been 'woven into a larger civilizational fabric by thousands of years of common living ... shared values, beliefs, customs, struggles, joy and sorrow' (BJP 2004).

The India imagined by the BJP is one rebranded as a centralized, economically and militarily powerful nation-state with a unitary culture based on *Hindutva*. *Hindutva* is described as a 'unifying principle which alone can preserve the unity and integrity' of India and 're-energize' its soul in order to build a 'strong and prosperous nation' (BJP 1996: 6). In 2004, the BJP reaffirmed its commitment to *Hindutva* by claiming that it could 'trigger a higher level of patriotism that can transform the country to greater levels of efficiency and performance' and thus make 'India a global economic power' (BJP 2004). *Hindutva*, in other words, is conducive to economic growth, and its ethics are the 'spirit of Indian capitalism' (Hansen 1998).

As Gurpreet Mahajan has pointed out, the agenda of Hindu cultural majoritarianism rests upon two assumptions. First, Hindu nationalists believe that nation-states can only be built around a shared cultural identity. Second, Hindu nationalists maintain that Hinduism is not a religion per se but a 'way of life' that is, and should be, the basis of a shared cultural and national identity (Mahajan 2002: 47). This assumption is borne out by an examination of the experience of most 'secular' nation-states in the West. Diverse religious traditions are tolerated in the modern West, and rights to freedom of worship are guaranteed, but the West, with the possible exception of ultra-secular France and the United States, continues to be defined with reference to Christian and post-Christian values.[3] By 'secularizing' Hinduism, Hindu nationalists claim that it is the shared identity of *all* peoples of India, irrespective of which *religion* an individual chooses to profess. The transformation of Hinduism into the shared identity of the people of India erases the differences between ethno-religious communities expressed in the Constitution.

The origins of Hindu nationalism lie in the Hindu revivalist movements of the colonial era, specifically the *Arya Samaj* in the Punjab and *Brahmo Samaj* in Bengal. Both movements attempted to redefine Hinduism as a religious tradition, intelligible to the colonial authorities and the proselytizing Christian missionaries. According to Chetan Bhatt:

> [t]he idea of revelation and the literal word of God embodied in a text (accurately speaking, itself foreign to Hinduism), the infallibility of sacred books, a singular already written truth and one organizational structure ('the Vedic Church') were seemingly borrowed from the 'semitic' religions.
>
> (Bhatt 2001: 18)

The politicization of Hindu identity dates to the First All India (*Akhil Bharatiya*) Hindu Mahasabha Conference held in 1914. The Hindu Mahasabha became the main organization for the articulation of a Hindu political identity in the colonial period and retained an uneasy relationship with the nominally secular Indian National Congress (INC) during the independence movement.

Central to the Hindu nationalist project is the concept of *Hindutva*, which stood in sharp contrast to the secular nationalism of the INC. Associated with the work of Veer Savarkar (1883–1966), who led the Hindu Mahasabha, the term *Hindutva* refers to an *ethnicized* Hindu identity. While Hinduism may be understood as a socio-religious philosophy based on the *Vedas* which is indigenous to India, *Hindutva* refers not only to the religious aspect of the Hindu people but 'comprehends even their cultural, linguistic, social and political aspects as well' (Savarkar 1998: 115). The 'Hindus' are thus imagined as both a religious and an ethnic community and, in Savarkar's writings, assume an almost racial dimension. For Savarkar, the Hindus 'are not only a nation but a *jati* [race], a born brotherhood' (Savarkar 1923: 89). *All* Indians, including those professing other religions, are considered Hindus, with the exception of Muslims and Christians: 'Every person is a Hindu who regards . . . this land from the Indus to the seas, as his fatherland as well as his holyland – i.e., the land of the origin of his religion, the cradle of his faith' (Savarkar 1998: 115). Muslim and Christians, however, were regarded as 'foreigners, since "Hindustan"[4] is not to them a holyland . . . [T]heir holyland is far off in Arabia or Palestine' (Savarkar 1998: 113). The hostility towards religious minorities, as seen in the recent attacks on Christians and periodic pogroms against Muslims, is coupled with a defence of the hegemony of the higher castes. For Savarkar, 'all the caste system has done is to regulate its noble blood on lines believed . . . by our saintly law-givers and kings to contribute most to fertilise all that was barren and poor, without famishing all that was flourishing and nobly endowed' (1998: 86).

Created by a resolution of the Hindu Mahasabha in 1932, the Rashtriya Swayamsevak Sangh (RSS) provides the institutional infrastructure for the articulation of this Hindu nationalist ideology. Although the RSS was briefly banned following the assassination of Gandhi by an ex-RSS member in 1948, today it can claim to be the largest voluntary organization in the world after decades of disciplined, well-managed organizational and ideological expansion. Others have seen it as a more sinister organization. Chetan Bhatt has claimed that 'it is the largest voluntary, private, paramilitary body existing in any nation' (Bhatt 2001: 113). The RSS's second leader, Golwalkar (1906–1973), is credited with playing a vital role in the development of Hindu nationalism by linking Savarkar's conception of *Hindutva* with an 'ideology of xenophobic racism' (Bhatt 2001: 126). The RSS considers itself the parent of the 'family' of affiliated organizations and movements: the Sangh Parivar. In 1964, the RSS formed the Vishwa Hindu Parishad (VHP) to mobilize Hindus throughout the world, and in 1980 the Bharatiya Janata Party (BJP), the political wing of the RSS, was formed out of the Jana Sangh.

The Jana Sangh[5] had been part of the governing Janata Dal coalition, but its share of the vote had declined to 7.4 per cent in the 1977 election, from 9.4 per cent in 1967. Although the BJP won only two seats in the 1984 Lok Sabha election it has steadily increased its share of the vote in every election it has contested whilst adopting a distinct Hindu identity and advocating policies of economic liberalization. Corbridge and Harriss (2000) have seen this as the beginnings of what they term an 'elite revolt' against the Nehruvian consensus of secularism and state socialism. In the 1989 general election, the BJP campaigned on a militant *Hindutva* agenda based upon the building of a temple to Lord Ram[6] in Ayodhya and scrapping Article 370 of the Constitution, which granted Kashmir exceptional status in comparison with other states. It correspondingly increased its representation to eighty-six seats in the Lok Sabha and became part of V.P. Singh's National Front Coalition. However, its opposition to the 1990 decision to implement the 1980 Mandal Commission report which recommended quotas for public sector jobs for the lower castes led to collapse of the coalition government. The BJP leader, Lal Krishna Advani, embarked on a *rath yatra*, a mass procession through North India in a Toyota jeep decorated as Ram's chariot, and in the 1991 election the BJP campaigned on the slogan 'Toward Ram *Rajya*',[7] winning 120 seats in the Lok Sabha and 20.1 per cent of the popular vote, capturing the states of Uttar Pradesh, Madhya Pradesh, Himachal Pradesh and Rajasthan. Its 1996 election manifesto committed the BJP to *Hindutva* as 'a unifying principle which alone can preserve the unity and integrity' of India and to building a temple to Ram in Ayodhya where the *Babri Masjid* once stood. Consequently, the BJP increased its share of seats to 161 in the 1996 elections and formed a government for two weeks before losing a vote of no confidence. By 1998, the BJP had emerged as the largest political party in India's governing coalition, winning 25.6 per cent of the vote. Its leader, Atal Behari Vajpayee, was India's prime minister from October 1999 to May 2004.

Although the BJP has appeared to dilute its *Hindutva* ideology since Vajpayee became leader in 1992, the rise of Hindu nationalism as articulated, amongst other organizations, by the BJP has been accompanied by a rise in communal violence between the different religious communities of South Asia. Perhaps the most notorious example was the 1992 destruction of the *Babri Masjid* by RSS *kar sevaks* (volunteers), which led to the dismissal of BJP-controlled state governments by the Congress-controlled central government. Hindu nationalists had long believed that the *Babri Masjid* mosque in Ayodhya in the heart of the 'Hindi belt' had been built on the site of a temple to Ram. Indeed, a lot of recent government 'scholarship' has attempted to scientifically prove this to be the case. The destruction of the mosque was followed by an unprecedented attack upon Muslim communities in late 1992 and early 1993 throughout India (Bhatt 2001: 196). In Mumbai, Shiv Sena, a regional party based in Maharashtra espousing a particularly virulent form of Hindu nationalism under the leadership of Bal Thackeray, systematically planned mob attacks upon Muslim individuals and businesses in India's financial capital.

Once in power, the BJP sought to distance itself from its more extreme supporters in the Sangh Parivar. However, the communal carnage in Gujarat led to allegations of the state government's alleged complicity in the violence. The burning of fifty-nine Hindus in the Sabarmati Express train at Godhra on 27 February 2002 led to a pogrom of Muslims in Gujarat. Over 2,500 were brutally murdered by Hindu mobs and 200,000 families displaced as the BJP-led state government refused to intervene (EIU 2003: 12). Some have considered it 'genocide', given the systematic and planned nature of the killings.[8] Certainly there were mass killings and rapes on grounds of religion. Muslims were sought out not because of any even imagined complicity in the precipitating event at Godhra, but simply because they were Muslims. Furthermore, there is evidence to suggest a degree of state complicity if not involvement.[9] Despite refusing to condemn the mass murder of some of his constituents, the Gujarat chief minister, Narendra Modi, was duly re-elected six months after the atrocities and he appeared to derive political capital from the events. Similarly, the Indian prime minister, Vajpayee, seemed to be condoning the massacre by telling the BJP Party Congress in Goa shortly after that, 'had a conspiracy not been hatched to burn alive the innocent passengers of the Sabarmati Express, then the subsequent tragedy in Gujarat could have been averted' (Vajpayee, cited in Nussbaum 2003).

The coexistence of extreme wealth and poverty unleashed by economic liberalization undoubtedly played a role in exacerbating communal tensions, particularly as it tends to reinforce the religious divide. Although in Hindu nationalist discourse Muslims are represented as foreign invaders, the majority of South Asia's Muslims were converts from lower-caste backgrounds. According to the 2001 Census, Muslims account for 12.2 per cent of the total Indian population of over 1 billion and, despite fifty years of state-sponsored 'secularism', Muslims remain underrepresented in both the public and the private sector, further education and levels of literacy. Conversely, Muslims have a higher or far higher than proportionate representation in terms of poverty, illiteracy and unemployment (Bhatt 2001: 197).The Muslim community in Gujarat, however, was one of the more prosperous in the country and there is evidence to suggest that economic motives lay behind the killings there, as Muslim businesses, factories and farms were targeted by Hindu mobs (*Communalism Combat* 2002).

The post-9/11 international climate, combined with the periodic attacks by Islamic insurgents in Kashmir and the manipulation of partition memories by Hindu nationalists, has created a climate in which indiscriminate murder of Muslims and other minorities can both take place and be condoned by India's political leaders. In Punjab, Amnesty International report that 'the vast majority of police officers responsible for human rights violations during the period of civil unrest . . . continued to evade justice despite the recommendations of several judicial inquiries and commissions' (Amnesty International 2006).

Globalization, regionalism and the 'new democratic alignment': an analysis of the 2004 elections

Despite having a clear vision of where it wanted to take India, of how to *rebrand* India, the BJP lost the 2004 Lok Sabha elections. The elections had been brought forward to capitalize on the 'feel-good factor' which had swept the nation, as reflected in the 2003 State Assembly elections, which the BJP won, and was captured in the BJP slogan: 'India Shining'. The increased tactical awareness of minority voters, its neglect of its traditional support base, its poor choice of electoral allies and the effects of its neo-liberal economic policies upon the rural masses which make up an estimated 80 per cent of India's population ultimately led to its defeat in the 2004 elections. The INC emerged as the largest party, winning 145 seats to the BJP's 138, and it captured 26.53 per cent of the popular vote as compared to 22.15 per cent for the BJP (Election Commission of India 2004: 122–125). Together with its allies in the United Progressive Alliance (UPA), it controlled 217 seats to the 186 of the BJP-led National Democratic Alliance (NDA) and formed the government with the support of the Left parties (*Tribune* 2004c). The return of the INC to power as the largest party in the UPA governing coalition should not, however, be seen as a vindication of the Nehruvian vision, or 'myth', of a democratic, socialist India, but evidence of the further *regionalization* and democratization of Indian politics following the demise of the Congress 'one-party dominance' system.

The imperatives of electoral politics in a quasi-federal, multi-religious, multi*national* and poly-ethnic society such as India meant that the BJP was reliant upon the support of regional coalition partners outside of its traditional heartland of the Hindi-speaking belt of northern India. This led to a contradiction which the BJP leadership under Vajpayee, despite its renowned coalition-building skills, ultimately failed to reconcile. On the one hand, the BJP needed to play down the *Hindutva* rhetoric in order to appeal to its coalition partners in the NDA, particularly in the south of India. On the other hand, any attempt to 'water down' its *Hindutva* ideology ran the risk of alienating its hard-core supporters in the Hindi belt of northern India. Indeed, the RSS criticized the BJP for neglecting its ideological commitment to *Hindutva* and considered this to be a primary reason for the BJP's defeat. Certainly, the BJP itself may be considered a victim of its own complacency with regard to its traditional supporters. Many *kar sevaks* may well have campaigned less vociferously for the BJP in the 2004 election or even stayed at home, since the polls had consistently shown the BJP in the lead. Staying at home or abstaining from campaigning may well have been a way for the rank-and-file members of the RSS to show displeasure at the government's 'inclusive' policies and may have cost the BJP forty-four seats (Price 2004).

Although the BJP performed poorly in the election, its election partners in the NDA performed worse. The NDA lost fifty-one seats in two states alone, Andhra Pradesh and Tamil Nadu, both of which lay outside the Hindi belt in the supposedly 'shining' South. In Andhra Pradesh, the Telugu Desam Party (TDP), headed by arguably the 'poster-boy' of the new 'shining' India, Chandrababu Naidu, lost twenty-four seats. Although not formally part of the NDA, the TDP had lent its support to the NDA, and its chief minister, Naidu, had been internationally lauded as a modern state leader, by succeeding in attracting much-needed foreign direct investment in the key IT sector of India's 'shining' economy. The fact that Chief Minister Naidu was the victim of a failed assassination attempt makes it all the more surprising that the TDP lost. Similarly, the BJP's decision to align itself with the All-India Anna Dravida Munnetra Kazhagam (AIADMK) in Tamil Nadu, after the withdrawal of the Dravida Munnetra Kazhagam (DMK) from the NDA coalition over comments by the BJP president, Venkaiah Naidu, cost the NDA dear. Despite winning a larger share of the popular vote than any other party in Tamil Nadu, the AIADMK lost ten seats and failed to win a single seat in the wake of the DMK decision to join the Congress-led UPA. Congress, the DMK and the smaller Communist parties gained seats at the AIADMK's expense (CSDS 2004; Election Commission of India 2004).

However, this begs the question of *why* the TDP and, to a lesser extent, the AIADMK performed so poorly. Were the reasons purely regional or can we see the rejection of key NDA allies as part of a *national* trend against the NDA? Although regional factors may have been uppermost in the minds of the electorate in Andhra Pradesh, the 2004 election can be read as a verdict against the pro-growth and anti-poor policies of the NDA. In the National Election Study of 2004 carried out by the Centre for the Study of Developing Societies (CSDS) more than two-thirds of the approximately 23,000 sample respondents stated that the reforms carried out by the NDA had benefited only the upper middle class, with 30 per cent of the very poor 'dissatisfied' – as opposed to 12 per cent 'satisfied' – with their current financial situation (CSDS 2004). The main beneficiaries of the BJP's failure to meet the perceived needs of India's poor have been the Communist-dominated Left parties, which captured fifty-nine seats, suggesting that the BJP's campaign to highlight India's rapid economic growth through its 'India Shining' campaign backfired. According to a Chatham House report, the 'India Shining' campaign merely highlighted that many Indians were being 'left out', with the country's successes concentrated geographically in urban areas in the South and West and among the 'new middle class' (Price 2004).

In conclusion, the 2004 elections saw a further consolidation of what Kothari had earlier termed a 'new democratic alignment' (Kothari 1998), which first emerged over a decade ago as part of a United Front government under the prime ministership of, first, H.D. Dewe Gowda (1996–1997) and, secondly, the Punjabi I.K. Gujral (1997–1998). This 'new democratic alignment' stood in opposition to neo-liberal globalization, 'the new national chauvinism in the name of religion', the erosion of faith in the political process, and state repression (Kothari 1998: 30). It consisted of a broad alliance of hitherto marginalized political actors, including Dalits, scheduled castes and tribes, lower-caste groups and ethno-religious minorities, which used the democratic system to challenge upper-caste and class hegemonies on a local level. These groups were also opposed to the centralizing tendencies of both the INC and the BJP and committed to 'resizing' and 'reshaping' the Indian state (Gurharpal Singh 2000) to give states greater autonomy within the Indian union.

Globalization, the SAD–BJP alliance and the reassertion of Punjabi identity in post-Blue Star Punjab

One of the BJP's more important regional allies is the SAD (Badal) in Punjab, which won eight out of the ten seats it contested in the 2004 elections (Election Commission of India 2004: 110). The SAD (Badal) had re-emerged as the dominant faction of the Shiromani Akali Dal after the reversion to what Gurharpal Singh refers to as 'hegemonic control' in the Punjab. Singh sees India as 'an ethnic democracy'[10] where 'hegemonic and violent control is exercised over minorities . . . thereby creating the conditions for the resilience of ethno-nationalist separatist movements in the latter regions' (Gurharpal Singh 2000: 35). Where ethnic groups have contested violently the nature of hegemonic control, which exists where the main ethnic group can 'effectively dominate another through its political, economic and ideological resources and can extract what it requires from the subordinated' (Gurharpal Singh 2000: 47), the Indian state has readily resorted to 'violent control'. This is best exemplified by the crushing of Sikh militancy by the Indian state between 1984 and 1992 which killed an estimated 25,000–30,000 people (Gurharpal Singh 2000: 125–179).

The post-Blue Star period was indeed characterized by massive state repression and the 'securitization' of Sikhism by the Indian state: that is to say, by the extension of the instruments of state power over the Sikh 'political system'. The widespread use of violence by the state and militants resulted in a complete 'de-politicisation of the social life and institutions of governance' (Jodhka 2005) which reduced the Punjab to silence. The physical elimination of the militants through staged police encounters and military operations such as Operations Woodrose[11] and Black Thunder[12] allowed the previously discredited moderate faction under the leadership of former Chief Minister Parkash Singh Badal to reassert control over the decimated Akali movement and rekindle their anti-Congress alliance with Hindu nationalists. Whereas previously Badal and the SAD had worked with the Jana Sangh, which had a following among those very urban Hindus who had opposed the creation of a *Punjabi Suba*, now they entered into an electoral alliance with the BJP. In order to accommodate their electoral partner, the SAD (Badal) had to distance itself from the separatist demand for *Khalistan*, as embraced by other Akali leaders such as Simranjit Singh Mann, and emphasize a regional identity which could transcend the historically contradictory class interests of the rural *Jat* landowners and the urban Hindu entrepreneurs.

This it has managed to do with considerable success. As part of a coalition with the BJP, it was able to win the 1997 Punjab Legislative Assembly elections, winning 75 out of a total of 117 seats and capturing 37.6 per cent of the popular vote (Election Commission of India 1997: 10). A decade later, Parkash Singh Badal was again re-elected chief minister as the SAD (Badal)–BJP alliance was returned to power in an election characterized by the almost complete absence of religious or *panthic* issues. The SAD–BJP alliance succeeded in getting 45.37 per cent of the vote compared to the INC's share of just under 41 per cent (*Tribune* 2007b). Aside from the personal battle, and mutual antipathy, between Badal and the INC chief minister, Captain Amarinder Singh, the major issues which dominated the elections were related to neo-liberal globalization, namely 'economic growth and development, unemployment, inflation and corruption, besides growing incidence of suicide among farmers due to mounting debts' (*Tribune* 2007d). The SAD (Badal) manifesto promised to 'unleash the State's developmental potential in all spheres' and to provide food to the poor at subsidized rates and free health insurance cover for farmers and landless labourers if returned to power (*Hindu* 2007).

On being re-elected chief minister for a fourth time, Badal pledged to 'put development, rule of law and civilized values in public life back on course' – a reference to the alleged corruption of Captain Amarinder Singh, who in turn had instigated legal proceedings against the Badals on the same charge when in power. No mention was made of Sikh or *panthic* issues. Instead, a *Punjabi* as opposed to Sikh identity was asserted: 'People have given us a direction to take Punjab forward and make it a spearhead in global development and progress. We will commit ourselves to these tasks from the day one of the new government' (*Tribune* 2007c). This (re)assertion of a Punjabi identity was in part a response to the efforts of Captain Amarinder Singh to 'rebrand the Congress Party from one obsessed with national issues to one rooted in the economy, history and culture of Punjab' (Pritam Singh 2007: 466). His efforts had paid dividends, as he ousted Badal, who had denied him a ticket as an Akali in 1997, to become chief minister in the 2002 elections. The INC won sixty-two seats as opposed to the SAD's forty-one, with the BJP losing fifteen seats to secure just three (Election Commission of India 2002). Captain Amarinder Singh had been able to win over many Akali voters who were impressed by his personal integrity in having quit the INC after Blue Star, and he repaid their trust by passing a river water bill in the Punjab assembly which unilaterally abrogated the previous river water treaties signed with Haryana and Rajasthan in 1981 – a key Akali demand since the ASR that the previous SAD administration had not even attempted. This left 'a deep impact on the consciousness of all sections of Punjabi people, especially the Sikh peasantry' (Pritam Singh 2007: 466). According to some observers, the Akalis had perhaps been more interested 'in re-establishing their credentials as a mainstream political formation, a party that believed in the sanctity of the Indian Constitution and the parliamentary system of democracy', than in fulfilling the key demands of their constituents. The general issues which concerned the Sikh community as a whole were 'relegated to the background' as the Akalis 'catered to their traditional class base, the agrarian rich' (Jodhka 2005).

The Akali neglect of the needs of the more disadvantaged sections of the community whose livelihoods had been destroyed by the commercialization and mechanization of agriculture cost the SAD (Badal) dear in the 2002 State Assembly elections. Although the traditional class base of the Akalis has benefited from the introduction of market-oriented agricultural reforms, the adverse consequences of economic liberalization and neo-liberal globalization have been particularly felt in the agricultural sector, with declining numbers of cultivators and agricultural labourers. The number of cultivators in the total number of workers in the Punjab declined from 31.44 per cent in 1991 to 22.60 per cent by 2001 and that of labourers from 23.82 per cent to 16.30 per cent. Altogether only 39 per cent of the working population of the state – as opposed to 58 per cent nationally – are involved in agriculture, despite the fact that over two-thirds of the population live in rural areas (Jodhka 2006). The changing nature of the region's political economy has furthermore transformed the Punjab's caste structure. Although caste had not previously played a significant role in Punjab politics, Punjab has the highest proportion of scheduled castes in India, accounting for nearly 29 per cent of the total population of the state (GOI 2001). Over the past two decades, a large proportion of Dalits in Punjab have consciously dissociated themselves from their traditional occupations and attempted to free themselves from locally dominant castes by distancing themselves from everyday engagement with the agrarian economy and building their own *gurdwaras* (Jodhka 2002). However, the Bahujan Samaj Party (BSP), the traditional party of the lower and scheduled castes, has been unable to capitalize on their discontent, and the INC has been the main beneficiary.

In sum, the 'return to region' (Jodhka 2005) under the INC further underlined the emergence of a regionalist discourse characterized by *Punjabiat*: an attachment to the Punjab which transcends religious boundaries. Candidates, such as Simranjit Singh Mann of the SAD (Amritsar) party, who raised *panthic* issues found themselves increasingly isolated from the mainstream of Punjabi politics. Mann fared poorly in the 2004 general elections, winning no seats and picking up only 3.79 per cent of the popular vote in the Punjab (Election Commission of India 2004: 129). This, in turn, allowed the Badal faction to reassert its hegemony within the Sikh 'political system' by further marginalizing its more militant opponents.

After Operation Blue Star, a power struggle developed at the heart of the Sikh 'political system' between the SGPC, headed from 1979 to 1999 by the late Gurcharan Singh Tohra (1924–2004), and successive Akali-led state administrations, headed respectively by Surjeet Singh Barnala, Gurnam Singh, and Badal in particular. Badal's election in 1997 allowed him to assert his authority over the SGPC by engineering Tohra's dismissal after a twenty-seven-year reign in February 1999.[13] Widely seen as a triumph of moderates over extremists within Sikhdom, the move served also to reinforce the centrality of the SGPC to the deployment and working of power in the Akali Dal. With the Sikh 'political system' under his control, Badal was able to further de-communalize Punjab politics, thus forcing his opponents to distance themselves from separatist demands. After splitting from the SAD (Badal) to form the Panthic Morcha, Tohra, described on his death as the 'most celebrated leader of the *Khalsa Panth* for about four decades' (*Tribune* 2004a), increasingly articulated Sikh demands in terms of changing centre–state relations within an all-India context. His new party committed itself to 'the development and strengthening of a truly federal India for the preservation and progress of various religious, linguistic and cultural denominations, particularly the minorities and regional identities' (Jodhka 2005). However, this was not enough to prevent it being 'wiped out in his bastion' of Amloh by finishing an embarrassing third in the 2002 state elections (*Tribune* 2002).

By 2007, Badal's position within the Sikh political system was unrivalled, and his election victory, coupled with the annihilation of the SAD (Amritsar) and Chauhan's Khalsa Raj party, removed the last vestiges of the *Khalistan* movement from Akali politics. In the election campaign, all major political parties reaffirmed the primacy of regional issues over the old divisive issue of religion and community by emphasizing their commitment to the further development of the Punjab. However, none mentioned 'the rapid commodification of life taking place in Punjab' (Pritam Singh 2007: 466) as a result of the intensification and deepening of the processes associated with neo-liberal globalization.

For many prominent Punjabis I interviewed in the intermediate aftermath of the 2007 elections, it is the reform process itself – or rather its mismanagement by successive state governments – which is the key issue facing the Punjab. According to Ravneet Kaur, a former financial commissioner for the Indian Administrative Service, globalization has 'increased the gap between rich and poor'. Although Punjab used to be a predominately 'middle-class' society, Kaur believes the 'middle-class is turning into the new poor' (personal correspondence, 23 March 2007). For Charanjit Singh Sethi, the key issue is 'unemployment and how to stop the youth migrating abroad' (personal correspondence, 23 March 2007). To these issues, Sharanjit Singh Kallah added the impending environmental catastrophe awaiting the Punjab caused by the depletion of water sources, particularly from the subsoil (personal correspondence, 23 March 2007).[14]

Although Punjab remains India's 'most prosperous and developed state with the lowest poverty rate', the state government remains 'impoverished' and its future 'uncertain' (World Bank 2004: 3). The World Bank has identified three main areas of growing concern: growth slowdown, fiscal crisis and deteriorating public services. The Punjab's per capita income grew at just 2.1 per cent in the 1990s – well below the national average and the third lowest of all Indian states (World Bank 2004: 3–4). Much of this growth slowdown has originated from the agricultural sector, although industrial growth remains relatively low, owing to a negligible share in India's total foreign direct investment. This has had an impact on state finances. The Punjab has the 'dubious distinction of being the most prosperous as well as one of the most indebted states in the country'. It has one of the most overstaffed and overpaid civil services in the country and has been borrowing to finance its current consumption. Furthermore, its tax performance compares unfavourably with that of other states in terms of both revenue raised and its growth. As a result, state finances are 'bordering on bankruptcy' (World Bank 2004: 4). Despite its high expenditure, Punjab, however, does not score well in terms of service delivery outcomes and has a high level of absenteeism among education and health workers (World Bank 2004: 5).

Conclusion

In conclusion, the two decades since the proclamation of *Khalistan* by the *Sarbat Khalsa* have seen a transformation in Punjabi politics from a 'politics of identity' to a politics of region. Back in 1986, Sikh militants, protected by prominent Akalis such as Tohra, were engaged in a war of 'national self-determination' against security forces controlled directly by the Indian state under the leadership of the INC. At the time of writing, most of the militants – and their backers inside the Sikh 'political system' – are either dead or content to articulate their demands from *within* the Indian political system. Although the demise of the *Khalistani* movement can be attributed to its physical elimination, as Gurharpal Singh (2000) and Joyce Pettigrew (1995) amongst others have suggested, it has been argued that globalization – and particularly the commodification of life which has accompanied the penetration of the market mechanism to the local level – has profoundly restructured both regional *and* national politics, making a return to the militancy of the 1980s and early 1990s unlikely.

At a regional level, all the main political parties now embrace a non-communal Punjabi identity, and there is evidence to suggest that the identification of political parties with various sectarian interests – Akalis with rural Sikhs and the INC or BJP with urban Hindus – is slowly changing. Indeed, the SAD put up a substantial number of Hindus as their party candidates for the first time in their history in the 2007 state elections. Although this was perhaps a strategy to capitalize on the fears which many urban Hindus harboured about Captain Amarinder Singh and his attempts to appeal to the rural Sikh *Jat* base of the SAD, this would have been unthinkable two decades ago. Furthermore, there is evidence to suggest that the strategy worked, as many Punjabi Hindus voted for, and joined, the SAD in 2007. On the one hand, many Hindus, it would seem, realize they need to 'hook their destiny with a Punjab-based regional party instead of being tied to "national" parties like the BJP and the Congress Party'. The SAD, for their part, appear 'to have realised that the long-term future of Akali politics lies in becoming inclusive of all sections of Punjabis'. On the basis of this newly emerging Hindu–Akali relationship it is thus possible to conclude that 'the transformation of Akali Dal from a Sikh party to a regional Punjabi party seems to be at last beginning to take place' (Pritam Singh 2007: 466). However, the existence of a Sikh politico-religious establishment committed to defending a tradition which the *Tat Khalsa* unconsciously helped to define in the colonial period places constraints upon the extent to which the SAD can go beyond *Khalistan* and represent the interests of all Punjabis, irrespective of religion.

At a national level, Sikhs seem to have 'assimilated into the democratic mainstream'[15] following the appointment of a Sikh prime minister. Although national politics has become increasingly dominated by a *Hindutva* discourse as articulated by the BJP, Sikh elites have been able to successfully elide the tensions which exist between a Hindu/Indian 'Self' and a, mainly Muslim, non-Hindu 'Other' by redefining Sikhs as a *regional* rather than *national* minority within India. Furthermore, the defeat of the BJP-led alliance in 2004 and the further consolidation of the 'new democratic alignment' (Kothari 1998) of subaltern regional, class and caste minorities have created space for the further restructuring of Indian politics along federal lines.

It would appear, therefore, as if – for most Sikhs in the Punjab at least – *Khalistan* is an idea whose time appears to have passed.[16] However, although the Akali Dal (Badal) and many former *Khalistanis*[17] have welcomed the appointment of Dr Singh as Prime Minister, the wounds inflicted upon the Sikh community by Operation Blue Star and the anti-Sikh riots in Delhi which followed Indira Gandhi's assassination have not yet healed and, as we shall see in the next chapter, are being kept alive online and in the diaspora. Although a step in the right direction, Manmohan Singh's response[18] to the government-appointed Nanavati Commission[19] has not gone far enough in assuaging Sikh anger and, unless the INC seriously addresses legitimate Sikh grievances, a return to the militancy of the 1980s remains a distinct, if distant, possibility.

5 'The territorialization of memory'

Sikh nationalism in the 'diaspora'

In modern, Western, 'developed' societies, we can isolate three interrelated discourses or 'master narratives' which locate the Sikhs as subjects. The first narrative identifies the Sikhs as followers of a universal world religion, such as Islam or Christianity (Dusenbery 1999: 127–142). The second narrative identifies the Sikhs as a nation. Sikh nationalism may be seen as relying on the interpellation of overseas Sikh communities as members of a Sikh nation, rather than as followers of a world religion or as Punjabis or Indians (see previous chapters). Finally, the Sikhs have recently been 'interpellated' (Althusser 1971), both by scholars of the Sikhs working in Western academic institutions and by diasporic organizations, as a 'diaspora'.

'Diaspora', derived from the Greek verb *sperio* (to sow) and preposition *dia* (over) (Cohen 1997: ix), has come to be used to describe any deterritorialized,[1] transnational[2] community. James Clifford has appropriately called it a 'travelling term in changing global conditions' (Clifford 1997: 244). One of the distinctive features of the contemporary age is that 'the language of diaspora is increasingly invoked by displaced peoples who feel (maintain, revive, invent) a connection with a prior home . . . Many minority groups that have not previously identified this way are now reclaiming diasporic origins and affiliations' (Clifford 1994: 301). Whilst in earlier times the term 'diaspora' was reserved for the Jewish and Armenian dispersion, it now, according to the editor of the journal *Diaspora*, 'shares meanings with a large semantic domain that includes words like immigrant, expatriate, refugee, guest worker, exile community [and] ethnic community' (Tölölyan 1991: 4–5). The narrative of diaspora as applied to the Sikhs relies upon what Brian Keith Axel terms *the place of origin thesis* (Axel 2001: 8–9). The argument is that the place or origin of 'homeland', regardless of birthplace, *constitutes* the diaspora. Sikh claims to being a diaspora are therefore contingent on securing a 'Sikh' homeland.

Most attempts at providing 'ideal-type' definitions of 'diaspora' subscribe to the place of origin thesis. For William Saffran, diasporas are expatriate minority communities, dispersed from an original 'centre' to at least two 'peripheral' places. They maintain a memory or myth about their original homeland; they believe they are not, and perhaps cannot be accepted by, their host country; and they see an ancestral home as a place of eventual return and a place to maintain and restore (Saffran 1991, 1999). Similarly, Robin Cohen suggests that dispersal from an original homeland, often traumatically, is the central characteristic of a diaspora community (Cohen 1997). Applying Cohen's typology to the case of the Sikhs, Darshan Singh Tatla has convincingly made the case for the inclusion of the Sikhs as a global diaspora (Tatla 1999: 5–8). Tatla, in his study of the Sikh diaspora, identified the Sikhs as a 'victim' diaspora,[3] which has been mobilized by what he considers to be a single critical event – the storming of the Golden Temple complex in Amritsar in 1984 by Indian troops (Tatla 1999: 6). From Tatla and Brian Axel's (2001) attempts to account for the formation of a Sikh diaspora, we can conclude that narratives of a Sikh diaspora are contingent on two factors: 1) the existence of a 'homeland'; and 2) 'forced' dispersion from it. Both of these factors are key features of the Sikh nationalist discourse in the diaspora.

This chapter considers the rise of Sikh nationalism outside of India after the storming of the Golden Temple complex by Indian troops in June 1984. It is argued that, whereas the military solution preferred by the Indian state to the 'Punjab Problem' may have succeeded in reducing the Sikhs of the Punjab to silence, it has opened up an alternative site for nationalist activity in the 'diaspora'. The nationalist discourse in the diaspora as articulated by nationalist organizations and the Punjabi media and increasingly through the Internet is then examined. It is argued that the violence of partition and the storming of the Golden Temple complex in 1984 are the 'critical events' (Das 1995) central to the imagination of *both* a Sikh 'nation' and a specifically Sikh 'diaspora'. Both narratives are based upon and play upon a 'politics of victimhood': the representation of Sikhs as 'victims' of two *ghallughara* or 'genocides', which drove them into either physical or emotional 'exile' from India. Central to the construction of a discourse of 'victimhood' is the selective use of *memory* by nationalists: how Sikhs in the diaspora 'remember' partition and 'Operation Blue Star' and what they, and more importantly Sikhs in the Punjab, choose to 'forget'.

A Sikh diaspora?

Only a few of the countries where the Sikhs reside contain any religious affiliation questions in their censuses, so only a rough estimate can be made of the population of Sikhs outside India. Although the boundaries between non-religious Sikhs and other South Asians, particularly Punjabi Hindus, are difficult to ascertain in a diaspora context, it is estimated that in 2005 there were probably between 1 million and 1.5 million Sikhs outside India, the vast majority of whom resided in Europe, particularly the UK, and North America. The worldwide Sikh population in 1991 was about 17,911,000. It is estimated that the current global Sikh population is around 20 million (see Table 5.1), although some organizations have put it as high as 25 million (Sikh Coalition 2007d).

Table 5.1 Global Sikh population, 2005

Region	Sikh population (2005)	Main areas/characteristics
Punjab	14,592,387	Mainly rural.
India (excluding Punjab)	4,623,343	Haryana (rural). Rajasthan (rural). Uttar Pradesh (urban). Delhi (urban) (post-partition migrants).
UK	336,179	London and Midlands (urban) (post-war migrants).
EU (excluding UK)	100,000 (approx.)	Germany, Italy, Belgium (urban) (post-1984 migrants and refugees).
USA	250,000 (approx.)	California (Stockton, Yuba City and San Francisco), Chicago, New York (urban) (mainly post-1984 professionals and some pre-war farmers).
Canada	278,415	British Columbia and Ontario (urban) (long history of Sikh settlement dating from colonial era).
Others	273,000 (approx.)	Middle East (temporary migrants). Australasia (professionals). South-East Asia (colonial migrants).
Total	20,453,324	

The Sikh presence in the overseas diaspora is proportionally far greater than that of other South Asians. Between a third and a half of all Britons of Indian origin, and the overwhelming majority of Indo-Canadians, are 'Sikh'.[4] Although the overwhelming proportion of this overseas Sikh population had migrated in the post-colonial era, the rise of Sikh mass migration outside South Asia can be traced to the posting of Sikh soldiers to British colonies by the British colonial army in the nineteenth century. Rural Sikhs, of the *Jat*, or agricultural, caste,[5] designated as a 'martial race' by the British colonial authorities, were stationed in South-East Asia (Hong Kong, Singapore and Malaysia) and East Africa (Kenya and Uganda). From there, Sikh migrants with army connections sought to settle in the West, particularly on the Pacific coast of North America where communities were established before the imposition of anti-immigration legislation in the early twentieth century. The partition of the Punjab following the creation of the independent, successor states to the British Raj, India and Pakistan, in 1947, had the effect of creating a large, internally displaced Sikh population within India who formed the backbone of post-war northern Indian migration to the UK. They were joined in the UK by 'twice-migrant' Sikhs of the *Ramgharia*, or artisan, caste, following political changes in East Africa in the early 1970s (Bhachu 1985).

The Sikh nationalist discourse in the diaspora

The Sikh nationalist discourse, as articulated by diasporic organizations such as the British-based Khalistan Council, the US-based Council of Khalistan and the various branches of the Babbar Khalsa International, Dal Khalsa and the International Sikh Youth Federation (see Table 5.2), identifies the Sikhs as an ethno-religious community, forced from their homeland of the Punjab by the violence of partition and the storming of the Golden Temple complex in 1984. Although initially disseminated throughout the diaspora through *gurdwaras* and via the Punjabi-language press serving the Sikh community in places of settlement, in recent years a Sikh 'nationalist' discourse has emerged online increasingly articulated in English and serving a global audience. On the Google search engine, there were approximately 5 million web matches for the word 'Sikh' in English (as of 2 February 2007). The most popular matches were websites designed for and by Sikhs in the diaspora (see Table 5.3). Even more significantly, there were 132,000 matches for 'Khalistan', the name given to the imagined Sikh nation-state. All of the main *Khalistani* organizations have websites in English with contact addresses based in the US, UK and Europe (see Table 5.4). As we shall see, this Sikh

Table 5.2 Main Sikh nationalist organizations in the diaspora

Name	Year founded	Location	Main leaders
Council of Khalistan	1986	USA	Dr Gurmit Singh Aulakh
Khalistan Council	1984	UK	Dr Jagjit Singh Chauhan (1984–2007)
Khalistan Affairs Center	1991	USA	Dr Amarjit Singh
Babbar Khalsa International	1978/81–2001/3	Canada (banned 2003), UK (banned 2001)	Talwinder Singh Parmar (1984–1992)
Dal Khalsa	1984	Punjab, UK, Canada	Gajinder Singh (1986–2005) Satnam Singh Paonta (2005–)
International Sikh Youth Federation	1984–2001/2/3	Punjab (banned 2002), UK (banned 2001), Canada (banned 2003)	Jasbir Singh Rode (1984–1988) Lakhbir Singh Rode (1988–2001) Satinderpal Singh Gill (1988–2001) Balwinder Singh Chaherhu (1988–2001)
World Sikh Organization	1984	USA, Canada	Ajit Singh Sahota (Canada) Dr Manohar Singh Grewal (US)

Updated and adapted from Tatla (1999: 116–123, 138–143).

Table 5.3 Selected Sikh websites

Name	Country of origin (if known)	URL
SGPC	India	http://www.sgpc.net/
The Sikhism Homepage	UK	http://www.sikhs.org/
Sikh.org	USA, Canada	http://www.sikh.org/
Sikhism Page	USA	http://www.sikhs.org/
Sikhnet	USA	http://www.sikhnet.com/
Sikh Awareness	UK	http://sikhawareness.com
Sikh.net	USA	http://www.sikh.net/
The Sikh Coalition	USA	http://www.sikhcoalition.org/
Sikh Foundation	USA	http://www.sikhfoundation.org/
Sikhe.com	N/A	http://www.sikhe.com/
Sikh History	N/A	http://www.sikh-history.com/
Sikh Lionz	UK	http://www.sikhlionz.com/
Sikh Unity Network	India	http://members.tripod.com/sikhunity
Sikh Nation	Singapore	http://www.sikhnation.com/
Sikhs in Australia	Australia	http://www.sikh.com.au/
Sikh Spirit	UK	http://www.sikhspirit.com/
World Sikh Organization	USA	http://www.world-sikh.org/
United Sikhs	USA, UK, India	http://www.unitedsikhs.org/
World Sikh Council – AR	USA	http://www.world-sikhcouncil.org

nationalist discourse simultaneously *globalizes* and *localizes* Sikh identity through its advocacy of a 'politics of homeland'.

The existence of a territorially defined homeland is central to the imagination of Sikh diaspora nationalism. Sikh diaspora nationalists, like other nationalists, do not, in the words of A.D. Smith, 'seek to acquire any territory. They want their "homeland", that is, an historic territory which their people can feel is theirs by virtue of a convincing claim of possession and efflorescence sometime in the past' (A.D. Smith 1999: 219). In the imagination of Sikh diaspora nationalists, 'the homeland' is *equated* with the Indian state of Punjab. The 'ancestral homeland' of the Sikh nationalist imagination, however, does *not* correspond to the present-day borders of the Indian state of Punjab. Some of the 'great events that formed the nation', to which A.D. Smith refers, and the place where 'the heroes, saints and sages of the community from which the nation later developed lived and worked and . . . are buried' (A.D. Smith 1996: 383) lie to the west in Pakistan. This includes the birthplace of the founder of the Sikh religious tradition, Guru Nanak. Sikh nationalist organizations in the diaspora do not lay claim to those lands but instead seek to invest those shared memories within the borders of the

Table 5.4 Selected Khalistani websites

Name	Country of origin (if known)	URL
Council of Khalistan	USA	http://www.khalistan.com/ http://www.khalistan.net/
Khalistan Government in Exile	UK	http://www.Khalistan.demon.co.uk/
Khalistan Affairs Center	USA	http://www.Khalistan-affairs.org/
World Sikh Organization	USA	http://www.world-sikh.org/
Burning Punjab	UK, Netherlands	http://www.burningpunjab.com/
Sikh Youth Federation	USA, Canada	http://www.syj.jaj.com/
Shaheed Khalsa	N/A	http://www.shaheedkhalsa.com/
International Sikh Youth Federation (ISYF)	UK	N/A (banned 29 March 2001)
Dal Khalsa International	India	http://www.dalkhalsa.org/
Panth Khalsa	USA, Canada	http://www.panthkhalsa.org
Khalistani Lionz	UK	http://www.khalistan.8m.com/
Maboli Systems	N/A	http://www.maboli.com/
Shaheed Khalsa	USA	http://www.shaheedkhalsa.com/

East (Indian) Punjab. Dr Gurmit Singh Aulakh, the president of the US-based Council of Khalistan, in his millennium message to the Sikh 'nation', writes of a 'sovereign, independent nation' established by Guru Gobind Singh. Sovereignty, given to the Sikh peoples by Guru Gobind, was 'lost' to the British and then the Hindu Raj in Delhi. Aulakh urges the Sikhs to reclaim their 'lost sovereignty' through the establishment of an independent Sikh state in the *Indian* state of Punjab (Aulakh 2000). Surjan Singh, of the Babbar Khalsa International, regards the Sikhs and the Punjab to be 'interchangeable elements'. The Sikhs are seen as the 'true sons of the soil', having defended the Punjab from 'the foreign Afghan' and having valiantly resisted the British until 1849 (Surjan Singh 1982: 15) – a view shared by the late Dr Jagjit Singh Chauhan, president of the Khalistan Council (personal interview, 2 January 2000). When interviewed by the author, Dr Chauhan described the *Khalsa* Sikhs as the 'vanguard of the Punjabi peoples' and conceived of *Khalistan* not as a theocratic but a pluralistic state where freedom of worship would be guaranteed.[6] *Khatri* Sikhs originally from West Punjab but resident in Vancouver, *Ramgharia* Sikhs from East Africa, and *Jat* Sikhs born and bred in Birmingham are enjoined to regard East Punjab as the 'homeland' irrespective of *actual* place of origin. The Sikh nationalist discourse in the diaspora therefore *territorializes* Sikh identity.

Sikh diaspora nationalism plays upon collective experiences of forced dispersal or 'flight following the threat of violence' (Gilroy 1997: 318) shared by other ethno-religious diasporas. Of key importance to the Sikh diaspora nationalist discourse is the concept of the *ghallughara*, translated in English as 'holocaust' or 'genocide'. While the Holocaust has been

> narrated by Jews and non-Jews alike as a collective (and sole) property of the Jews, as something to be left to, or jealously guarded by, those who escaped the shooting and the gassing, and by the descendants of the shot and the gassed
>
> (Baumann 1989: viii–ix)

The term 'genocide', however, has acquired a wider currency and has been applied to a variety of different atrocities from the concentration camps of the Nazis, the 'killing fields' of Kampuchea, the massacre of Tutsis by Hutus in Rwanda, up to the present crisis in Darfur. Originally defined by the Polish jurist Raphael Lemkin during the later stages of the Second World War as the 'coordinated and planned annihilation of a national religious or racial group by a variety of actions aimed at undermining the foundations essential to the survival of the group as a group' (Hansen 2002: 24), genocide became the pretext upon which Axis leaders were tried and hanged. Article II of the UN Convention on the Prevention and Punishment of the Crime of Genocide, one of the first post-war international declarations, distinguished between five different meanings of genocide:

> In the present Convention, genocide means any of the following acts committed with intent to destroy, in whole or in part, a national, ethnical, racial or religious group, as such:
>
> a) Killing members of the group,
> b) Causing serious bodily or mental harm to members of the group,
> c) Deliberately inflicting on the group conditions of life calculated to bring about its physical destruction in whole or in part,
> d) Imposing measures intended to prevent births within the group,
> e) Forcibly transferring children of the group to one another.
>
> (UN General Assembly 1948)

As Tatla points out, the term *ghallughara* is not used lightly in the Sikh tradition and its use is restricted to just two episodes: the *Chhota Ghallughara* ('Small Holocaust') of 1746 and the *Vadda Ghallughara* ('Great Holocaust') of 1762. The first or 'smaller' *ghallughara* refers to the massacre of more than 10,000 Sikhs by Diwan Lakhpat Rai in 1746 in retaliation for the murder of his younger brother by a Sikh *misl* or unit led by Jassa Singh Ahluwalia. Ahluwalia, the commander-in-chief of the *Dal Khalsa*, was also present at the *Vadda Ghallughara* of 1762 where the forces of Ahmad Shah massacred an estimated 25,000–30,000 Sikhs, including many women and children. Tatla then applies the term, with important qualifications, to the consequences of Operation Blue Star some two centuries later. The application of this terminology to the storming of the Golden Temple by Indian troops 'suggests a community's search for its attending redemptive value of quick recovery from such massacres as also to use it as a resource to challenge the accompanying hegemonic discourse by the Indian state'. However, Tatla admits that 'by drawing a parallel to earlier holocausts it also . . . obscures the more complicated and tragic consequences of the third, as both the Sikhs and the Indian state have evolved into far more complex structures since the eighteenth century' (Tatla 2006: 61).

Although it is debatable whether any of the historic *ghallughara* outlined above meet the internationally agreed definition of genocide, since Sikhs were engaged in battle with their adversaries, their impact on the development of a Sikh narrative of *victimhood* enables comparisons to be made with other 'genocides'. The existence of the concept of *ghallughara* simultaneously furnishes nationalists with a conceptual vocabulary with which to legitimize the establishment and defence of a sovereign *imagined* homeland internationally and also enables Sikhs to make sense of, redefine and *remember* the traumatic events which befell the Sikhs in the twentieth century. Two historical events in particular are referred to as *ghallughara*: partition, and the storming of the Golden Temple in 1984. Both these events have served to facilitate the construction of cultural and religious boundaries between the Sikhs and the other main ethno-religious communities in the Punjab, and are central to the imagination of both a Sikh 'nation' in the diaspora and a specifically *Sikh* 'diaspora'.

Partition

> In this unique moment, their souls had merged, as it were, with the souls of their ancestors. Time had again come to cross swords with the Turks. The Khalsa was again facing a crisis created by the Turks. Their minds had been transported to earlier times . . . every 'Singh' in the congregation was ready for sacrifice . . .
>
> Everyone in the congregation, man or woman, intensely felt that he or she was a link in the long chain of Sikh history, an integral part of it and, at that moment of crisis, like the ancestors was ready to lay down his or her life.
>
> (Sahni 2001 [1970]: 228–229)

The partition of the Punjab province of the British Empire into two new successor states, India and Pakistan, caused one of the 'greatest human convulsions of human history' as between 10 million and 12 million people (Brass 2003: 75) moved either side of the Radcliffe line. Partition was marked by a high level of organized communal violence, and hundreds of thousands were slaughtered whilst travelling between West and East Punjab. A recent study has estimated that 5.4 million Muslims left East Punjab and 4 million Sikhs and Hindus left West Punjab and that an estimated half a million[7] died in the carnage that swept through the province during the summer and autumn of 1947 (Hansen 2002: 1). Partition may be seen as the most violent process of ethnic cleansing in recent history and foreshadowed contemporary genocidal conflict in the Balkans and central Africa.[8]

Gyanendra Pandey has distinguished between three different conceptions of partition that went into making the partition of 1947 (Pandey 2001: 21–44). The first conception of partition can be discerned in the Muslim League demand for Pakistan from 1940 onwards. Pakistan was envisaged as a Muslim-majority state to balance Hindu-majority Hindustan in a loose, federal structure. The plan did not, until 1946–1947, require the migration of Muslims into Pakistan or Hindus and Sikhs into India but merely for the principle of Muslim rule in Muslim-majority states to be conceded. However, this conception of Pakistan, although acceptable to the majority of Muslim Punjabis and Bengalis, who were anxious to preserve the territorial unity of their regions, was opposed by Punjabi Hindus and Sikhs in particular, who feared that their identity would be submerged under Muslim rule. Furthermore, this conception of Pakistan failed to appease the primary supporters of the Muslim League, the educated, UP Muslim elite centred around Aligarh who had campaigned vociferously for a homeland for *all* Muslims in the subcontinent.

The second conception of partition involved splitting up the Muslim-majority provinces of Punjab and Bengal. This, the British authorities hoped, would allay Punjabi Hindu and particularly Sikh fears of being swallowed whole into a Muslim-majority state. Support for this 'partition' came from the Hindu Mahasabha and, in what must be considered one of the most myopic and biggest miscalculations in Sikh history, from the Sikh leadership under Master Tara Singh. Despite opposition from many Sikhs, the Shiromani Akali Dal allowed the *panth* to be effectively partitioned in 1947, leaving the 'regroupment'[9] or 'reterritorialization' of the Sikh community in East Punjab the only effective strategy for survival as a distinct community in Hindu-dominated India. Whether the Akali leadership foresaw the consequences of the partition of the province or not is a moot point. Although every Sikh member of the eastern section of the Punjab Assembly voted in favour of partition in July 1947, the president of the SAD, Giani Kartar Singh, claimed that the Sikhs had not in fact consented to the existing plan. The Sikh position, according to Kartar Singh, was to oppose any 'partition that does not maintain the solidarity of the population in the East Punjab and does not consolidate their shrines in the East Punjab' (Pandey 2001: 33). In other words, the Akalis accepted the principle of the partition of the Punjab into East and West but sought to include the majority of the Sikh population and shrines in the East. This would unsurprisingly be rejected by the Muslim League eager to incorporate all Muslim-majority districts of the Muslim-majority province into West Punjab.

The final 'partition' was the violence associated with the 'official' partition: the massacres, the nightmares, 'those other partitions that people would have to live with for decades to come' (Pandey 2001: 35). Violence was central to partition and the generation of partition memories. As Paul Brass has pointed out, violence did not result only as a consequence of, but was the principal mechanism for creating the conditions for, partition (Brass 2003: 76). The deliberate use of violence allowed the terms of partition itself to be changed. Partition, by forcibly displacing religious minorities, had implications that were carried to their logical conclusion: 'the concentration of all peoples in categorical terms as belonging to particular religious groups on opposite sides of the partition line' (Brass 2003: 82).

Partition violence differed from communal violence in three respects. First, it was dominated by national discourses and issues of state formation. The 'old' multiethnic discourse of coexistence amongst Hindus, Muslims and Sikhs was challenged by a 'new' national discourse that finally prevailed and became a driving force for the violence (Hansen 2002: 29). The violence that accompanied partition facilitated the construction of national boundaries between the two new states and *legitimized* their claims to state sovereignty. This was particularly so in the case of Pakistan, which only after partition could claim to be a homeland for all South Asia's Muslims. Before partition, the Muslim League had been unable to command an overwhelming majority of the Muslim vote in Muslim-majority states, particularly the Punjab where the regionalist Unionist Party was strong. The violence which accompanied partition 'ethnically cleansed' the Punjab of its Hindu and Sikh minorities and, in so doing, enabled hundreds of thousands of Muslim refugees from East Punjab to relocate. Partition violence also tarnished the secular credentials of the Congress Party, as it was unable to guarantee the safety and property of Muslims. Its failure to create a Sikh-majority state after independence further cemented it in minority perception as predominately a 'Hindu' party, although it continues to rely heavily on Muslim votes in independent India.

Second, partition violence spread beyond urban areas, traditionally the site of communal violence, to engulf rural areas. An early example includes the riots in March 1947 in Rawalpindi district, which included villages such as Bewal, Dubheran and, infamously, Thoa Khalsa. The intention was to force religious minorities to migrate to East Punjab, Delhi or Uttar Pradesh, leaving Muslims in control of their property and businesses. Finally, partition intruded into the private sphere of the family by inflicting sexual violence on a massive scale (Hansen 2002: 194). The 'ethnic cleansing' of East and West Punjab of religious minorities was facilitated by widespread sexual savagery, with an estimated 75,000 women abducted and raped by men of religions different from their own, which served to reinforce communal boundaries (Butalia 2000: 3). Although Sikhs played an active role in 'cleansing' East Punjabi villages of Muslims, the nationalist discourse portrays the Sikhs exclusively as *victims* rather than participants in this 'ethnic cleansing'.[10]

March 1947 in particular seems etched in the Sikh consciousness. The riots in Rawalpindi and the surrounding districts, recorded for posterity as fiction in Bhisham Sahni's *Tamas*, 'crossed the threshold between *traditional* and *genocidal* violence' (Hansen 2002: 194, italics in the original). 'Genocidal' differs from 'traditional' communal violence in two crucial respects. First, genocidal violence is marked by a greater propensity to *kill* members of an opposing ethnic or religious group. As Hansen has shown, figures compiled from fortnightly reports and governors' letters show that the number of killed in the first five months of 1947 by far exceeded the numbers of injured, thus pointing towards genocidal intent (Hansen 2002: 193). Second, genocidal violence is characterized by its *systematic* organization. In many respects, genocidal violence may be seen as a more 'modern' form of communalism, as the principal mechanism though which the genocide has been carried out has been the modern, bureaucratic state. This is true of Nazi Germany, Ataturk's Turkey, the German colonization of South-West Africa, Belgian colonization of the Congo and arguably Pol Pot's Kampuchea.[11]

Partition, however, was characterized by the very *absence* of direct state involvement. Indeed, it was the inability or unwillingness of the departing colonial authorities to maintain law and order which is often cited as a contributory factor for the escalation of violence. However, it will be argued, following Hansen, that a genocidal conflict can also occur when the state is either unwilling to counter or incapable of countering the violence. Hansen bases his argument on the premise that 'communalism needs to be recognized as a structure giving possible rise to conflicts that can attain genocidal proportions' (Hansen 2002: 197). According to Harff and Gurr, there exist three preconditions for genocide: structural change, sharp internal cleavages and lack of external constraints (Harff and Gurr 1988: 32). Applying Harff and Gurr's criteria to the Punjab, Hansen convincingly demonstrates that decolonization, coupled with the sudden withdrawal of the British, brought about a situation in which power was usurped by armed, 'communal' organizations. The private armies of all three religious communities, the Muslim League National Guard, Rashtriya Swayamsevak Sangh (RSS) and Akal Fauj, provided ready-made opportunities of employment for recently demobbed soldiers. This helps explain the systematic nature and military character of the killings.

However, the fact that it was the Muslim League that started this process of ethnic cleansing by attempting to drive Sikhs (and Hindus) out of Rawalpindi and its surrounding districts in March 1947 is significant for the development of a 'nationalist' narrative which is simultaneously 'Indian' and 'Sikh'. Beginning on the night of 6–7 March and lasting for a week, armed Muslim gangs attacked a number of Sikh and Hindu villages in the Rawalpindi area, leaving more than 2,000 dead (Ahmed 2002: 15). The events of one particular village, Thoa Khalsa, where ninety Sikh women committed suicide by jumping into a well rather than run the risk of falling into the hands of Muslim assailants, became embedded into the collective Sikh memory as a tale of epic resistance in defence of faith and nation. As recounted by prominent survivors, including the leader of the local Sikh community, whose wife was the first to jump, the actions of the women are interpreted as having been motivated by a desire to maintain the 'honour' of the women of the village. When Muslims surrounded the ninety women and children bathing in a well, the wife of the village leader Sant Gulab Singh, Sardani Lajwanti, took a 5-year-old granddaughter by one hand and a grandson by the other and, calling out 'Sat Sri Akal', leaped into the well so that her husband would not have to witness, in his words, 'the dishonouring of any daughter'. The rest of the women by the well followed suit, leaving the Muslim mob 'to flee in terror'. Upon hearing what had transpired, the Sikh men and women cried out in one voice 'Danya Guru Kalgidhar' (Blessed is the Guru Kalgidhar – a reference to Guru Gobind Singh), and the leader of the Thoa Khalsa Sikhs, Sant Gulab Singh, allegedly saw an apparition of Guru Nanak himself, entrusting him with the protection of the surviving members of the community (Pandey 2001: 84–85). As we see by the above account based on Gulab Singh's recollections, the suffering and self-sacrifice of the women of the village become translated into martyrdom. The women become martyrs not just for the village and the patriarchal code of honour which Sikhs shared with other Punjabis, but also, through the narrator's invocation of the Sikh Gurus, for the *panth*.

The 'memorialization' (Edkins 2003) of Thoa Khalsa in the Sikh nationalist narrative proceeded from the publication of an SGPC report, *Muslim League Attack on Sikhs and Hindus in the Punjab*. Published three years after the event, the report praises the 'epic resistance' of the Sikh women of Thoa Khalsa who saved the honour of their faith and village by committing suicide or 'entreating their husbands and fathers to kill them'. In contrast, most of the Hindus of the village succumbed and 'under pressure accepted Islam' (Talib 1991 [1950]: 352). This theme, of Sikh courage and martyrdom and Hindu duplicity and cowardice, re-appropriated from colonial accounts, has become prominent in later accounts of what transpired at Thoa Khalsa. The experiences and 'resistance' of the mainly *Khatri* Sikhs in West Punjab, most of whom lived in Hindu communities, became part of a homogenized, militaristic national discourse built around the *Jat* soldier-farmers of East Punjab. This was partly in response to attempts by the Indian national leadership to appropriate the memory of Thoa Khalsa for its own purposes and to weave it into a new anti-Pakistani (and thus implicitly anti-Muslim) nationalist narrative.[12]

It would be tempting to conclude that Thoa Khalsa has thus been transformed into what Pierre Nora has termed a *lieu de mémoire* (Nora 1996), a place whose very mention invokes 'memories' of martyrdom and self-sacrifice in the service of the *panth* or *qaum*. However, based upon my own conversations[13] with partition survivors about their memories of partition, Sikhs from Rawalpindi and other surrounding villages who lived through and witnessed the partition violence had equally chilling stories, which they were, initially, reluctant to speak about. One woman from a small village of Kuri surrounding Rawalpindi and now living in Delhi recalls being abducted with her two sisters by Muslim mobs and held 'captive' for two weeks. Although understandably unwilling to elaborate on her experiences in 'captivity', she admits to having had her head shaved, a sign of 'dishonour' in the Sikh tradition, and to fearing her father's reaction when she eventually 'returned'. Indeed, after fleeing her captors with the help of a local Muslim doctor who was a friend of the family, she went to stay with her uncle in Rawalpindi rather than return home, painfully aware that she had unwittingly 'shamed' the family.

Another, a student at Khalsa College in Rawalpindi at the time, remembers the gruesome murder of his warden and the vicious gang-rape of his pregnant wife by a Muslim League mob. Having heard of the riots in the surrounding villages, the warden, his wife and their non-Muslim students had elected to flee the city before the mob arrived, but having left in the middle of the night they were betrayed by the woman's high-pitched voice. A Muslim youth, emerging from the darkness, viciously killed the warden, and the stunned and traumatized students watched in terror as his wife was raped repeatedly by the mob before their very eyes. Now resident in Birmingham, the former student adds, almost as an aside, that he 'thinks' the woman died soon afterwards because of her injuries. Another man from the village of Kahuta, near Rawalpindi, recalls with bitterness the bravery of the women of his village who, like the women of Thoa Khalsa, jumped in the well to avoid capture and humiliation. He also recalls the story of his uncle, who was the only man to escape when a Muslim mob surrounded his village. His uncle, a wealthy man, managed to do so only by intentionally dropping his money so his pursuers would stoop to pick it up, thus enabling him to flee.

In all cases, the commitment to their 'faith' of those who had 'witnessed'[14] first-hand the brutality of partition was strengthened. 'Partition made me feel stronger religiously. That was the only good thing to come out of the whole sorry event', said one man now living in Uttar Pradesh. In most cases, this commitment to one's own faith was paralleled with hostility towards the 'other', in this case Islam. Although most of those interviewed claimed that their experiences had not altered the way they felt about Muslims and many continue to lay the blame at the door of the 'politicians' of both sides (and the British), it is difficult for them to 'forgive' the Muslims for what happened or 'forget' their experiences. A familiar claim made by the survivors was that the 'Muslim' strategy was to 'slaughter all non-Muslims', for 'that was the only way they would get Pakistan'. Commenting on partition after the events of 11 September 2001, which had seemingly legitimized Islamophobia in the Western press, another Midlands-based Sikh commented to me that, as far as Muslim mentality was concerned, nothing much had changed for they only 'understood the language of force'.

A dissenting view, however, was offered by another partition survivor, who having left Rawalpindi in March settled in Jullunder in East Punjab. He recalls playing with his neighbour's children when his uncle exhorted him and his friends to 'occupy' their neighbour's house. Puzzled, he asked his uncle why he wanted him to do so, considering that the house belonged to a friend of his father. He was told that he should do so before 'other refugees' from West Punjab did, for his neighbour, a Muslim, was 'preparing' to go to Pakistan. The man, then a child of 11, remembers helping them pack and watching his own father touch the feet of his friend as a mark of respect. The neighbour then entrusted the boy's father with his house and all the possessions he could not load on to his cart. Then his father wished his friend a safe journey and, having prayed to their respective Gods, his neighbour and his family left as part of a convoy of Muslim families for the railway station. With tears in his eyes, he recalls that they never made their train to Pakistan, as a mob of Sikhs and Hindus butchered every one of the convoy. Although more than fifty years have passed, he admits to still being haunted by the look of resignation on his father's friend's face as he left the only home he had ever known.

What emerged following the Rawalpindi massacres and the identification of Muslim League cadres as the culprits was an anti-Muslim discourse which underpinned regional nationalist narratives. Before the Lahore Resolution of 1940, Indian nationalism was defined primarily in terms of an anti-colonialism, which, despite frequent Hindu communal overtones, was inclusive of all ethno-religious 'communities'. The development of Muslim nationalism as articulated by the Muslim League dramatically altered the situation. Just as the term 'Muslim' was appropriated by the Muslim League to signify a political identity, 'Hindu' and 'Sikh' became synonymous in official discourse with Congress and Akali positions. Although the RSS and its related political organizations 'defended' the Hindu communities from attack in West Punjab and provided for relief for refugees from West Punjab in the aftermath of partition, in the process gaining a great deal of support from these communities, they were effectively marginalized on a national level as a result of the electoral mandate which allowed Congress to 'speak' for *non-Muslims*. Thus, whilst the Rawalpindi riots were taking place, the All-India National Congress Committee passed a resolution demanding the division of Punjab into two provinces so that 'the predominately Muslim part may be separated from the predominately non-Muslim part' (Ahmed 2002: 15). The nationalism which Congress espoused following the passage of this resolution (which also called for the partition of Bengal) would, therefore, be an ethno-cultural one which implicitly recognized and legitimized the Boundary Commission's categories of Muslim and non-Muslim. India was re-imagined, despite its secular veneer, as a non-Muslim nation, albeit with the largest Muslim minority in the world. Sikh identity was, furthermore, submerged into the category of 'non-Muslim', thus blurring the boundaries between Sikhism and Hinduism.

The participation of the SAD in the deliberations of the Punjab Boundary Commission was significant in two respects. First, it recognized the existence of a Sikh community with an identity and interests distinct from those of the Muslims and Hindus. Second, it legitimized the position of the SAD as the sole representative of the Sikh community. The SAD could, by its participation in the talks, 'speak for' and 'interpellate' an ideology derivative of Jinnah's 'two-nation' theory. The Sikhs, according to the Akali leader, Master Tara Singh, constituted a nation or *qaum* in their own right. If Pakistan was to be created on the grounds that the Muslim *qaum* constituted a 'nation', then the Sikhs too were entitled to their own 'homeland'. The Cabinet Mission Plan had been 'greatly impressed by the very genuine and acute anxiety of the Muslims lest they should find themselves subjected to a perpetual Hindu majority rule'. 'This feeling has become so strong and widespread amongst the Muslims', they concluded, 'that it cannot be allayed by mere paper safeguards.' They proposed, therefore, that 'if there is to be internal peace in India it must be secured by measures which will assure to the Muslims a control in all matters vital to their culture, religion, and economic or other interests' (Cabinet Mission Plan Statement, in Tara Singh 1946). This laid the basis for the creation of a territorially defined Muslim homeland: Pakistan. For Master Tara Singh and the Akali leadership, there was an important lesson to be learned:

> So the course left for the Sikhs is to prove their 'very acute and genuine anxiety', and further that there can be no internal peace, not at least in the Punjab, unless some effective power is given to the Sikhs to defend 'their culture, religion and other economic interests'.
>
> (Tara Singh 1946: v)

Sikh participation in the (Indian) nationalist struggle (redefined as a struggle against the Muslim League) was conditional on assurances from the Congress that the Sikhs would be permitted a homeland in independent India. Two factors militated against the Congress's concession to Akali demands. In the first place, the Sikhs were territorially dispersed and did not constitute a majority anywhere in the Punjab. This was the precisely why the Sikhs could not expect anything from the Boundary Commission. Furthermore, the religious boundaries between Sikhs and Hindus, particularly in the *Khatri* communities of West Punjab, were by no means clearly demarcated. Master Tara Singh, for instance, was himself born into a Hindu *Khatri* family in West Punjab. Secondly, the concession of a Sikh 'homeland' would qualify the commitment of Congress to secularism. Congress would thereby cease to be a 'national' and become a 'communal' party representing the interests of the majority Hindu community. In order for Congress to preserve the veneer of secularism and, therefore, assuage the fears of Muslim subjects who could not – or might not want to – emigrate to Pakistan, as well as lay claim to being a genuinely 'modern' nation-state which could play a key role in the emerging international society, it was imperative for the Nehruvian leadership to deny the Sikhs a 'homeland' once the Sikh community had regrouped in East Punjab. Partition, therefore, set the parameters over which the battle for the Punjabi *Suba* and, eventually, *Khalistan* would be fought.

'Operation Blue Star'

The second 'holocaust' suffered by the Sikhs was 'Operation Blue Star': the storming of the Golden Temple in Amritsar by the Indian government in 1984. For Darshan Singh Tatla, 'the Indian army's assault on *Harimandir*, the holiest shrine in Sikh perception, constituted a "sacrilege", a slur on a nation's dignity and integrity, an act of *genocide*' (Tatla 1999: 28, italics mine). The assassination of the prime minister, Indira Gandhi, on 31 October 1984 by her Sikh bodyguards precipitated the worst communal riots in India since partition. As with partition, the communal violence was highly organized, and attacks upon Sikhs in Delhi were orchestrated by the ruling Congress Party. More than 2,000 Sikhs died in the Delhi suburbs alone as Sikh homes and businesses were targeted (Khilnani 1997: 53). The actions of the Indian state gave rise to the view among overseas Sikhs that the very existence of the Sikh *panth* was in danger. The homepages of both Burning Punjab and Khalistan.com, two of the most popular sites, explicitly refer to state repression of Sikhs in India, which they claim has resulted in the deaths of a quarter of a million people in the last two decades, by the term *genocide*. For Dr Gurmit Singh Aulakh, president of the Council of Khalistan, 'after the Golden Temple attack in June 1984 by the Indian government it was clear to the Sikhs that the Indian government is determined to destroy Sikhism completely' (Aulakh 2000; Osan 2000a). According to Colonel Partap Singh Ajrawat, Operation Blue Star was a 'massive act of state terrorism' whose 'sole purpose' was to reduce Sikhs to servility. The November 1984 anti-Sikh riots were, however, 'an even bigger exercise in state brutality' and similarly constituted a genocide (Ajrawat 1997).

The ethnic boundary created by violence in the Punjab helps explain the transformation in the consciousness of Sikhs living overseas. Indeed, it can be argued that a specifically Sikh identity in the diaspora only emerged as a result of violence *in* the Punjab. In her analysis of Punjabi/Sikh/*Jat* migrants in early-twentieth-century California, Karen Leonard refers to a *Punjabi*, not a Sikh, diaspora (Leonard 1990: 120). For Verne A. Dusenbery, a localized territorial identity based upon the village coexisted with a deterritorialized religious identity in overseas communities for much of the last century. Members of the same Punjabi village settled overseas might share a sense of community with their local *bhum bhai* (brothers of the earth) without expecting all villagers to be *guru bhai* (coreligionists) (Dusenbery 1995: 23–24). The boundary created by violence served to sever the links between *bhum bhai* whilst reinforcing the links that bound *guru bhai* together. The violence in the Punjab led many Sikhs in the diaspora to re-examine their relations with other South Asian immigrant communities, particularly with their Punjabi Hindu neighbours and, in many cases, relations. In the UK, this was reflected in the rise of *Khalistani* organizations. When Dr Jagjit Singh Chauhan first demanded a Sikh state in India in the early 1970s in an advertisement in the *New York Times* (12 October 1971), the response amongst the Sikh population was muted. Sikh politics in the diaspora, as in the Punjab, continued to be dominated by the various factions of the Akali Dal, all of which were in favour of remaining within the Indian union. Chauhan was subsequently ostracized by the Akali Dal and refused entry to *gurdwaras* in the UK where he was resident. By 1984, however, the Akali Dal itself had been discredited and 'swept aside' by Chauhan's newly elected Khalistan Council (Tatla 1999: 140). Indeed, the violence in the Punjab was constitutive of a specifically Sikh diaspora. Sikhs became conscious of constituting a separate, culturally distinct community in the diaspora only *after* the events of 1984. A localized, Punjabi identity, therefore, gave way to a *globalized* Sikh identity in the diaspora.

At the heart of the Sikh nationalist discourse there is what Jenny Edkins refers to as a 'struggle over memory'. According to Edkins, 'some forms of remembering can be seen as ways of forgetting: ways of recovering from trauma by putting its lessons to one side, refusing to acknowledge that anything has changed, restoring the pretence' (Edkins 2003: 16). It is significant that, whilst Operation Blue Star, like partition before it, is the event which the 'victims' themselves, in this case the victimized community of Sikhs in India, choose to 'forget', Sikhs in the diaspora choose to 'remember' the events of 1984 by *memorializing*[15] it. Whilst, for the former, 'forgetting' is a strategy used to cope with the trauma of being victimized by their *own* government in their own homeland, for the latter remembering is constitutive of *community*, a way of asserting their own identity as Sikhs. Thus, the Sikhs in India I interviewed were reluctant to speak about 1984.[16] Even though many had been physically threatened by rioting mobs in Delhi, and one had been forced to remove his *pagh* (turban) in order to 'pass' as a Hindu, the only response I got from those interviewed was that of 'shock'. Indeed, all of the Sikhs I met who were willing to speak about 1984 used variations of the very same word. Operation Blue Star was either 'shocking' or 'very shocking', yet the violence of the Indian state was perceived as 'irrational'. Sikhs, most asserted, had not been discriminated against before or after Operation Blue Star, and Mrs Gandhi's assassination, which ironically led to the orchestrated attacks upon Sikhs, had 'removed' the problem.[17] They were thus free to get on with their lives and continue to practise their 'faith' in 'secular' India.

Sikhs in the diaspora, many not even born in 1984,[18] were, however, more willing to speak about an event which they had only experienced or 'witnessed' through the media. Prominent Sikh political activists I interviewed[19] admitted that they had been radicalized by Operation Blue Star[20] and in some cases had only become *Kes-dhari* Sikhs after the 'critical event'. Operation Blue Star thus enabled them to rediscover their 'Sikh' roots. The violence of 1984 was, for them, perfectly in keeping with an Indian state strategy of oppression of ethno-national minorities. The Sikh 'genocide' was, therefore, perfectly 'rational'.

For Edkins, the memorialization of war is a practice that reproduces stories of national glory and heroism, producing a linear time, the time of the state. Memorials to war, even to defeat, can inscribe the national myth or imagined community (Edkins 2003: 16–17). Sikhs in the diaspora have chosen to memorialize an event they never witnessed and to reinscribe it in a nationalist narrative that interrupts the homogenizing narrative of the Indian nation-state. They have sought to do so because they consider *their* nation, the *Khalsa* or Sikh *qaum*, to be at war with the 'pseudo-secular' Brahmanical Indian state. Thus 1984 is part of a narrative that legitimizes the creation of an independent Sikh state, *Khalistan*, by highlighting the repressive state policies of 'torture and genocide' employed by the Indian state in the Punjab. In recent years, this nationalist narrative has become increasingly mediated through graphic images of tortured political prisoners and an obliterated *Akal Takht* on the Internet, in an attempt to unite Sikhs living as far apart as London, Vancouver and Singapore and instil a sense of Sikh 'nationhood' in the diaspora.

As Brian Axel has pointed out, images of men valorized as martyrs (or *shahid*) circulate widely on the Internet along with historical narratives of the Sikh *qaum*. These images and narratives, according to Axel, 'interarticulate' with those that have circulated through other means, such as books, pamphlets, and audio-cassettes of Bhindranwale's speeches, and form a central part of an emergent archive of Sikh struggles. Consequently, Axel maintains that the 'pure' image of the gendered *amritdhari* Sikh has become twinned with the image of the tortured body in a new diasporic politics. 'Circulating globally by means of Internet technology, disparate images of gendered Sikh bodies have thus been brought together with discourses about a homeland, Khalistan, which, itself, has never existed as an empirical delimitation' (Axel 2002: 10). Although Axel is correct to draw attention to the symbolism of the tortured body of the male *amritdhari* Sikh, the body does not operate in a vacuum but derives its emotive power from the graphic representations of the *Akal Takht* reduced to rubble. For it is the *Akal Takht*, the site of all temporal authority within the Sikh tradition, which represents the Sikh 'nation'. By reducing the *Akal Takht* to rubble, the Indian state sought to destroy the Sikh 'nation' or, rather, Sikh aspirations to nationhood. The *shahid*[21] are in fact 'witnesses' to the martyring of the nation. As Mahmood explains, the *amritdhari* Sikh, in simply being there, is using his or her own body as a witness to the truth. In this 'perpetual challenge', *amritdhari* Sikhs disrupt the homogenizing narrative of the 'secular' Indian nation-state. The five Ks, as 'symbols of truth' in which people have invested their lives, become the critical aspects of witness, for relinquishing them under any circumstances, including torture, appears to *amritdhari* Sikhs as 'unforgivable capitulation'. The martyr is thus defined by Mahmood as one *whom terror does not silence* (Mahmood 1997: 24–25).

By logging on and downloading images of 1984 from the comfort of our own home, we also become witnesses to the terror of 1984. Indeed, witnessing is a recurrent theme in the cybernationalist discourse. Khalistan.net (http://www.khalistan.net), operated by sympathizers of the Council of Khalistan in the US, offers us 'glimpses of genocide', including 'a *Sikh* burnt alive', 'a Sikh tortured and butchered' and 'Avtar Singh, a candidate for Punjab Assembly brutally tortured (with hot iron and electric shock) and murdered by the Indian police' (Ajrawat 1997).

Maboli[22] Systems (http://www.maboli.com), which controls the Khalsa.net network, provides a detailed gallery of photos detailing 1984 under the trope 'human rights'. The gallery is divided into five sections: 'Operation Blue Star', 'Torture', '1984 Riots', 'Harassment' and 'Rape Victims' (Maboli Systems 1995). The first section details the immense damage that was inflicted upon the *Akal Takht* during Operation Blue Star. These pictures show pilgrims[23] being rounded up, arrested and even killed, although the army denies taking any pilgrims captive. We are thus witnesses to an event which the Indian army denied ever took place. Pride of place in the pantheon of Sikh *shahidi* goes naturally to Sant Jarnail Singh Bhindranwale[24] and his cohorts, Bhai Amrik Singh and General Shabeg Singh. The dead body of Shabeg Singh, the man who planned the 'defence' of the Golden Temple complex against the army of which he was formerly a general, lies in the bottom left-hand corner and is immediately followed by one of his 'Indian' counterpart, General K.S. Brar, walking into the holiest shrine in Sikhism with his shoes on, the biggest sign of disrespect in a Sikh *gurdwara*, which General Brar claims he never committed. We witness, therefore, not only the 'martyrdom' of General Shabeg Singh but also the lies and insensitivity of General Brar. On Khalistan.net, the disrespect shown to the *Khalsa* is illustrated by photos of Indian army officers posing in front of the *Akal Takht* after its destruction, a smile visible on their shaven faces (http://www.khalistan.net/obs.htm).

The most extensive collection of pictures, however, depicts graphically the 'genocide' of Sikhs in Delhi between 31 October and 3 November 1984. Maboli Systems devote seven separate pages to the November 1984 massacres, including gruesome photos of dogs picking at the remains of dead Sikh bodies and a large mob armed with sticks, poles and kerosene walking past a Sikh man who is burning alive. Many of the same photos are available on Khalistan.net and two websites set up especially to commemorate the twentieth anniversary of Operation Blue Star: Shaheed Khalsa (shaheedkhalsa.com) and Witness 84 (witness84.com). Whilst the former website makes the case explicitly for *Khalistan* and devotes three galleries to 'freedom fighters of Khalistan', the latter 'seeks to bring a new perspective to the Sikh campaign through means of communication that can invite interest and enquiry' (Witness 84 2004). These means of communication include organizing a year-long screening of films in the UK to highlight the Sikh struggle, a theatre production that will relate the stories and accounts of eyewitnesses during the storming of the Golden Temple, the Delhi anti-Sikh riots and subsequent atrocities against the Sikhs committed by the Indian state, and a visual arts show about the 1984 'experience'.

Although not strictly part of the 1984 'experience', photographs of the atrocities committed by the Indian and state security forces against Sikh militants are also exhibited in most of the major Sikh websites. The first picture on Maboli.com shows Amarjit Singh and Ajit Singh, two men who were taken into police custody and died of torture at the hands of the police. Other photographs show a Sikh youth who was taken into police custody and had his forearm damaged beyond repair and the partially decomposed body of a Sikh youth who has had his hair cut, head scalped, fingers cut off, limbs twisted and body burned. Similar photographs can be found on other websites, such as Burning Punjab or Khalistan Lionz, of torture victims exhibiting their wounds or their dead bodies thrown into trucks like rubbish. Almost as significant as the tortured body of the *amritdhari* male is that of the 'dishonoured' woman. Included in the category of 'rape victims' is 24-year-old Manjit Kaur, whose house was broken into by policemen on 22 February 1992 and who was raped repeatedly, despite being four months pregnant, and Amandeep Kaur, the 19-year-old sister of suspected militant Harpinder Singh Goldi who was repeatedly 'raped, tortured, mistreated' at various police stations throughout Bathinda district. When she reported her case to the Punjab Human Rights Organization, she was killed on 24 January 1992 (Maboli Systems 1995).

The online exhibition of victims of torture and rape may be seen not as a radical innovation but as a continuation of the post-1984 tradition of what Mahmood terms 'massacre art'. Usually, these images are exhibited outside *gurdwaras* or in rooms next to congregation halls, especially when the *ardas*, the daily prayer, is recited. 'In their very gruesomeness', Mahmood remarks, these images 'assert themselves in a room; they are impossible to ignore, and intrude in conversation, meditation, and everyday activities' (Mahmood 1996: 189). In other words, they serve to remind the community of the sacrifices made in defence of the *qaum*. The Internet has enabled graphic images of tortured political prisoners and an obliterated Golden Temple, previously exhibited outside *gurdwaras*, to be transmitted to a younger generation, many of whom do not go regularly to *gurdwaras* or know about the events of 1984. Like the Jewish or the Armenian holocaust, or the slave trade for African-Americans, it is this 'chosen trauma' that has enabled a Sikh *diaspora* to be imagined.[25]

Conclusion

It has been argued during the course of this chapter that territory and memory are intrinsic to the construction of nationalist *and* diaspora narratives. Diasporas, however scattered and dispersed, are usually defined in terms of common *memories* of a *territorially* defined 'homeland' or place of origin. These memories are necessarily selective. Following Edkins, some forms of 'remembering' can be seen as ways of 'forgetting'. The selective memory of the nationalist discourse 'remembers' the violence which the (Muslim/Hindu)

'Other' inflicted upon the (Sikh) 'Self' but 'forgets' both the complicity of the 'Self' in the violence of partition and the events leading up to 1984. The political use of the memories of partition by post-independence Sikh elites both 'naturalized' partition, that is, made it seem an inevitable consequence of 'primordial' religious differences, and, subsequently, made the imagination of a Sikh homeland or *Khalistan* in the diaspora possible. Centuries of peaceful coexistence between the three main religious communities of the Punjab were conveniently forgotten as *memory was territorialized*. Memory was itself partitioned between a Muslim 'Pakistan', a predominately Hindu 'India' and, after the similarly 'genocidal' violence unleashed by the Indian state following Operation Blue Star, a Sikh 'Khalistan'.

Furthermore, the existence of the concept of *ghallughara* in the Sikh tradition and its translation as 'holocaust' or 'genocide' allows Sikh nationalists to both construct a discourse of 'victimhood' and legitimize the 'imagined community' (Anderson 1991) of the nation internationally. Through the 'massacre art' exhibited outside *gurdwaras* and increasingly available online as a result of the ICT revolution, Sikhs are able to 'witness' the 'martyrdom' of the *shahid* in the Punjab and, most importantly, the desecration of the Golden Temple complex. It has been argued that the destruction of the *Akal Takht*, in particular, is (correctly in the author's opinion) interpreted as an attack upon Sikh sovereignty by the Indian state. Consequently:

> the movement for the preservation of Sikh identity is framed in a language which immediately places it in the context of modern nation states, for it is replete with references to the rights of minorities, international covenants and the centrality of territory of preserving identity.
>
> (Das 1995: 121)

This will be examined in the subsequent chapters of the book.

6   The politics of recognition

From a Sikh 'national' to a Sikh 'diasporic' identity in a post-9/11 world?[1]

> The politics of difference is full of denunciations of discrimination and refusals of second-class citizenship. This gives the principle of universal equality a point of entry within the politics of dignity. But once inside . . . its demands are hard to assimilate to that politics. For it asks that we give acknowledgment and status to something that is not universally shared.
>
> (Taylor 1994: 39)

This chapter examines the tensions that exist between a nationalist 'politics of homeland' and a diasporic 'politics of recognition', which are frequently conflated in practice. It will be argued that this tension, seen in the appropriation of the language of 'nationalism' by Sikh diasporic organizations and vice versa, stems from a common dynamic: the rift between *location* and *identity* within states in modern, Western, racialized societies. To a certain extent, the participation of many Sikhs in the *Khalistan* movement may be seen as motivated not only by a concern with Indian state repression in the Punjab, but also by a desire to gain *recognition* of their ethnic and religious particularity in their place of settlement.

The politics of recognition is predicated on the assumption that, far from being primordial, identity is formed in a continuing dialogue and struggle with significant 'Others' (Lacan 1977). The lack of recognition of the collective 'Self' by significant 'Others' can damage a group's moral and psychological well-being: its self-confidence, self-respect and self-esteem. In the case of the Sikhs, the significant 'Others' include 'white' people and other ethnic minorities, including Muslim and Hindu fellow Punjabis. The politics of recognition demands that the Sikh *qaum*'s particularity, as well as equal entitlements to collective rights, is recognized by the state, thus bringing into play a politics of difference not easily reconcilable with mainstream liberal thought. Whilst mainstream liberal thought, or the 'politics of equal dignity' in Taylor's words, 'fights' for forms of non-discrimination that are 'blind' to the ways in which citizens differ, the 'politics of difference' redefines non-discrimination as requiring that these distinctions are made the basis of differential treatment (Taylor 1994: 39–40).

The 'politics of recognition' has often been contrasted with an egalitarian 'politics of redistribution' and has been described as the dominant paradigm of justice of the 'postsocialist condition' (Fraser 1997). While claims for redistribution seek the alleviation of injustices which are rooted in 'exploitative' socio-economic relationships, claims for recognition seek the alleviation of cultural injustices which have their origins in social patterns of representation, interpretation and communication. Some view claims for 'recognition' and 'redistribution' to be contradictory and, in order to facilitate greater equality of opportunity, have called for the abandonment of the former in order to facilitate the latter. Brian Barry in particular has seen the granting of special rights to minority groups as inconsistent with an egalitarian commitment to the equalization of opportunities for all (Barry 2001). However, others have seen the two as interdependent; Nancy Fraser, for example, has shown how the two 'paradigms of justice' are, at an empirical if not a philosophical level, mutually interconnected (Fraser 1997). Struggles for recognition can be addressed by changing our cultural patterns of interpretation, communication and representation. These have *distributive* consequences, in that the transformation of the cultural status of misrecognized groups may have tangible socio-economic benefits, in the extension to them of entitlements to welfare, education, health care, housing, voting rights and their inclusion in the public sphere. For Selya Benhabib, *all* claims for distribution involve recognition. To distribute X (goods, services, entitlements) to Y (persons) always implies recognizing Y to be a certain kind of Gm (group member) in virtue of which Y is entitled to X. As members of one kind of social group, we have an entitlement to certain rights claims and not to others: as citizens we are entitled to vote; as foreigners and residents, we are not. Therefore, although redistribution and recognition are analytically distinguishable, in practice they are interdependent (Benhabib 2002: 69–71).

Recently, a plethora of groups have emerged in the diaspora committed to representing the interests of Sikhs in their places of settlement, and their activities will be briefly analysed below. Using the case studies of the Sikh Federation in the UK and the Sikh American Legal Defense and Education Fund (SALDEF) and the Sikh Coalition in the US, it is suggested that these groups are in the process of articulating a *diasporic* Sikh identity which encompasses claims for both recognition *and* redistribution, in response to the retreat from multiculturalism in the wake of the events of 11 September 2001 (hereafter 9/11) and 7 July 2005 (hereafter 7/7). This 'diasporic' identity is made possible by the mobilization of the Sikh community through the nationalist project but is opposed to its territorializing, reifying imperatives and, despite its homogenizing tendencies, may be considered counter-hegemonic. For, as Singh and Tatla have pointed out, if in the recent past 'the Sikh diaspora has been the main driver of the Sikh nationalism and homeland project, today it is also the site of creative alternatives' (Singh and Tatla 2006: 25). However, all three organizations operate *within* the boundaries and laws of their places of settlement and accept the nation-state as the basic and natural unit of world politics. Therefore, although the Sikh identity which they defend is implicitly *transnational* in that sovereignty is conferred on the *Khalsa panth* and not on any territorialized state, they cannot strictly be termed *transnational* organizations in the same way as the World Sikh Council or UNITED SIKHS (see Chapter 7).

Location and identity: the dynamics of Sikh diaspora nationalism

Although a closer examination of Sikh demands for a 'homeland' within India at the time of partition undermines the view that Sikh nationalism is an entirely diasporic phenomenon, Sikh diaspora nationalism does appear to have outlasted the militant separatism in the Punjab. Whilst, as Chapter 5 illustrated, Sikh militancy was crushed by police counterinsurgency operations[2] – part of a strategy of 'violent control'[3] by the Indian state which facilitated the re-emergence of the Badal faction of the Akali Dal as the premier political force within the Punjab – the Sikh diaspora continue to provide 'the ideological underpinning for the demand for a separate Sikh state' (GOI 1984: 35).

To some extent, Sikh diaspora nationalism may be seen as having its origins in a rift between location and identity within states in advanced capitalist societies, which has given rise to a 'politics of homeland' articulated through nationalist organizations. This is not to deny that linkages exist between nationalist organizations in the diaspora and militant organizations within the Punjab nor to downplay the genuine shock and anger felt as a result of the *ghallughara* of 1984, but merely to assert that *Khalistani* sympathizers have hitherto exerted a disproportionate degree of power and influence within the diaspora. Whilst the Sikh diaspora may not have radically restructured Sikh nationalism, which, for the most part, remains territorialized, it did not 'simply mirror homeland developments' as Gurharpal Singh has claimed (Singh 1999: 297). The 'politics of homeland' was constitutive of a specifically Sikh diaspora and may be seen as an outcome of the various localized 'politics of recognition' that preceded it.

As we have seen in Chapter 5, home, in the Sikh diasporic imagination, refers to the 'ancestral homeland', the mythic place of return rather than the lived experience of a locality. The concept of a Sikh diaspora thus 'opens up' what Paul Gilroy termed 'an historical and experiential rift between the place of residence and that of belonging' (Gilroy 1997: 329). The rift between location and identity may be seen in the disjuncture between a diaspora Sikh's legal identity as a citizen of a territorial state and his/her political identity, as a member of the transnational Sikh *qaum*. Location may be defined in terms of citizenship. Citizenship may be seen as a legal category as opposed to description of political identity. The citizen is linked intrinsically to the state insofar as it is only the state which can bestow this status upon the individual. However, as Benedict Anderson notes, a passport has become a mark of economic status far more than any political attachment (Anderson 1994: 324). For many South Asians, possession of US citizenship, in particular, not only greatly enhances employment prospects but increases the eligibility in the marriage market within the transnational *jati*.[4] With respect to many Punjabi immigrants, Anderson is quite right in stating that the 'segregated queues all of us experience at airport immigration barricades mark economic status far more than any political attachments' (Anderson 1994: 324).

Sikh political identity in places of settlement takes on the form of a diaspora consciousness: a 'homing desire', which may, but may not necessarily, take the form of a desire for a 'homeland'. The concept of diaspora, according to Avtar Brah, inscribes a homing desire while simultaneously critiquing discourses of fixed origins (Brah 1996: 193).The 'homing desire' of the Sikh diaspora can be seen in the variety of linkages that exist between diaspora Sikhs and the 'ancestral homeland'. The growth in the number of *gurdwaras* built around Sikh settlements, in particular, is indicative of this 'homing desire'.[5] Following Brah, the *gurdwara*, the site of religious, social, educational and political activity within the *panth*, may be seen as a 'diaspora space'.[6] Although the *gurdwara*, as a place of worship, is theoretically open to all denominations, it is also the locus of all religious/political power within the Sikh community and thus constructs religious boundaries between Sikh and non-Sikh. Political parties contest elections to the SGPC, which controls the *gurdwaras* in the Punjab.

The SGPC acts as the 'Sikh Parliament': its influence extends beyond the borders of the Punjab, facilitating the creation of a Sikh *national* consciousness. Furthermore, the Punjabi- and English-language press has played a vital role in the *imagination* of both a Sikh national identity and a specifically Sikh diaspora. At the turn of the millennium, there were over twelve daily newspapers (four in the UK) and thirteen periodicals (eight in the UK) published in either Punjabi and/or English published outside India serving the Sikh community (Tatla 1999: 72–73). The publications reflected the rising tide of an emerging Sikh national consciousness increasingly articulated and disseminated through the Internet and institutionalized in organizations such as the Khalistan Council in the UK, the World Sikh Organization and Council of Khalistan in North America, and various factions of the Babbar Khalsa International, Dal Khalsa and International Sikh Youth Federation throughout the diaspora (see Table 5.2).

This 'long-distance nationalism' keeps the dream of an imagined homeland alive. Its lingering image, according to Benedict Anderson, is of a Sikh, in Toronto or Vancouver (or London), who, unable or unwilling to participate in Canadian (or British) politics, keeps in touch with terrorist groups within India through e-mail.

> Canada indeed, by its profound indifference to him and to his fellows, encourages him to sikhify himself, and to live out a suburban dream politics of his own. His political participation is directed towards an

imagined *heimat* in which he does not intend to live, where he pays no taxes, where he cannot be arrested, where he will not be brought before the courts – and where he does not vote: in effect a politics without responsibility or accountability.

(Anderson 1992: 11)

For Anderson, it is this 'profound indifference' or alienation from the place of settlement which encourages the *cyberkhalistani* nationalist to take an active interest in the politics of 'the homeland', the Punjab. Put differently, Canadian *multiculturalism* (Taylor 1994; Kymlicka 1995) facilitates the emergence of Sikh diaspora nationalism. Verne A. Dusenbery goes so far as to suggest that Sikh identity in Canada may be seen as a product of state policies of multiculturalism (Dusenbery 1995, 1999) in the same way as Richard Fox had previously suggested that the Sikh self-image during the colonial period was a result of their treatment as a separate 'race' by the colonial state (Fox 1985). The discourse of multiculturalism as employed in modern Western states holds that society is naturally divided into a series of culturally distinct communities each with their way of 'trying to get the world right'. The Sikhs constitute one such community with their own distinct ethno-religious identity and appearance, yet in order to be recognized as such, and be eligible for state grants for university chairs, they need to differentiate themselves from other 'East Indians', to 'sikhify' themselves in Anderson's words. Like the Quebecois and First Nations, Sikhs affirm a separate identity, which cannot be attained within anglophone Canada. Unlike both 'nations without states' (Guibernau 1999), the Sikhs, however, do not lay claim to territories inside Canada and were encouraged to engage in 'long-distance nationalism' in order to gain the recognition of their particularity from the Canadian state, at least until the more violent manifestations of their long-distance nationalism threatened Indo-Canadian relations.

Such a simplistic explanation, however, ignores *both* the transnational links which exist between *Jat* Sikhs from East Punjab, particularly from Jullunder Doab (Ballard 1994), and the degree to which Sikhs in Canada[7] and elsewhere *are* participating in politics in their place of settlement. Despite considerable differences in the upward mobility, class composition and sheer numbers between British and North American Sikhs, Sikh organizations have sprung up on both sides of the Atlantic articulating a politics of recognition and difference in their place of settlement. It furthermore ignores the extent to which Sikhs and ethno-religious minorities have, through successful and coordinated political mobilization, made multiculturalism in North America and Europe possible. While Canada may 'encourage', in Anderson's words, the Sikhs to 'sikhify' themselves through a policy of multiculturalism, this is the case neither in the US, where Sikhs are expected to *de*-sikhify themselves by assimilating to the 'melting pot' (Glazer and Moynihan 1975) or core Anglo-Protestant 'American' values (Huntington 2004), nor in Britain, where Sikhs have 'played a crucial role as a bridgehead community which has "pioneered" British multiculturalism, but in so doing have also expanded its remit to include greater public recognition of the culture and traditions of other ethnic minority communities' (Singh and Tatla 2006: 210).

In the sections that follow, the rise of Sikh organizations articulating a 'politics of recognition' in, first, the UK and, secondly, the US will be examined. It will be argued that, following 9/11 in the US and 7/7 in the UK, the prospects for multiculturalism in both countries look bleak, with a sharp increase in racially motivated attacks upon Sikhs and an increased 'securitization' of daily life[8] making the need for a post-nationalist, *diasporic* 'politics of recognition' all the more pressing.

Britain: from 'nation-state' to 'community of communities'?

Four 'ideal-types' of institutional arrangements by which immigrants are invariably incorporated into the host country may be identified (Tambiah 2000: 167–168; Modood 2005). They are assimilation, exclusion and integration, with a fourth category of multiculturalism, which intersects with integration but highlights issues relating to the recognition of difference within plural societies whilst holding them together as viable polities. Whilst assimilation involves the creation of a 'melting pot', as in the US as described in the 1970s by Glazer and Moynihan (1975), where immigrants are expected to take the initiative in adapting to a de-ethnicized, market or secular culture as in France, exclusion involves the participation or incorporation of migrants only into the selected and marked-off sectors of the host society, as in Germany and Japan. Neither involves the state and majority community in change. In contrast, integration is a 'two-way' process of social interaction which requires members of the majority community as well as immigrants and ethno-cultural minorities to facilitate the emergence of an integrated society.

Multiculturalism is where processes of integration are seen both as two-way and as working differently for different groups. It differs from integration because it recognizes the *social reality* of ethno-cultural groups, not just of individuals and organizations. As Modood points out, this reality can be of different kinds, for example a sense of solidarity with people of similar origins or faith or mother tongue. It might be an act of imagination but may also be rooted in lived experience and embodied in formal organizations dedicated to fostering group identity and keeping it alive (Modood 2005). Philosophically, it is based on the premise that we are all 'cultural beings, born and raised within a thick culture, which we no doubt can revise and even reject but only by embracing some other culture' (Parekh 2002: 141). Politically, a commitment to multiculturalism tends to involve *active* state policies, in both the public and the private sphere, designed to accommodate immigrants in their host market through equal opportunities legislation, granting full access to social services, education and housing and, finally, access to citizenship whilst not requiring immigrants to 'give up' or *privatize* their pre-existing ethno-cultural identities. In so doing, it *legitimizes* the role of ethno-cultural groups in the political process.

The ideal of a multicultural society sees British society, in the words of John Rex, as 'involving simply a confrontation between private familial and communal cultures on the one hand, and the shared political culture of the public domain on the other' (Rex 1991: 13). The distinction between private and public domains corresponds to Tonnies's distinction between *gemeinschaft* and *gesellschaft*. Whilst the private domain is the space occupied by the socio-religious institutions of particular communities, the public domain is occupied by the political, educational, economic and legal systems that are shared by 'a multitude of natural and artificial individuals' from different communities bound together by a contractual relation (Tonnies 1955: 87). However, in much of the public debate on immigration and integration, the confrontation is seen as being between 'British public culture' in the public domain and 'the culture of immigrants in the private sphere'. The political culture of the public domain is not so much shared as constructed out of the 'myths and memories' (A.D. Smith 1999) of the 'British' (i.e. white) public.

Generally speaking, the British model of managing post-war immigration from former colonies since the mid-1960s has been, in the words of one of its principal architects, the former British home secretary Lord Jenkins, to avoid 'a flattening process of uniformity' as broadly favoured in continental Europe and the US, in favour of 'cultural diversity coupled with equality of opportunity in an atmosphere of mutual tolerance' (Singh and Tatla 2006: 209). However, the only 'cultural' distinctions recognized by the state were *racial* and not religious. The British state recognized the distinction between 'white' and 'non-whites' and, following political mobilization by minority groups employing a discourse of 'blackness', reluctantly passed legislation which outlawed overt racial discrimination.[9] However, it did not make distinctions *between* different groups of 'non-whites' and, when it finally did, it did so on the basis of *ethnic* background. Indeed, the Race Relations Acts of 1976 and 2000 do *not* include religion as a component of 'race', which is defined exclusively in terms of (skin) colour (Modood 2005: 113). Cultural difference, in other words, needs to be *racialized* in order for discrimination to be claimed.

The employment of what Modood (2005) terms this 'Atlantocentric' model of ethnic relations has led some theorists, such as Avtar Brah, to suggest that Sikhs and other former colonial immigrants can *never* be British because they are not seen as being native to Britain: Sikhs can be 'in' Britain, but not 'of' Britain (Brah 1996). For, although 'the membership of people with backgrounds in Africa, Asia and the Caribbean are accorded formal recognition', this recognition, as Harry Goulbourne has pointed out, 'is constructed in such a manner that their legitimate presence and participation in Britain are nearly always questioned' (Goulbourne 1991: 2). However, this view ignores the impact of globalization on *both* national and ethno-cultural identities. In particular, globalization has facilitated the emergence of 'hybrid' and 'multiple' identities, characterized by 'the refusal to be defined by any one or even a limited number of core identities'. At the same time, increased transnationalism has allowed local communities or ethno-religious groups 'who are keen to emphasise one or at least a limited number of core identities' to mobilize as political actors and seek 'quasi-corporate representation at local, national, and perhaps even transnational levels' (Modood 2005: 18).

An attempt to re-conceptualize British identity along multicultural lines to take account of the impact of globalization was made by the Commission on the Future of Multi-Ethnic Britain (2000). Chaired by Lord Parekh, a Labour peer and a leading theorist of multiculturalism, it concluded that Britain should be both a 'community of citizens and a community of communities' and 'both a liberal and a multicultural society'. While acknowledging the tension between liberalism and multiculturalism, the authors of the report felt that their sometimes 'conflicting requirements' could be reconciled (Runnymede Trust 2000: 1–2).

However, the report's recommendations, including the establishment of a new human rights commission and an equality commission as well as a single equality Act to cover all unlawful discrimination, met with a cool response from the government, and only two-thirds have been implemented (Runnymede Trust 2004).[10] Subsequent developments have only reinforced the marginalization of ethno-cultural minorities, particularly from the subcontinent, in Britain. The summer 'race' riots in Bradford, Burnley and Oldham involving mainly South Asian (Muslim) youth and 9/11 led to what Gurbux Singh, the former 'Sikh'[11] chair of the Commission for Racial Equality, termed a 'backlash against people who look different – Asians in particular' (Gurbux Singh 2001). The Cantle Report on the summer riots of 2001 proposed a loyalty test for all immigrants: an oath which, based on the Canadian model, would describe the 'responsibilities of citizenship' and include a promise to learn English and obey UK laws (UK Government Home Office 2001). According to the then home secretary, David Blunkett, the Cantle Report showed 'that too many of our towns and cities lack any sense of civic identity or shared values'. Blunkett warned that 'we have norms of acceptability and those who come into our home – for that is what it is – should accept those norms' (*Daily Telegraph*, 10 December 2001). In the 2002 White Paper on Immigration (UK Government Home Office 2002a), Blunkett outlined plans for 'light touch' naturalization programmes, including obtaining a 'modest grasp' of English in order to encourage immigrants to become 'more British', and a clause was inserted into the first paragraph of the new Nationality, Immigration and Asylum Act 2002 requiring immigrants to acquire 'sufficient knowledge about life in the United Kingdom' before becoming citizens (UK Government Home Office 2002b).

Writing at the time of the Iraq war, Singh and Rex concluded, in the light of the publication of the Cantle Report and the demise of the 'Leicester Model' of civic multiculturalism,[12] that, 'whereas the United Kingdom had been a place where multiculturalism could be sympathetically discussed and shown to be compatible with a modern society and a welfare state, it was now seen as a danger' (Singh and Rex 2003: 15). This perception of multiculturalism as a danger was greatly exacerbated by the events of 7 July (and also 21 July) 2005. On 7 July 2005 terrorist attacks on London Transport left fifty-two people dead.[13] The four young Muslims who carried out the 7/7 attacks, Mohammed Siddeque Khan, Hasib Hussein, Shazad Tanweer and Jermaine Lindsay, were all British citizens. Although there is still uncertainty about whether the attacks were conceived locally or planned abroad, the spectre of 'home-grown' terrorism has led many to lay blame at the door of what were viewed as 'multiculturalist' policies.[14] In conclusion, the establishment of a non-racially stratified society 'in which non-white migrants and their progeny can come to have a genuine sense of belonging to Britain without having to disavow their ethnic identities' (Modood 2005: 6) remains some way off.

In the section that follows, we will examine the history of Sikh political mobilization in the UK. It will be argued that, although this mobilization has taken different forms, the objectives have been consistent: to gain *recognition* of the Sikh community as a distinct ethno-religious or cultural group in their place of settlement. Consequently, a distinction between a 'politics of home-land' and a 'politics of recognition' is difficult to sustain, as the movement for *Khalistan* may, to some extent, be seen as *part of a broader politics of recogni-tion*. Finally, the emergence of the Sikh Federation (UK) will be examined in the light of a new, post-9/11 *diasporic* identity which encompasses *both* a 'politics of recognition' *and* 'distribution' (Fraser 1997; Benhabib 2002).

The politics of recognition: Sikh political mobilization in the UK

> Within the empire, the Sikhs had achieved status and stature. But when Sikh immigrants arrived on British soil they encountered a wall of racism and discrimination. Regardless of their qualifications or colonial contri-butions, Sikhs found themselves grouped together with other Asians, Africans and Afro-Caribbeans as 'black, foreign and inferior'.
>
> (K.D. Hall 2002: 4)

Britain is home to the largest community of Sikhs outside the subcontinent. Between a third and a half of a total of approximately 1 million overseas Sikhs live in the UK. According to the 2001 Census, there were 336,179 Indian-Sikhs in the UK (National Statistics Online 2001) but, since there is no census category for Sikh as an *ethnic group*, others have put the figure as high as 500,000 (Tatla 1999: 43) and 600,000 (British Sikh Federation 2003).[15] Although the Sikhs are one of the most upwardly mobile ethnic minorities, with a standard of living in line with the national average (Singh and Tatla 2006: 145–164), they remain, together with other ethnic minorities, under-represented in public life.[16] Although there are 'Sikh' Members of Parliament[17] and there have been Sikh Lord Mayors of Leicester,[18] there still exists what

Johan Galtung has termed a 'structural disequilibrium' (Galtung 1971) between the upward mobility of immigrants of South Asian descent in the economic sphere and their inability to find corresponding levels of social respectability and political power within metropolitan societies. This 'structural disequilibrium' may be seen to have given rise to a 'politics of recognition' (Taylor 1994), which in the case of Sikh organizations in Britain initially took the form of a desire to preserve the external symbols of the faith.

The status of the turban as an external symbol of Sikh identity in particular has been contested by the state in advanced capitalist societies keen to regulate increasingly multiethnic societies through 'difference-blind' liberal principles (Barry 2001). The case of G.S. Sagar, whose application for the position of a bus conductor with Manchester Transport was turned down because he wanted to wear his turban rather than the uniform cap prescribed by the municipality for all its transport workers, illustrates the clash between the 'politics of difference' and the 'politics of equality'. Sagar argued that the wearing of a turban was an essential part of his religious beliefs – an assertion which may well have been contested by the transport authorities given that the *Khalsa Rahit* does not explicitly instruct Sikhs to wear turbans. Instead of contesting the status of the turban as a symbol of Sikh identity, the transport authorities argued that 'if an exception to the rules of wearing the proper uniform were allowed there was no telling where the process would end. The uniform could only be maintained if there were no exceptions' (Cohn 1996: 106–107). Sagar enlisted the help of his local *gurdwara* and the Sikh community in Manchester and eventually, after seven years, the decision was reversed. After the Sagar ruling, Sikh organizations became increasingly assertive. The subsequent case of a Sikh bus driver in the Midlands, T.S. Sandhu, dismissed for wearing a turban and thus violating the customary code of the Wolverhampton Transport Authority, gave rise to *morchas*, petitions and threats of self-immolation in the 1960s and eventually led to a direct intervention on his behalf by a senior Akali leader, Gurnam Singh, who exerted pressure on the transport authorities by lobbying Indira Gandhi (Tatla 2001: 165). This was followed in the 1970s with the Motorcycle Crash Helmets (Religious Exemption) Act of 1976 which exempted *Kes-dhari* Sikhs from having to wear crash helmets when riding a motorcycle. Although merely symbolic, the passing of the Act,[19] after a successful campaign led by Sardar Baldev Singh Chahal which saw many *Kes-dhari* Sikhs attempting to ride a motorcycle for the first time,[20] was viewed as a public affirmation of the separate identity of the Sikhs and helped first construct ethno-religious boundaries between Sikhs and other South Asian minorities in the popular British imagination.

Finally, the exclusion of a *Kes-dhari* Sikh boy, Gurinder Singh Mandla, from an English public school for wearing a turban and the subsequent court ruling that the Sikhs were indeed an 'ethnic group' gave legal recognition to the hegemonic narrative of Sikh identity. In making it possible for Sikhs to enter educational institutions without having to abandon the external symbols of their faith, the *Mandla* v. *Dowell Lee* (1983) case 'marked a major landmark in the development of the community and anti-discrimination legislation in the UK' (Singh and Tatla 2006: 130–133). Initially, the case brought by Mandla's father, with the support of the newly established Commission for Racial Equality (CRE), against the headmaster of the school, A.G. Dowell Lee, was dismissed by the county court on the grounds that Sikhs did not constitute a 'racial group' and so were not covered under the Act. This decision was upheld by the Court of Appeal, yet following a concerted campaign of demonstrations orchestrated by the various chapters of the SAD in the UK the case was referred to the House of Lords, where the decision was overturned. Sikhs, the law lords claimed, resembled an 'ethnic' group as they possessed a 'long shared history' and a 'cultural tradition' of their own (Singh and Tatla 2006: 130–133). Sikhs were thus brought, like Jews but *unlike* other religious groups, within the protection of the Race Relations Act, and Sikh religious identity was *ethnicized* or even *racialized* in much the same way as in colonial times. Consequently, although the Act was a great victory for the Sikh community, it did not change the fundamental paradigm of British ethnic relations, which remained constructed on racial lines and sought to relegate non-Christian religious identities to the 'private' sphere, where they could not be covered by existing legislation.

More recently, the reasoning and significance of the *Mandla* v. *Dowell Lee* case has been contested by proponents of multiculturalism and advocates of a 'difference-blind' liberal egalitarianism. On the one hand, for Parekh and other multiculturalists, Sikhs should be allowed to wear turbans in schools on the 'grounds of equality of opportunity and respect for difference' (Parekh 2002: 147). On the other hand, advocates of a difference-blind liberalism such as Brian Barry may concede the right to wear turbans in schools as an *exception* to a general rule which should emphasize uniformity. Students, the reasoning goes, should be allowed to wear turbans in schools as it does not interfere with the effective functioning of the school. However, Barry contends that workers should *not* be allowed to wear turbans on construction sites as it does not offer adequate protection. So where Parekh views religious 'beliefs as significant components of a fulfilling life, and urges exemption for that reason, Barry sees them as at best irrelevant, and at worst significant impediments to a fulfilling life' (Mendus 2002: 40). Broadly speaking, the latter view is more representative of the British approach to managing diversity. However, with respect to the wearing of turbans on construction sites, once again Sikhs were able to secure an exception to the general rule as a result of political mobilization. Section 11 of the Employment Act 1989 granted a Sikh immunity from having to wear a safety helmet 'at any time when he is wearing a turban'.

The politics of homeland: the movement for **Khalistan**

The second phase of the 'politics of recognition' was marked by an increasing identification with the 'politics of the homeland', significantly by the same organizations and individuals active in the motorcycle campaign. This is the outcome not *only* of the impact of what Darshan Singh Tatla terms the 'critical event' of 1984 on the Sikh diaspora, but also, albeit to a lesser degree, of the changes taking place in British political life. The Falklands war of 1982 marked the beginning of a revival of a British ethnic nationalism, espoused by politicians from the mainstream Conservative right, articulated by the tabloids and characterized by the infamous Tebbit 'cricket test'. Increasingly, British South Asians became the alternating 'Other' (with other non-white ethnic minorities) against which British ethnic identity was constructed. In such a political climate, public displays of multiple political identities were difficult. Draconian immigration rules appeared to target subcontinental immigrants, yet failed to stem the tide of those seeking to be reunited with their extended families in the UK. Becoming British entailed a choice: identifying with the invented traditions of Britain's imperial past, with one's place of settlement, over one's place of origin. Those unwilling or unable to do so were left on the margins of British political life and 'encouraged' to identify with collective identities suppressed in their place of origin.

Economically, however, many Sikhs were able to make the transition from industrial workers and council tenants to entrepreneurs and homeowners.[21] Thus, perhaps paradoxically, the economic reforms and ethnic nationalism associated with Thatcherism led to the creation of a Sikh middle class willing and able to mobilize in support of a homeland but reluctant or unable to participate in British political life. Of particular significance for the 'sikhification' of diaspora politics was the demise of the Indian workers' associations (IWAs) in the light of these structural changes.[22] During the late 1950s and 1960s, the IWAs sprang up in almost every industrial city in the UK with a large *Jat* Sikh population and were in the vanguard in the unionization of Asian labour and the fight against racial exclusionism within the trade union movement. By the mid-1980s, the secular ideology of the IWAs no longer appealed to militant Sikh activists, who flocked to join the various *Khalistani* movements. The most significant of these were the Khalistan Council, International Sikh Youth Federation (ISYF), Babbar Khalsa (BK) and Dal Khalsa (DK) (Singh and Tatla 2006: 106).

Of these organizations, the most representative and influential was the Khalistan Council. Led by the charismatic ideologue Dr Jagjit Singh Chauhan (1927–2007), the Council was elected on 23 June 1984 in Southall and included Gurmej Singh of the Babbar Khalsa, Sewa Singh of the spiritual Akhand Kirthani Jatha, youth leader Kharamjit Singh, and Harmander Singh of the Akali Dal. Although Gurmej Singh left in 1986 to form his own 'government in exile' in the Midlands, the Khalistan Council replaced the SAD as the main political organization representing Sikhs in the UK (Tatla 1999: 140). Eschewing violent means, Chauhan consistently advocated a secular vision of *Khalistan* and returned to the Punjab in 2001 to continue his campaign for the establishment of a sovereign Sikh state through the Khalsa Raj party. His death, following his party's overwhelming defeat in the 2007 state elections, robbed the *Khalistan* movement of its most eloquent and charismatic leader and was covered in the international press.[23]

Towards a 'diasporic' political identity? The Sikh Federation (UK)

The establishment of the Sikh Federation (UK) in 2003 marked a new phase in the 'politics of recognition'. A non-governmental organization, it claims to be, and is registered as, 'the first ever Sikh political party in the United Kingdom', with the stated aim of giving Sikhs 'a stronger political voice by taking an increasing interest in mainstream politics in the UK' (Sikh Federation (UK) 2003a). Specifically, it is charged with implementing the Sikh Agenda, which was produced for the UK government in 2001. The key features of the Agenda are grouped into eight headings: Sikhs and the British establishment; government funding and Sikh organizations; the promotion of the Sikh identity and the Punjabi language; the establishment of state-funded Sikh schools; preserving Sikh heritage; the protection of the human rights of Sikhs and humanitarian aid; self-determination for the Sikh 'nation'; and, finally, lifting the ban on the International Sikh Youth Federation (Sikh Federation (UK) 2003b).

The first item on the Sikh Agenda is:

> to seek fair representation of British Sikhs in the establishment at local and national levels including local and central government and in Parliament and further to ensure fair recruitment and employment policies and practices in the public and private sector services.

The objective is to 'encourage British Sikhs, particularly practising Sikhs, to actively participate in British politics at national and local levels with a view to securing a greater Sikh representation of MPs, MEPs, Lords and councillors' (Sikh Federation (UK) 2003c).

The second item on the Agenda is government funding for Sikh organizations. The Sikh Federation (UK) seeks to 'secure for Sikh organisations and Sikh projects a "fair" share of Government funding made available to voluntary, charitable, community and religious organisations' (Sikh Federation (UK) 2003d). It seeks to achieve this by undertaking research regarding direct and indirect UK government funding available to voluntary, charitable, community and religious organizations and, with the help of the UK government, raising the awareness of Sikh organizations about the different sources of funding for Sikh projects by providing them with advice and assistance on how best to obtain funds from different sources within government.

The next item on the Agenda, the promotion of 'a distinct Sikh religion, history, culture and ethnic identity while respecting other religions and cultures', more closely reflects the new language of globalized identity politics within the discourse of multiculturalism. Greater recognition for Sikh identity, however, is seen to necessitate greater recognition for the Punjabi *language* in the UK, thereby underlining the importance of a language shared by many, perhaps even the majority of, South Asian immigrants in the UK, in the construction of a distinct Sikh identity and the transmission of 'Sikh' values. The Sikh Federation (UK) seeks to achieve this by working with the UK government to ensure, first, a better understanding of the Sikh religion in government institutions and, second, that the UK legislative and legal framework fully recognizes the right of Sikhs to practise their religion 'and fully respects the visible Sikh identity and articles of faith that are an essential part of the Sikh religion' (Sikh Federation (UK) 2003e). Specifically, the British Sikh Federation (UK) seeks the recognition of the 'British Sikh Community' as a separate *ethnic* group with a distinct *identity* embodied in the Five Ks so that any legal or social pressures to part with 'their articles of faith at work and at any public or business place' would fall under existing legislation on *racial* discrimination.

The fourth item on the Sikh Agenda, the call for the establishment of state-funded Sikh schools, clearly illustrates the *distributive* consequences of the 'politics of recognition'. Although it is claimed that Sikhism is the 'third largest faith in the UK', there is only one Sikh denominational school compared to almost 7,000 for other faiths. Consequently, the Sikh Federation (UK) seeks 'the establishment of a network of State funded Sikh schools in locations where there is a need in terms of promoting spiritual and cultural awareness of Sikh principles' in line with existing state policy on the funding of denominational schools and pledges to lobby the UK government to provide 'maximum financial assistance for the establishment and operation of Sikh schools' (Sikh Federation (UK) 2003f).

Preserving Sikh heritage is the fifth item on the Agenda (Sikh Federation (UK) 2003g). This involves the establishment of Sikh museums, the conservation of the *Guru Granth Sahib* manuscripts, and the lobbying not only of the UK government but also of relevant UN bodies to designate appropriate Sikh sites as World Heritage sites. The (trans)*nationalist* nature of the Sikh Agenda is clearly illustrated by the subsequent items on the Agenda: protecting the human rights of Sikhs, self-determination for the Sikh nation, and lifting the ban on the ISYF. Although the Sikh Federation seeks to protect the human rights of Sikhs in general, the wording makes it clear that the rights of Indian Sikhs are seen as particularly at risk (Sikh Federation (UK) 2003h).[24] This strategic use of the 'politics of victimhood' creates space for the explicit articulation of the nationalist position in the seventh item on the Agenda, which seeks the UK government's support for 'the Sikh Nation's right to self-determination' (Sikh Federation (UK) 2003i). In order to do so, the Sikh Federation, among a plethora of other Sikh organizations across the diaspora including the British Sikh Federation, British Consultative Forum, SAD (UK), National Council of Gurdwaras (UK), and Council of Khalistan, contributed to a March 2005 report of the Human Rights Advisory Group of the Panjabis in Britain All Party Parliamentary Group (HRAG 2005) which makes the clearest statement yet of the (British) Sikh diaspora's (continued) support for *Khalistan*. Using the language of universal human rights, HRAG concludes that the Sikhs have a 'lawful right' to self-determination and calls on the 'international community' to intervene so Sikhs can 'secure their lawful rights' (HRAG 2005: 16).

In conclusion, the Sikh Agenda illustrates the tension between the two narratives of 'nation' and 'transnational community'. The politicization of Sikh identity by the Sikh Federation suggests a potential challenge to the hegemonic narrative of the nation-state which constructs British subjects as citizens with equal rights and relegates religious and ethnic identity to the 'private sphere'. In this sense, the Sikh Federation's narrative may be considered 'diasporic', referring to a form of community consciousness and solidarity that maintains identifications outside of the nation-state 'in order to live inside, with a difference' (Clifford 1997: 251). In so doing, it points to what Sayyid describes as 'the impossibility of the nation', here defined as the British state, 'to provide a common "home" for all its inhabitants' (Sayyid 2001: 36). However, the Sikh Federation operates within the confines of the British political system and articulates its demands to the British state, in the space opened up for it by the state's discourse of multiculturalism.[25] The Sikh Federation utilizes, and thus implicitly *legitimizes*, the categories of 'religion' and 'ethnic group' in order to represent its interests to the British political system despite the fact that the Sikhs are 'at home' in neither category.

Furthermore, the elucidation of a 'diaspora' narrative – one which interrupts the closure of the nation-state and which implicitly challenges its primacy as the basic unit of international political life – is undermined by the Sikh Federation's commitment to seeking the UK government's support for 'self-determination for the Sikh Nation'. Indeed, according to Bhai Amrik Singh, the chair of the Sikh Federation (UK), the establishment of 'an independent sovereign Sikh state' remains the Sikh Federation's 'ultimate goal', since it will provide 'a solution to many difficulties faced by the Sikh community' in the diaspora (Gurjeet Singh 2007). This seems to suggest that the Sikh Federation cannot be considered a strictly *diasporic* organization in Clifford's sense, as it cannot go beyond *Khalistan* and envisage a Sikh identity in a non-territorial form.

Who are we? *Khalistan*, 9/11 and Sikh-American identity

> As witnesses to the 1984 riots in India and as immigrants in a post 9/11 America, Sikh immigrant youth from India face unique challenges as they make America home during emergent and changing social and political climates.
>
> (R.S. Verma 2006: 89)

For many Sikh immigrants to the US, pre-9/11 America represented their *Khalistan*:[26] a multicultural 'melting pot' (Glazer and Moynihan 1975) of different races, creeds and ethnicities where Sikhs were free to practise their religion without fear of persecution or state interference. Unlike the situation in the UK, Sikhs are not bound to Americans by a history of colonization; there is no established church, monarchy or other symbols of empire. Neither was there a post-war labour shortage, and the US seemed prepared to accept only well-educated, skilled professionals. Consequently, a perception has arisen that there is no significant Sikh-American working class and that American Sikhs, along with other South Asian Americans, have found fewer impediments to their entry into the American middle class than their relatively more numerous but less affluent British brethren, who initially found themselves marginalized by racialized discourses of Britishness.

However, a closer analysis of Sikh migration in the US will reveal that Sikhs have always faced legal challenges to the recognition of their distinctive identity and their very presence on American soil ever since the US Supreme Court ruled against Bhagat Singh Thind in 1923 (*US Supreme Court* v. *Bhagat Singh Thind* 1923).[27] Furthermore, those Sikhs who have managed to become US citizens have experienced racial stigmatization, physical abuse and employment discrimination as a result of their distinctive, and by implication 'un-American', appearance. This has intensified since 9/11, spawning the establishment of a plethora of organizations which have sought, first, to protect Sikhs from racially motivated attacks or 'hate crimes' and, second, to protect the civil rights of Sikhs from the increased 'securitization' (Buzan *et al.* 1998) of American society. In so doing, groups such as the Sikh Coalition, the Sikh American Legal Defense and Education Fund (SALDEF) and UNITED SIKHS have built upon the experiences of advocacy, lobbying and institutionalizing legal networks established by nationalist organizations such as the World Sikh Organization, Council of Khalistan and Khalistan Affairs Center, in order to articulate a post-nationalist 'politics of recognition' encompassing redistributive demands, which may be described as *diasporic* (Clifford 1997).

Sikh migration to the US

Although the beginning of Sikh immigration to North America is attributed to army connections, by the beginning of the last century an increasing number of Sikh Punjabi 'sojourners' came to work as labourers along the Pacific coast. Between 1904 and 1923 over 10,000 Sikhs lived in California, with a significant number around Yuba City, California, where a thriving Sikh community remains.[28] However, this number dwindled to just 3,000 in 1947 as a result of the introduction of discriminatory legislation which was aimed at stemming the tide of Asian immigration (Tatla 1999: 54). The 1917 Immigration Act banned further migration from Asia. Sikhs and other Asian immigrants had earlier been barred under the California Alien Land Act of 1913 from owning land and, under the *US Supreme Court* v. *Bhagat Singh Thind* 1923, from even becoming American citizens on the grounds of race.[29] Unable to gain recognition as 'Americans' (i.e. as 'free, white persons'), many

Sikh Punjabis succeeded, through intermarriage and Hispanicization, in assimilating themselves into the mainly Mexican rural working class (Leonard 1992).

After the Second World War, the Luce–Cellar Act of 1946 lifted restrictions on Asian immigration and granted naturalization rights to Asian Indians, no doubt in partial recognition of the sacrifices which many Indians, including a significant number of Sikhs, had made to the Allied cause. The increase in immigration allowed chain migration to take place as Punjabi Sikh men brought their wives and extended families to the US. The immediate post-war years saw the making of rural Sikh communities along the Pacific coast as *gurdwaras* were built enabling Sikh religion and culture to be reproduced and transmitted to Sikh youth. These communities, however, resembled isolated cultural islands and, despite the election of a shaven Punjabi Sikh, Dalip Singh Saund (1889–1973), to the US Congress in 1956, Sikhs remained, like other 'coloured Others', on the margins of an American society bifurcated on racial lines.

The civil rights movement succeeded in drawing government and public attention to the racialized nature of American democracy, and the Civil Rights Act 1964 sought to redress the grievances of discriminated-against minorities through the creation of the category of 'protected groups'. However, with the exception of African-Americans, it was unclear which groups were eligible to be classified as 'protected groups'.[30] The Civil Rights Act brought into existence the American welfare state, which, unlike its European counterparts, is, according to Benhabib, 'unique in that it has both typical redistributionist policies in the areas of social security, unemployment compensation, retirement, medical and housing benefits, and policies dedicated to completing the Civil Rights movement's agenda of racial, gender and ethnic equality' (Benhabib 2002: 72). Consequently, attaining the status of 'protected group' became highly desirable for disadvantaged minorities, as material benefits accrued from government recognition of that status.

The passing of the Civil Rights Act facilitated the emergence of a South Asian-American urban middle class, drawn from a 'third wave' of younger, skilled and more professional immigrants who settled in urban areas and were both fluent in the English language and well versed in their constitutional rights as US citizens. This wave of immigration accounted for half to two-thirds of Asian Indians now settled in the United States, with an annual rate of 14,376 immigrants per year between 1966 and 1981 (Gonzales 1986: 48). They were joined in the US in the 1980s and early 1990s by predominately rural immigrants, many of whom had requested political asylum from India or were refugees fleeing the troubles in the Punjab. As is to be expected given the disparities in cultural and socio-economic capital, considerable differences in outlook do exist between these two classes of Sikh migrants. According to Gurinder Singh Mann, 'Sikhs from urban backgrounds in the Punjab tend to stress the importance of devotional activity, while those from rural backgrounds are interested in the political agenda as well' (Mann

2000: 267). However, the establishment of *gurdwaras* has facilitated the emergence of a distinctly *Sikh*, as opposed to Punjabi or South Asian, community in the US with shared concerns. This community also includes a number of European converts to Sikhism. Followers of the late Harbhajan Singh Yogi, they 'constitute a small but visible segment of the community' (Mann 2000: 261).

Long-distance nationalism: the Ghadar movement and the movement for Khalistan

The history of Sikh diaspora nationalism in North America is almost as old as the Sikh community in the US itself and can be traced back to the *Ghadar* movement in the early years of the last century. The *Ghadar* (literally meaning 'revolt' or 'mutiny') movement has its origins in the experiences of Punjabis who migrated to North America in search of labour opportunities between 1905 and 1913. Harish Puri estimates that over 95 per cent of the movement was made up of Punjabi immigrants, mostly Sikhs, who worked on the Pacific coast of North America as unskilled labourers, farm workers, owner farmers and contractors (Puri 1993: 3). Confronted by the racism of white settlers and the exclusionary practices of North American states, many loyal Punjabis, some of whom had served 'King and Country' in the British army, looked to the *Ghadar* newspaper, published by Har Dayal from San Francisco, for a suitable explanation. The *Ghadar* effectively made the link between the poverty in the Punjab from which they had fled and economic exploitation by the British. For Puri:

> Their real life experiences in North America and their early organised community activity made it possible for the revolutionary nationalist propaganda to effectively link the existing oppressions of these people with their oppressions back home. That underlined the fact that India's interests and those of the British empire were not irreconcilable. There was only one answer: Ghadar i.e., violent revolutionary change.
>
> (Puri 1993: 3)

Juergensmeyer similarly argues that 'the hostility towards the prejudice of North Americans was transferred into hostility against the British, as the immigrant community identified itself with the nationalist struggle against the oppression in India' (Juergensmeyer 1977: 2).

Seventy years later, the reality of racial discrimination and increasing intolerance within Europe and North America reinforced the feeling of marginality, alienation and nostalgia amongst immigrant populations. In both cases, 'the cry for a homeland can be interpreted as a demand for "honour" and "respect" or a wish to be seen as equals among the world of nations' (Tatla 1999: 208). Sikh participation in the *Khalistan* movement, just like Punjabi participation in the *Ghadar* movement, may be seen as an attempt to change the political map of South Asia in order to gain honour or respect in their place of settlement. The Sikhs need an independent 'homeland' in order to 'feel at home' in a world of nation-states. However, whereas the 'imagined community' of the early settlers was India, free India itself later became the 'evil empire' from which liberation was sought.

In the United States, three organizations in particular have sought to articulate a 'politics of homeland' since 1984: the World Sikh Organization (WSO), the Council of Khalistan and the Khalistan Affairs Center (KAC). The WSO was founded on 28 July 1984 in Madison Square Gardens, New York, at a gathering attended by representatives of Sikh organizations from around the world. The goal was to create an organization that would be the representative voice of the Sikhs, and an international council was established. The WSO General Assembly presently has fifty-one members selected from among five regions of the world in which Sikhs are concentrated. The regional breakdown of General Assembly members is eleven from India, ten each from Canada, the USA and the UK, and ten from the rest of the world (WSO, 4 August 2007). However, despite its transnational organizational structure, it remains a primarily North American-based organization[31] committed to 'strive, through peaceful means, for the establishment of a Sikh nation, KHALISTAN, in order to protect the Sikh identity and faith as ordained by the Guru Panth in the daily prayer RAJ KAREGA KHALSA' (WSO 2007, capitalization in original). Its bilingual weekly, *World Sikh News*, published from Stockton, California, aims to 'project the voice of the Sikhs across the world' by giving news of the 'independence struggle' while highlighting Sikh participation in America's social and cultural life (Tatla 1999: 118).

The Council of Khalistan emerged from a factional split within the WSO and has been run since its inception by Dr Gurmit Singh Aulakh from an office in Washington, DC. Dr Aulakh,[32] who has built up a reputation as an effective lobbyist, is the president of the Council of Khalistan and is widely accepted as the unofficial spokesman for the Sikh 'nation' in the US, where he has tirelessly campaigned for the establishment of an independent Sikh homeland. Originally a member of the WSO, Dr Aulakh left in 1986 to establish the International Sikh Organisation. After having been appointed to represent the Sikhs in North America by the Panthic Committee in the Punjab, Dr Aulakh founded the Council of Khalistan and has managed to attract the support of, and more importantly funding from, American *gurdwaras* (Tatla 1999: 121). The Council of Khalistan is registered with the Department of Justice (DOJ) in Washington, DC, under the Foreign Agents Registration Act as an agent of the Council of Khalistan, Golden Temple, Amritsar, Punjab (Council of Khalistan 2007).

Dr Aulakh's strategy, in common with that of other nationalist organizations including the Khalistan Affairs Center, has been to highlight India's systematic human rights abuses in the Punjab and elsewhere. He has managed to do so by building contacts within Congress. Whereas earlier support came from members of Congress representing constituencies with a significant number of Sikh voters,[33] Edolphus Towns of New York, together with Cynthia A. McKinney and Dan Burton (chairman of the US House Government Committee), has emerged as the most vocal critic of the Indian state's treatment of the Sikhs and most vocal supporter of the Council of Khalistan. Representative Towns has frequently praised Dr Aulakh for his organizational work and has openly introduced press releases from the Council of Khalistan in Congress, thereby cementing Dr Aulakh's position within the Sikh diaspora as the leading representative of the Sikh nation.[34] Another strategy favoured by Dr Aulakh is the publication of 'open letters' to public figures which are posted on the Council of Khalistan website. Recent letters have been sent to the prime minister of Pakistan (16 November 2006), the *Jathedar* of the *Akal Takht* (9 January 2007) and President Bush (30 May 2006). In an 'open letter' to Prime Minister Manmohan Singh (10 October 2006), Dr Aulakh attempts to invert the discourse of 'victimhood' used by India in relation to cross-border terrorism from militant groups operating in Pakistan by making the familiar claim that India is a terrorist state itself engaged in supporting cross-border terrorist activities and in the repression of its minorities. The letter concludes with an assertion that there is 'no place for Sikhs in a supposedly secular, supposedly democratic India' and that the establishment of *Khalistan* is imminent:

> Our moment of freedom is closer than ever. Sikhs will continue to work to make certain that we shake ourselves loose from the yoke of Indian oppression and liberate our homeland, Khalistan, so that all Sikhs may live lives of prosperity, freedom, and dignity.
>
> (Aulakh 2006)

Dr Aulakh's work in Washington, DC, has been assisted by Dr Awatar Singh Sekhon from Edmonton, Canada. An internationally renowned scientist in the field of medical mycology, Dr Sekhon is also editor of the *International Journal of Sikh Affairs* and author, with Dr Harjinder Singh Dilgeer, of a *White Paper on Khalistan* (Sekhon and Dilgeer 2006). The *White Paper* was prepared in response to the infamous Indian government *White Paper* of 1984 which attempted to deflect criticism of its decision to storm the Golden Temple by asserting that the movement for *Khalistan* was exclusively a diaspora phenomenon (GOI 1984). The *White Paper on Khalistan* rehearsed the reasons needed for the establishment of *Khalistan*: Punjab as the 'historic homeland of the Sikhs'; the loss of Sikh 'sovereignty' to the British in 1849; the transfer of the Punjab from British to 'Hindu India' in 1947 against the will of the Sikh people; the colonization and persecution of Sikh and other minorities by the Indian state; Operation Blue Star and the genocide of the Sikhs after 1984; and the betrayal of the Sikh 'nation' by the Akali and SGPC leadership of Badal and Tohra (Sekhon and Dilgeer 2006).

The Khalistan Affairs Center (KAC) was established under a mandate by the Panthic Committee to promote the vision and creation of a sovereign Sikh state. Dr Amarjit Singh was appointed as the Panthic Committee spokesman in November 1991 and chartered to lead the KAC. Under his direction, the Center focuses its activities on advocacy for *Khalistan* by publicizing the 'atrocities committed by the Indian State against Sikhs'. In common with the Council of Khalistan, the KAC holds *Khalistan* to be 'the only solution to curb future atrocities against the Sikhs and to put an end to the current colonial policies instituted by the Indian State in Punjab' (KAC 2007). Dr Amarjit Singh publishes a weekly column, 'Khalistan Calling', in *Chardhi Kala* newspaper which addresses the significant events of the week and their affect on the Sikh 'nation'.

In an interview with the author,[35] Dr Amarjit Singh likened the KAC to Sinn Fein. Although not implicated in the armed struggle, the KAC acted as the *Khalistan* movement's 'political wing'. Following the liquidation of the *Khalistani* militants and the return to some form of democratic rule in the Punjab, the KAC has sought to support those political parties and groups most committed to defending Sikh interests in the Punjab, most notably Simranjit Singh Mann's SAD (Amritsar). However, unlike Sinn Fein, the KAC does not seek to play any direct role in Punjabi or Sikh politics, since it views existing institutions, including the SGPC,[36] as discredited and independence as the 'only solution for the Sikh nation'. There is no problem, Dr Amarjit Singh contends, which can be solved 'in the Indian map' (i.e. within the territorial nation-state of India). India is seen as an 'artificially created' multinational state on the brink of implosion, as happened in the post-Cold War Soviet Union (USSR) and Federal Republic of Yugoslavia (FRY). Like the USSR and FRY, it relies upon state repression to keep national minorities such as the Sikhs, Nagas, Kashmiris and Miripuris in check and is 'at war with its own people'. Despite the appointment of Manmohan Singh as prime minister, the fundamentally repressive nature of the Indian state is not seen as having changed, as power remains firmly in the hands of India's Brahmanical elite. Although Manmohan Singh is seen as an 'honest and capable minister', he is merely a 'seat warmer' and is ultimately loyal not to the *Khalsa panth* but to the Nehru–Gandhi dynasty which appointed him in the first place. His impotence can be seen in his failure to dismiss Jagdish Tytler, the minister of state for overseas Indian affairs, for his involvement in organizing the anti-Sikh Delhi pogroms of 1984.[37] When Tytler was eventually forced to resign, he did so not to the prime minister of India but to Congress president Sonia Gandhi.

In Dr Amarjit Singh's view, Manmohan Singh, like India's Sikh chief of army staff Lieutenant-General Joginder Jaswant Singh, owes his position to the *Khalistan* movement which exposed the repressive Brahmanical nature of the Indian state and thus made tokenism necessary in order to preserve the territorial integrity of India. Seen in this light, the *Khalistan* movement is not a failure since at least now there is a 'name for Sikh sovereign aspirations' and a pantheon of icons, heroes and martyrs with whom to identify. *Khalistan* is envisaged, in accordance with the Constitution adopted by the *Sarbat Khalsa* on 29 April 1986 which proclaimed the independence of *Khalistan*, not as a theocratic state but as a state based on the Sikh principle of *miri-piri*, where the rights of all citizens would be guaranteed without 'distinction of caste, colour and creed'.

From stigmatized 'Other' to Sikh-Americans: 9/11, SALDEF and the Sikh Coalition

For many Sikh immigrants to America, 9/11 was chillingly reminiscent of 1984. Just as Operation Blue Star may be described as the 'critical event' (Das 1995; Tatla 1999) which convinced many Sikhs that India was not their homeland and made the imagination of a Sikh nation possible, 9/11 led to a re-imagining of American national identity. In the light of the racist backlash unleashed on the Sikh community in the aftermath of 9/11 which claimed the life of Balbir Singh Sodhi,[38] American Sikhs were once again forced to ask themselves the question: who are we (Huntington 2004)?

For many American Sikhs, the US could no longer be considered 'home'. The purportedly universal rights which Americans enjoyed were redefined as 'Anglo-Protestant values' (Huntington 2004). The PATRIOT Act greatly increased state powers of surveillance over the individual and curtailed the civil liberties of citizens and non-citizens alike through the establishment of the Department of Homeland Security. The 'War on Terror' furthermore subordinated these rights to the exigencies of 'national security' (Shani *et al.* 2007). Moreover, India's transformation from 'nuclear pariah' to important strategic ally of the US made it more difficult for diaspora Sikh groups to make their grievances heard. More perniciously, owing to their perceived physical resemblance to members of the Taliban and Al-Qaeda, turbaned male Sikhs became – at least for some uneducated, white Americans – the 'enemy within': a stigmatized and racialized 'Other' against which the imagined community of America and the West defined themselves. It thus became more difficult to be a *Kes-dhari* Sikh in the 'home of the free'. Branded as terrorists because of their *dastaar* (turban), Sikhs have since 9/11 'lived in constant fear of hate crimes and discrimination' (Sikh Coalition 2006). Under these circumstances, many young Sikhs who had previously regarded themselves as Americans became convinced that a sovereign Sikh homeland was necessary for Sikhs to be allowed to follow the teachings of the Sikh Gurus and the *Guru Granth Sahib*.[39]

For others, however, the challenge was to make America 'home' once again by constructing a new category of American: *Sikh*-American. Unlike 'American Sikh', the term 'Sikh-American' is a hyphenated identity articulating both belonging and difference. Sikh-Americans are simultaneously Sikh *and* American yet also different from *other* Sikhs and *other* Americans. The hyphen not only suggests the fusion of two previously separated identities but also the tension which results from the *insolubility* of the 'Sikh' in the American 'melting pot'. It is as if 'the right-hand side of the hyphen can barely contain the unruliness of the left-hand side' (Appadurai 1996: 172). For Appadurai:

> The United States, always in its self-perception a land of immigrants, finds itself . . . no longer a closed space for the melting pot to work its magic but yet another diasporic switching-point to which people come to seek their fortunes though no longer content to leave their homelands behind.
>
> (Appadurai 1996: 172)

The term 'Sikh-American' may be seen as an example of what Appadurai calls a 'disjunctive' identity located at the intersection of the ethnoscapes, mediascapes, technoscapes, financescapes and ideoscapes which characterize the globalized world (Appadurai 1996: 33–36). It connotes the 'in-betweenness', 'border-crossing' and 'hybridity' which results from globalization (Pieterse 2004: 44–50). By inhabiting an 'in-between' space, Sikh-Americans highlight the borders between 'Self' and 'Other' in the American consciousness. Sikhs are simultaneously 'inside' and 'outside' post-9/11 America. On the one hand, they are inside in that they make claims to the same civil liberties and rights as other Americans and in so doing reaffirm the universality of American values. On the other, they remain outside an American mainstream defined by its whiteness (Appadurai 1996: 168) and Anglo-Protestant heritage (Huntington 2004) by drawing attention to their ineradicable alienness through a politics of recognition which demands recognition of their *difference*.

Although the term 'Sikh-American' was used before 9/11, its significance changed in the light of the tragic events of the day. Whereas before it was used to differentiate Sikhs from Indians in the American consciousness, after it was used to reaffirm their presence in America *as American citizens*. Consequently, Appadurai's assertion that 'diasporic communities become doubly loyal to their nations of origin and thus *ambivalent* about their loyalties to America' (Appadurai 1996: 172, italics mine) appears dated at best. At worst, it is pernicious in that it reproduces the binary or 'Self/Other' distinction which it is attempting to transcend by suggesting that identity is a zero-sum game. Sikhs, by affirming their membership of the Sikh 'nation' through the Five Ks are in no way 'ambivalent about their loyalties to America'. Rather, it is (white, mainstream) America which has proved itself ambivalent about the Sikh (and Muslim) presence in the United States. The rest of this section will analyse the activities of two organizations which, in attempting to protect American Sikhs from hate crimes and employment discrimination, have articulated a Sikh-American identity.

Founded in 1996 as the Sikh Mediawatch and Resource Task Force (SMART), the Sikh American Legal Defense and Education Fund (SALDEF) is the oldest Sikh-American civil rights and advocacy organization in the United States.[40] Initially focusing on media analysis and education, SMART immediately began responding to civil rights, legislative, employment and accommodation issues in response to the needs of the Sikh community and changed its name to SALDEF in 2004. Its mission is 'to protect the civil rights of Sikh-Americans and ensure a fostering environment in the United States for our future generations'. It seeks to do this by empowering Sikh-Americans through legal assistance, educational outreach, legislative advocacy and media relations (SALDEF 2007).

First, SALDEF provides free legal assistance to Sikh-Americans who have been victims of civil rights violations and arranges for legal representation of Sikh-Americans in instances where litigation is necessary. It also maintains 'one of the largest Legal Databases of judicial opinions affecting the Sikh community for the use of lawyers, scholars, reporters, and other interested persons' (personal correspondence, 25 February 2007). Second, SALDEF has developed professional training programmes for public and private agencies, including over 25,000 law enforcement officials, on Sikh cultural and religious practices in order to promote more awareness of the community. SALDEF officials have also entered into dialogue with local, state and federal government and have co-produced posters on turbans and *kirpans* with the Departments of Justice (2004) and Homeland Security (2006) as well as producing a Sikh-American law enforcement training video (2007). Furthermore, SALDEF conducts outreach to local Sikh-American communities in order to increase awareness of their rights. Third, SALDEF has worked on legislative issues affecting the Sikh community, including support for the following legislation: the Workplace Religious Freedom Act, which requires employers to reasonably accommodate the religious needs of employees at work; the Local Law Enforcement Hate Crimes Prevention Act, which ensures federal support for local law enforcement officials in combating hate crimes; and the End of Racial Profiling Act, which will formally ban racial profiling by law enforcement officials as the sole determining factor of investigations. Finally, SALDEF's Office of Media Relations monitors the media for misrepresentation of Sikh-Americans.

Although SALDEF is the oldest civil rights and advocacy organization for American Sikhs, nascent Sikh-American identity is perhaps best articulated by the Sikh Coalition, which seeks to represent the 'voice of a people' (Sikh Coalition 2007a). Founded in the weeks following 9/11 by a group of young Sikh professionals from diverse professional backgrounds in response to the dramatic increase in the number of hate crimes and religious and racial profiling, the Coalition of Sikh Organizations set out to 'create an organization that would act as a clear and accurate voice on behalf of Sikh Americans' (Sikh Coalition 2007b). Based in New York City, the Sikh Coalition, as it came to be known, developed affiliations in Toronto, Boston, Washington, DC, Chicago, Houston, Seattle, San Francisco and Los Angeles through its website (http://www.sikhcoalition.org/), which was set up with the help of activists in Chicago. According to its mission statement posted on the web, the Coalition seeks to:

- Provide all citizens with the information and tools necessary for them to safeguard their fundamental rights as free citizens and make the most of the democratic process
- Advocate cultural diversity and stand against racism while advocating social justice, equality for both sexes, and human rights for all peoples
- Foster organization and civic engagement within the Sikh community to enable local empowerment and activism
- Provide Sikh organizations, Sikhs, and others with the skills and resources necessary to help organize, coordinate, and implement an effective and sustained Coalition effort.

(Sikh Coalition 2007c)

It has been active in community relations, education, government affairs and legal affairs and, under a banner of education, advocacy and protection, has scored some notable successes. Immediately after its establishment, it successfully lobbied for the introduction of legislation condemning hate crimes against Sikh-Americans in the wake of the post-9/11 backlash. The resolution (Senate Congress Resolution 74), introduced by Senator Richard Durbin (Democrat, Illinois) and co-sponsored by thirty-seven other senators, was passed unanimously and specifically calls upon local and law enforcement authorities to 'prosecute to the fullest extent of the law all those who commit crimes' against Sikh-Americans (Sikh Coalition 2001). More locally, the Sikh Coalition has worked with a member of the New York City Council to develop two post-9/11 discrimination bills, Intro 576, which would require the city of New York to create a plan to mitigate backlash violence against Sikhs, Arabs, Muslims and other minorities, and Intro 577, which would ban discrimination on the basis of religious garb in New York City uniformed agencies. Consequently, *Kes-dhari* Sikhs, for the first time, are able to serve in the New York City Police Department (NYPD) and Metropolitan Transit Authority (MTA) without being forced to remove their turbans and *kirpans*. These bills mark the first time that a bill drafted by the Sikh community to address the concerns of Sikh-Americans has ever been introduced by a city, state or federal legislature (Sikh Coalition 2007c).

The Sikh Coalition has, furthermore, provided assistance to over sixty Sikhs concerned that they were victims of employment discrimination, including the cases of Amric Singh (Rathour) and Kevin Harrington (Sathari Singh). Harrington, a convert to Sikhism, had worked as an MTA train operator for over twenty years when he was demoted to a position where he would be hidden from public view for not removing his turban. Amric Singh, meanwhile, was actually fired from the NYPD for refusing to do so. Both men were reinstated following the Sikh Coalition's intervention (Sikh Coalition 2005:

13–15). The Coalition has also been involved in providing assistance to the victims of over forty hate crimes, including that of Rajinder Singh Khalsa, whose assailants were sentenced to perform community service with the Sikh Coalition (Sikh Coalition 2005: 9).

The success of the Sikh Coalition may be attributed to the vision of its dynamic young executive director, Amardeep Singh, and its ability to mobilize the community at grassroots level. The Sikh Coalition has worked with all of the *gurdwaras* in the New York area and has encouraged members of the community to be involved in the political process. The election of five Sikhs[41] to the Queens Democratic County Committee in New York proved a 'huge milestone' for the Sikh community marking the beginning of the Sikh community 'not just being perpetual outsiders, but insiders . . . who have a place at the table when policy affecting the community is enacted' (Sikh Coalition 2007c).

Conclusion

In conclusion, this chapter has examined Sikh identity in the diaspora. Using the case studies of the United Kingdom and the United States, it has been argued that Sikh immigrants have faced challenges to maintaining the external symbols associated with their faith in their places of settlement. Consequently, many Sikh migrants were initially forced to choose between, on the one hand, succumbing to the assimilationist pressures of the nation-state and abandoning the Five Ks and, on the other hand, exclusion from the national 'mainstream' and stigmatization as alien outsiders. Many Sikhs frequently also experienced (and, in some cases, continue to experience) employment, educational and other forms of discrimination on the basis of their religion and/or ethnicity and sought to counter this through political organization and mobilization.

It has been argued that the objective of Sikh political activity has been consistently to gain *recognition* of their ethno-religious particularity, or *difference* from other groups, from the state in their places of settlement. According to Taylor, the politics of recognition 'asks that we give acknowledgment and status to something that is not universally shared' (Taylor 1994: 39). Seen in this light, the demand for a sovereign state of *Khalistan* has been consistent with this broader 'politics of recognition'. For although Sikh diaspora nationalism was undoubtedly motivated by homeland developments and the violent struggle for a sovereign Sikh state in the Punjab between 1984 and 1992, it was also motivated by a desire to gain 'acknowledgment and status' for Sikhs in their places of settlement. Putting Sikhs 'on the map' internationally through the establishment of a sovereign Sikh state has important *domestic* consequences. In the first place, it helps differentiate Sikhs in the public consciousness and media discourses from other immigrant communities, particularly the (South) Asian, Indian or Hindu community. This, in turn, affects how the state views the Sikhs and facilitates the institutionalization of Sikh identity *within* the state. If Sikh identity is recognized and institutionalized by the state, it is easier for groups representing Sikhs (and other ethno-religious minorities) to make the case for 'special exemptions' to be occasionally made in order to accommodate the requirements of the Sikh faith and, moreover, to secure access to a 'fair share' of political representation and government funding in order to facilitate their integration into the national 'mainstream'. In those societies, such as contemporary France and much of continental Europe, where such recognition is not forthcoming, it is much more difficult to be both a practising Sikh *and* a citizen of the state. Consequently, the 'politics of homeland', or what Anderson (1992) calls 'long-distance nationalism', should *not* be seen as necessarily precluding participation in the political process in places of settlement.

Indeed, as illustrated by our case studies of the emergence of post-nationalist organizations representing Sikhs in the diaspora such as the Sikh Federation in the UK and Sikh Coalition and SALDEF in the US, 'long-distance nationalism' has *facilitated* the emergence of a *diasporic* Sikh identity. This embryonic *diasporic* identity encompasses claims for both recognition *and* redistribution and has been articulated in response to the retreat from multiculturalism in both countries following 9/11 and 7/7. This 'diasporic' identity is made possible by the mobilization of the Sikh community through the nationalist project but seeks to find a place for Sikhs 'inside' the nation-state without having to abandon the requirements of the Sikh faith or severing the ethno-national bonds with other members of the transnational Sikh *qaum*. By maintaining identifications outside the nation-state, diasporic identities, in Clifford's words, allow minorities to 'live inside, with a difference' (Clifford 1997: 251).

However, a clear distinction between a 'politics of homeland' and a 'politics of recognition' or between a nationalist and diasporic politics is not always possible. Many of the young Sikh activists involved in the post-nationalist movements are themselves supporters of *Khalistan*. The reasons they give, however, do not make reference to the Punjab but concern the difficulties which they face in maintaining their symbols of faith in their places of settlement after 9/11. Although organizations such as the Sikh Coalition do not take a position on *Khalistan*, their executive director, Amardeep Singh, personally believes that the existence of a sovereign Sikh homeland would help prevent hate crimes and discrimination against Sikhs, thus facilitating the work of organizations such as SALDEF or the Sikh Coalition. Referring to his attempts to lobby members of Congress after the murder of Balbir Singh Sodhi, Amardeep Singh stated:

> It is one thing for someone who is under 30 to go around Congress saying do something about hate crimes, [yet] it is another for an ambassador of a Sikh country to go around Congress saying do something about hate crimes . . . because the way the law of the world is set up . . . those groups who have been given the legal status of recognition by the United

Nations as a nation have legal protection which those groups that do not have recognition just don't have.

(Amardeep Singh, 24 February 2007, Palatine Gurdwara,
Illinois, USA)

It is to this 'law of the world', and attempts by transnational religious actors to change it, that we will turn in the next chapter.

7 Beyond *Khalistan?*

The Sikh diaspora, globalization and international relations [1]

The state-building process in the Westphalian era produced territorial concentrations of power. Centralized political institutions established a complex ensemble of monopoly powers over clearly defined territorial frontiers and aimed, with varying levels of success, to create homogeneous national units. Territorialized nation-states employed nationalist symbols to bring political and cultural boundaries into close alignment and to accentuate the differences between 'insiders' and 'outsider'. Neo-realism, the dominant perspective in international political theory, is testimony to the success of the totalizing project in creating the sharp divide between domestic and international politics.

Recently, however, increasing globalization and fragmentation in the post-Cold War world have led to the return of religion, culture and identity to international relations theory (Lapid and Kratochwil 1996; Petito and Hatzopoulos 2003). Fragmentation has highlighted the disjunction between the boundaries of cultural and political communities in many parts of the world, whilst globalization casts doubt on the supposition that the nation-state is the only significant political community. The impact of global social and economic change on the territorialized nation-state now means that the notion of a bordered, self-contained community that is at the heart of international political theory has become difficult to sustain. International relations (IR) is increasingly seen as constituted by thought on issues of 'inside–outside' (Walker 1993) or 'inclusion–exclusion' (Linklater 1998). This creates space for the articulation of a deterritorialized Sikh diasporic identity which challenges the Westphalian order in its rejection of sovereign statehood and its assertion of the sovereignty of the *Khalsa panth*. Unlike *Khalistani* discourses, Sikh diasporic discourses do not place territorial limits on the sovereignty of the *Khalsa panth* and, thus, may be seen to go beyond Westphalia.

It will be argued that realism,[2] the dominant perspective in international political theory, has 'naturalized' the Westphalian order, which in turn has territorialized Sikh identity. However, the Westphalian order of secularized, territorialized nation-states has recently been challenged by a global religious resurgence. I will then examine the possibilities which globalization opens up for the Sikh diaspora by examining two transnational religious actors representing the *Khalsa panth*: the World Sikh Council (WSC) and UNITED SIKHS. Finally, an attempt will be made to analyse the extent to which Sikh communities have indeed moved beyond *Khalistan* and embraced a 'diasporic' Sikh identity by using empirical data from interviews and Internet discussion groups.

The Westphalian order and IR theory

The contemporary world order may be described as an 'inter*national*' or 'inter-state' order, an order composed of territorialized nation-states. A nation-state claims 'the monopoly of the legitimate use of physical force within a given territory' (Weber 1991: 78) and seeks to unite the people subjected to its rule by means of cultural and linguistic homogenization (Guibernau 2001: 242). Bull defined international order as 'a pattern of human activity that sustains the elementary or primary goals of the society of states, or international society' (Bull 1977: 8). A society of states exists:

> when a group of states, conscious of certain common interests and common values, form a society in the sense that they conceive themselves to be bound by a common set of rules in their relations with one another, and share in the working of common institutions.
>
> (Bull 1977: 13)

A society of states, or international society, presumes the existence of a system of states 'formed when two or more states have sufficient contact between them, and have sufficient impact on one another's decisions to cause them to behave . . . as parts of a whole' (Bull 1977: 9–10). The primary or elementary goals of a society of states are, for Bull, 'the preservation of the system and the society of states itself' (Bull 1977: 16). This is to be achieved through 'maintaining the independence or external sovereignty of individual states' (Bull 1977: 17). The contemporary international order is conventionally understood to have its origins in the 1648 Peace of Westphalia, which gave rise to a European system or society of sovereign states. The norms and practices of this European system or society of states were then imposed upon the non-Western world by European imperial powers. Anti-colonial movements, by casting their claims to independence in terms of a demand for their own sovereign states, made the 'expansion of international society' based upon an international order of territorialized sovereign states possible (Bull 1984). For Jackson, the rules constitutive of Westphalian international society include the following: 1) sovereign equality; 2) refraining from the threat or use of force; 3) inviolability of frontiers; 4) non-intervention in internal affairs; 5) respect for human rights; 6) equal rights and self-determination of peoples; 7) cooperation amongst states; and 8) fulfilment in good faith of obligations under international law (Jackson 2000). Jackson refers to state sovereignty as *the* most important norm of international relations.

Nationalism is constitutive of the contemporary international order. According to the norms underpinning international regimes governing sovereign statehood, sovereignty is seen to reside with the nation. The nation-state continues to be the primary internationally recognized structure of political association. Only nation-states are admitted into the United Nations or other international organizations. Chapter XI, Article 73 of the UN Charter affirms the principle of equal rights and self-determination of peoples. This was echoed by the General Assembly, which declared in its resolution in 1960 (UN General Assembly 1960) that 'all peoples have the right to self-determination'. However, this right to self-determination is confined to claims by state elites.

After decolonization, the language of self-determination was used to legitimize the post-colonial state, although the post-colonial state boundaries did not always coincide with *national* boundaries. For Mayall, the post-war international order institutionalized the principle of national self-determination and, in so doing, 'tamed' it by 'freezing' the political map. In this sense 'the world has been made safe for nationalism' (Mayall 1990: 50). The nationalist world order is dependent upon the continued existence of the sovereign state system. Nationalism, as Meadwell has pointed out, 'continues to be about territory, and territorial politics presupposes states in the modern era' (Meadwell 1999: 262). The territorial configuration of the Westphalian world order impacts upon personal identity by privileging one form of collective identity, belonging to a nation, over others, i.e. class, gender and locality. Consequently, in order for the Sikh *qaum* to be recognized internationally, its self-appointed elites are forced to employ discourses of 'nationhood' and 'territoriality', which reinforce traditional conceptions of the international order. Sikh identity in the diaspora is, therefore, *territorialized* by a nationalist narrative that seeks to narrate Sikh identity in Westphalian terms.

The Westphalian world order has been 'legitimized' or 'naturalized' within the discipline of IR by the emergence of first 'realism' and later 'neo-realism' as the dominant perspective in international political theory after the Second World War (Carr 1962 [1939]; Morgenthau 1967; Waltz 1979, 1986, 1990). Although the hegemony of realism has recently been eroded by the purported globalization of liberal values and systems of political and economic organization following the collapse of the Soviet Union, most conventional theories of international relations are anchored in the same 'realist' assumptions. First, conventional theories view the state both as the key actor in international relations and as the legitimate representative of the collective will of a community/nation. International relations are seen as inter-state relations, and only those communities in possession of a state of their own can lay claim to sovereignty. The sovereign state, as Young points out, has two important features. First, it requires that no other centre of political power may legitimately exist; and, secondly, it demands that there be nothing outside the scope of the state and its power (Young 1995: 529). Both realist and liberal conceptions of the international order take the territorial sovereign state to be the basic unit of international political activity. Whilst most realists would agree with Waltz that, on the international stage, 'states set the scene in which they, along with non-state actors stage their dramas' (Waltz 1986: 89), liberals seem to limit state sovereignty through a network of regimes and institutions designed to promote universal standards of conduct necessary for the creation and maintenance of an international society. These standards include the formalization of the consent of the governed in representative institutions, the maintenance through the rule of law of individual guarantees to life, liberty and property, and the creation of a market economy regulated by the 'invisible hand' of multinational capital, all of which require the disciplinary power of the state. As Agnew notes, 'the merging of the state with a clearly bounded territory is the geographical essence of the field of international relations' (Agnew 1998: 80).

Second, state leaders' primary responsibility is to ensure the survival of their state in an international system characterized by *anarchy*: defined by Wendt as 'the absence of authority' (Wendt 1996: 52). In the absence of a world government, states have to rely upon themselves to ensure the survival of their state. The absence of a common power affords international politics a structure which helps explain the persistence not only of separate territorially bounded units of international political activity but also conflict between these units. The anarchic structure of an international system composed of territorialized nation-states is seen to make conflict between these units inevitable. For realists, the best method of managing these conflicts is through maintaining a balance of power, whilst liberals believe that cooperation under anarchy is best achieved through the maintenance of international regimes and institutions based on 'universal' liberal principles.

Third, conventional theories of international relations share the neo-realist assumption that a strict separation of domestic (intra-state) and international (inter-state) relations is possible. Neo-realism, according to its main exponent, Kenneth Waltz, 'establishes the autonomy of international politics and thus makes a theory about it possible' by depicting 'an international political system as a whole, with structural and unit levels at once distinct and connected' (Waltz 1990: 27). Whilst, for Waltz, the 'ordering principle' of domestic politics is *hierarchic*, with power and authority exerted upwards through legal and political institutions, in international politics it is *anarchic*, given the absence of an overarching authority regulating the behaviour of states ('like-units') towards each other. This structure is seen as 'immutable', having endured since the days of Thucydides, the historian of the Peloponnesian War. For realists, the task of IR theory is therefore to *explain* the persistence of the state system and the features associated with it, namely war, in terms of its anarchic structure.

'A revolt against the West': the global religious resurgence

However, as recent events have shown, the Westphalian international order predicated on the territorialization of political communities and the privatization of religion has been under siege from deterritorialized faith-based communities. The rise of politicized collective religious identities in the Middle East,[3] North Africa[4] and South and South-East Asia[5] during the 1990s has shattered the assumption, most famously – and crudely – espoused by Francis Fukuyama (1992), that the ending of the Cold War has created a worldwide consensus in favour of secular liberal-democracy.[6]

As Scott Thomas has argued, three main interrelated reasons may account for the global religious revival, particularly in the South (Thomas 2000, 2005). In the first place, the global religious revival may be seen as having its origins, particularly in the South, in the legitimacy crises of the postcolonial secular state. The secular nationalism of first-generation post-colonial leaders such as Nehru, Nasser, Nkrumah and Sukarno conspicuously failed to bring economic development or freedom from the structural constraints of the world economy. Their failure, although not acknowledged in their lifetimes, became clear with the abandonment of their legacies by their successors. 'Political decay', the decline of politics into authoritarianism, corruption and patrimonialism since the late 1960s, was followed, in sub-Saharan Africa, by 'political collapse': state disintegration of some states. By the early 1990s, the third-generation post-colonial elites had abandoned secularism, democratic socialism and non-alignment in favour of economic liberalization, a pro-Western stance on international affairs and, most importantly, the use of a religious vocabulary to mobilize mass support (or, at least, maintain mass acquiescence). In India, the emergence of the 'Hindu right' under the leadership of the BJP, largely accomplished through strategic regional alliances, was seen, prior to the 2004 elections, as the final nail in the coffin of Nehruvian secularism. India's democratic structures, rather than resulting in the demise of religious identities as predicted by India's post-colonial leaders, have led to the emergence of a pan-Indian Hindu cultural nationalism with local variations.

This begs the question of why 'religion' continues, to use a modernist term, to be the language of public discourse. At a deeper level the global resurgence or 'politicization' of religion may be seen to 'reflect a deeper and more widespread disillusionment with a "modernity" which reduces the world to what can be perceived and controlled through reason, science, technology, and bureaucratic rationality, and leaves out considerations of the religious, the spiritual or the sacred' (Thomas 2000: 816). It reflects a disillusionment with but not a rejection of modernity, for, as Mark Juergensmeyer has pointed out, religious nationalism has a contradictory attitude towards modernity. Secular ideas but not secular politics are rejected.

> At the same time, however, they [religious nationalists] see no contradiction in affirming certain forms of political organization that have

developed in the West, such as the democratic procedures of the nation-state, as long as they are legitimised not by the secular idea of a social contract but by traditional principles of religion.

(Juergensmeyer 1993: 7)

Even 'fundamentalism' – a term coined to describe (and stigmatize) conservative religious movements advocating a 'return' to a 'traditional' (and, in the case of monotheistic religions, textual) approach to religion – bears the imprints of modernity. According to contributors to the Fundamentalisms Comprehended project, funded by the American Academy of Arts and Sciences, fundamentalism is a 'hybrid' religious mode:

> While fundamentalists claim to be upholding orthodoxy (right belief) or orthopraxis (right behaviour), and to be defending and conserving religious traditions and traditional ways of life from erosion, they do so by crafting new methods, formulating new ideologies, and adopting the latest processes and organizational structures.

(Almond *et al.* 1995: 353)

Lastly, the global resurgence of religion in the South may be seen as the latest wave of 'revolt against the West'. According to Hedley Bull, 'the struggles of non-western people to throw off the cultural ascendancy of the western world so as to reassert their identity' (Bull 1984: 217) – the resurgence of indigenous cultures in the post-colonial world – was the third 'wave' of revolt against Western domination of the international system, following on from 'the struggle for sovereign equality' (the anti-colonial struggles of the 1940s to 1960s) and 'the struggle for racial equality and economic justice' (the campaigns against apartheid, Zionism and the attempts to reform the international economic order in the 1970s and early 1980s). As a result of the failure of secular nationalism to fulfil its promises to 'the people' it invented out of the cultural mosaic of colonial societies, state elites have had to respond to more popular perspectives which in turn have challenged the assumptions of Western cosmopolitan modernity. Bull's observation that 'as non-western peoples have assumed a more prominent place in international society it has become clear that in matters of values the distance between them and western societies is greater than in the early years of . . . decolonisation' (Bull 1984: 217) seems to be supported by the global 'religious' revival.

Beyond Westphalia? Globalization, transnational religious communities and international relations

The global religious resurgence has been sustained by the processes associated with the contemporary phase of globalization. As a result of globalization, faith has 'obtained greater significance as a non-territorial touchstone of identity in today's more global world' (Scholte 2005: 245). Three developments in particular have provided a context for a religious resurgence on a global scale. In the first place, globalization – through economic restructuring programmes which necessitate reduced public expenditure – has impacted upon the relative power of the secular state, decreasing its capacity to impose its secular vision of the nation to the exclusion of other identities. Increasingly national identities coexist and compete with other forms of collective identities on an individual level. The assertion of a national identity no longer necessitates a rejection of pre-national, *communal* identities, particularly those based on ethnicity and religion, so that it is now possible to articulate a 'hybrid' (Pieterse 2004) British Sikh or 'hyphenated' Sikh-American identity as suggested in Chapter 6.

Second, globalization has decreased the salience of *territory* in the construction of individual and collective identities. Identity is no longer exclusively defined in terms of place: where one is from no longer allows us to define who one is. As Scholte points out, 'territorialism as the previously prevailing structure of social space was closely interlinked with nationalism as the previously prevailing structure of collective identity' (Scholte 2005: 225). However, one of the significant consequences of contemporary globalization has been to sever the connections between the state, a coercive apparatus of governance defined in terms of its monopoly of organized violence, and the nation, an 'imagined political community' (Anderson 1991), to the point where 'many national projects today no longer involve an aspiration to acquire their own sovereign state' (Scholte 2005: 228). The *deterritorialization* of nationalism has created space for the reassertion of transnational religious identities. Indeed, religious identities seem particularly suited to the needs of a rapidly globalizing world since, despite the attachment to a territorially defined 'holyland' which is often the site of pilgrimage, the core tenets of most religions are in principle universal and can be embraced and practised anywhere on earth.

Finally, globalization has, through the ICT revolution in particular, facilitated the dissemination of these universal core beliefs and tenets on a global scale. Most religious organizations maintain websites to introduce non-believers to the faith and to provide spiritual guidance to the faithful. Sikhism is no exception, and the SGPC maintains a bilingual website which offers Sikhs in the diaspora a chance to read a daily *hukamnama* (edict from the Gurus) and even listen to live *kirtan* from *Harmandir Sahib* without having to visit Amritsar (SGPC 2007)! Information Technology has, thus, provided followers of transnational religious communities with the opportunity to communicate across the boundaries and transcend the limitations of the territorially defined national community. In the words of Nicholas Negroponte:

> In the same way that hypertext removes the limitations of the printed page, the post information age will remove the limitations of geography. Digital living will include less and less dependence upon being in a

specific place at a specific time, and the transmission of place itself will start to become possible.

(Negroponte 1995: 165)

According to Jose Casanova:

> ongoing processes of globalization offer a transnational religious regime like Catholicism, which never felt fully at home in a system of sovereign territorial nation-states, unique opportunities to expand, to adapt rapidly to the newly emerging global system, and perhaps even assume a proactive role in shaping some aspects of the new system.
>
> (Casanova 1997: 121)

Casanova goes on to suggest that in Catholicism globalization finds expression primarily in three new directions. First, it finds expression in the ever widening publication of papal encyclicals dealing not only with doctrinal matters but also with secular issues affecting all of humanity. The second direction in which it finds expression is in the increasingly active role of the papacy in issues dealing with international relations, as can be seen in the opposition of Pope John Paul II to communism and the Iraq war. Finally, globalization has increased the public visibility of the person of the pope 'as the high priest of a new universal civil religion of humanity as the first citizen of a global civil society' (Casanova 1997: 125).

Globalization has – given the absence of a highly centralized, hierarchical Church – arguably had an even greater impact upon Islam, and the development and proliferation of ICTs in particular have facilitated the dissemination not only of fundamentalist ideologies associated with political Islam (Kepel 2004) but also of a *critical* Islamic identity which challenges both the homogenizing logic of the nation-state system and the 'jihadist' version of political Islam. According to Peter Mandaville, globalization and the ICT revolution have permitted the *reformulation* of Islam and the reconceptualization of the *umma*. It has done so by giving rise to a condition which he terms 'translocality' whereby political identities 'no longer inhabit the exclusive container of the nation-state and must be seen as configured in and between multiple political spaces' (Mandaville 2001: 188). Consequently, Islam has been allowed to 'travel' between these multiple political spaces and, in so doing, has been transformed.

Mandaville identifies two interrelated and apparently contradictory ways in which translocality has contributed to the reformulation of Islam:

> On the one hand, translocality brings together Muslims of diverse sociocultural, sectarian and theological backgrounds. By forcing Islam to hold a mirror up to itself, translocality makes it aware of the many differences (and disunities) within. On the other hand, however, translocality and globalization are providing Muslims with a greater capacity to

communicate, interact and otherwise bridge the distances between them. In this sense, translocality resonates with the Qur'anic injunction to Muslims of different nations to get to know one another.

(Mandaville 2001: 187)

One of the effects of translocality on 'traditional' Islam has been the emergence of what may be termed a 'critical' Islamic discourse. Previously, in 'traditional' Islamic societies, the *ulema* were the custodians of the faith and tended to interpret sacred texts in ways which would reproduce their own privileged position within society. However, the development of first 'print' and then 'digital' capitalism has created space for the articulation of alternative Islamic narratives. Muslims are increasingly willing 'to take Islam into their own hands', relying upon their own interpretations of classical sources and sacred texts which are more widely available in print or digital form. Consequently, the traditional position of the *ulema*, as the privileged source of religious knowledge within Sunni societies, has been undermined. For, as Mandaville writes:

(t)he authority of the written word is no longer the sole reserve of a select few, and the religious elite cannot compete with the myriad range of Muslim voices reading, debating and, effectively, *reformulating* Islam on the Internet, on satellite television and in a plethora of widely-distributed books and pamphlets.

(Mandaville 2001: 179)

This interpretation of Islam, with its emphasis upon dialogue with other faith-based communities and on recognizing internal differences, is radically different from the 'jihadist' vision, particularly its Wahabite Sunni version, which prioritizes the capture of state power and espouses a literal, orthodox interpretation of Islam as a set of homogeneous, universally agreed doctrines, laws and sacred texts. One such critical voice is that of Ramadan, for whom the challenge is to articulate an internally differentiated but coherent Islamic identity which simultaneously rejects the assimilationist project of the nation-state and the violent and homogenizing logic of the *jihadist-salafists*. Ramadan locates the 'diaspora' as the site for the articulation of a critical Islamic discourse:

We are currently living through a veritable silent revolution in Muslim communities in the West: more and more young people and intellectuals are actively looking for a way to live in harmony with their faith while participating in the societies which are their societies, whether they like it or not.

(Ramadan 2004: 4)

In conclusion, Islam is developing its own version of *critical* theory, which can only be understood within the wider context of 'reconstructing Muslim civilization' (Sardar 2003) from *within*. Tension, however, still exists between the claims of the universal 'community of believers' and those of the homeland, the *watan*. Indeed, as is obvious to any casual observer, the *umma* is neither homogeneous nor monolithic, and considerable regional, doctrinal and cultural variations exist among Islam's 1 billion believers. However, a clear distinction – at least for non-Arabs – can still be made between the religious community, centred on the 'holyland', and 'homeland'. This distinction cannot, as we have seen, be so easily made in the case of the Sikh community. The extent to which the global Sikh community has indeed gone beyond *Khalistan* will be examined in the next sections, through an analysis of the activities of Sikh *transnational* religious actors and Sikh discussion groups on the Internet.

Serving the *qaum*: Sikh transnational religious actors

The intensification of the processes associated with contemporary globalization has permitted the further institutionalization of *transnational* religious activities, which – potentially at least – both challenges the ontological foundations of secular modernity and brings the territorial limits of the Westphalian world into question. Improved communications, the greater mobility of capital and the acquisition of organizational skills and techniques have allowed transnational religious actors, such as the Vatican, Al-Qaeda or the Organization of the Islamic Conference (OIC), to play an increasingly visible role in international relations (Haynes 2001). In this section, two transnational actors seeking to represent the *Khalsa panth* will be examined: the World Sikh Council and UNITED SIKHS.

The World Sikh Council

The World Sikh Council (WSC) was originally established by the acting *Jathedar* of the *Akal Takht*, Manjit Singh, in September 1995. It was founded on the belief that the global Sikh community needed an 'umbrella organisation which would unite Sikhs around the world in prayer and service to humanity' (WSC 2007). The constitution of the Council did not specify which Sikh institutions could participate, and initially it consisted of a group of people nominated by the organizing committee selected by the *Jathedar* himself. However, many Sikhs felt that the World Sikh Council ought to be representative of all Sikh organizations which accepted the Sikh *Rehat Maryada* and accepted the sovereignty of the *Akal Takht*. This, it was argued, could best be accomplished if the WSC was divided into regions which each had its own representative Council to 'cater to the national/regional needs and interests of the Sikhs belonging to that country/region while working with the World body' (WSC 2007).

The World Sikh Council – America Region (WSC-AR) was established to represent the interests of American Sikhs. Established in April 1996, it is a representative and elected body of Sikh *gurdwaras* and institutions in the US. Its members include more than thirty-eight *gurdwaras* and other Sikh institutions across the nation, which work under the overall guidance of the Council. It aims to 'promote Sikh interests at the national and international level focusing on issues of advocacy, education, and well-being of human-kind' (WSC 2007). Specifically, it seeks to achieve the following goals: the preservation of and respect for a distinct Sikh identity; safeguarding the cultural heritage of the Sikhs; the advancement of their social and economic interests; the promotion of 'quality education among Sikhs'; the promotion of Sikh studies in general and religion, theology, liturgy and history in par-ticular; the promotion of public awareness of Sikh beliefs and practices in order to enhance educational and employment opportunities for the Sikhs; the development of programmes for the proper upbringing of Sikh children and youth and imparting to them sound knowledge of, and inspiring in them real pride in, the Sikh identity, religion, culture, tradition and history; the acceptance and implementation of the Sikh *Rehat Maryada* as notified by the SGPC; the propagation of the awareness of, and strengthening of faith in, fundamental human rights and the dignity of the human person; equality of all human beings as preached by the Sikh Gurus and ensuring equal rights to men and women; the harmonization of relations among various social and religious groups, associations and institutions in order to establish a strong and forward-looking international brotherhood, firm in Sikh spirit and reso-lutely committed to the Sikh way of life; and, finally, cooperation with national and international organizations in maintaining the rule of law, estab-lishing peace and security, and promoting the basic Sikh tenet of *Sarbat Da Bhala* (well-being of all people) (WSC 2007).

Although no mention is made of *Khalistan*, the conflation of the advocacy of Sikhism with the specific material interests of the Sikhs illustrates the tensions which exist between *qaum* and *panth*.[7] Furthermore, it is unclear *how* the various regional councils relate to one another and *whether* the *Akal Takht* exercises anything other than nominal control over the organization.[8] Nevertheless, the establishment of the WSC is clearly an attempt to institution-alize a *transnational* Sikh identity which goes beyond *Khalistan* to represent the interests of Sikhs globally – albeit from a regional perspective.

UNITED SIKHS

Whereas the WSC operates – albeit autonomously – within the Sikh 'political system' centred on the *Akal Takht* and the SGPC, UNITED SIKHS is a more strictly apolitical organization operating outside it. Often referred to as the Sikh 'Red Cross',[9] UNITED SIKHS aims to 'transform underprivileged and minority communities and individuals into informed and vibrant members of society through civic, educational and personal development programs, by fostering active participation in social and economic activity' (UNITED

SIKHS 2007a). Like the WSC, it is a coalition of autonomous organizations with its origins in North America, but is arguably a more *transnational* organization. Founded in 1999 by a group of Sikhs from the New York metropolitan area who banded together to assist in the 'socio-economic development of immigrant communities in Queens, New York', it now has 'chapters in America, Asia and Europe that pursue projects for the spiritual, social and economic empowerment of underprivileged and minority communities' (UNITED SIKHS 2007a). Chapters are in the process of being registered in Africa and Australasia (Mejindarpal Kaur, interview, 25 March 2007).

Its various activities are grouped together into six main project areas: International Civil and Human Rights Advocacy (ICHRA), Sikh Aid, Empowerment and Education, Community and Multifaith Awareness, Community Service, and Heritage and Culture. Its ICHRA helps advance the 'economic, social and spiritual empowerment of minorities and other marginalized groups and individuals in need, *regardless of race, religion, gender, sexual orientation, social status, age or ability*'. This is achieved 'by protecting and enforcing the civil and human rights of minorities and marginalized groups in the Americas, Europe and Asia' (UNITED SIKHS 2007b, emphasis mine). UNITED SIKHS, furthermore, provides global humanitarian disaster relief service through its Sikh Aid team, which also runs projects to eradicate poverty. Its activities have helped provide relief to survivors of the Asian tsunami, South Asian earthquake and American hurricanes Katrina and Rita whilst importantly raising the profile of Sikhs. Through its Empowerment and Education project, UNITED SIKHS seeks to empower individuals and groups to 'help them attain their full potential and become active participants in society' through involving themselves in the decision-making processes in their local communities 'as well as taking their place in the international arena' (UNITED SIKHS 2007b). Like the WSC, UNITED SIKHS is moreover committed to working with other faiths and traditions and has been an active participant in international dialogue on multi-faith issues. Specifically it has sought to improve the understanding and treatment of minority religions, traditions and beliefs through its participation (UNITED SIKHS 2007b).

Although UNITED SIKHS is also involved in projects in the areas of community service and heritage and culture, it is the 'Right to the Turban' (RTT) campaign which has attracted the most media attention. It seeks to provide advice, counsel and legal representation to those whose rights to wear the articles of faith are threatened by local, state or national legislation. The RTT campaign 'covers any turban issue in any country where Sikhs are denied their right to wear their Turban' (UNITED SIKHS 2007c). Its activities in working together with other Sikh organizations to overturn the ban on the wearing of turbans and other religious symbols in French schools in particular has brought its transnational aspirations in conflict with the Westphalian world order of the secular, territorialized nation-state.

In March 2004, the French state passed a law which bans conspicuous religious symbols and attire in public schools in order to uphold the principle of *laïcité*.[10] Although the law does not explicitly target the Sikh community, Sikh schoolchildren are most affected by the ban, since the wearing of the Five Ks is an integral part of *Kes-dhari* Sikh identity and is arguably more important to the maintenance of the Sikh faith than the cross is to Christianity, the skullcap to Judaism or the headscarf to Islam. Consequently, many of the 5,000-strong Sikh community in France have been faced with a stark dilemma: either to cease wearing the religious symbols which are the very *embodiment* of their faith or to face exclusion from state schools. French (and other European) Sikhs have thus been forced to choose between 'faith' and 'nation'. Despite the French government's assurance that a 'satisfactory' solution for the Sikh community in France would be sought,[11] the ban on religious symbols in the classroom has led to the expulsion of six Sikh schoolboys.[12] Furthermore, two adult French Sikh citizens – Shingara Singh Mann and Ranjit Singh[13] – were unable to renew important documents, as they declined to remove their turban for the ID photo.

Led by a legal team including Judge Mota Singh, QC – the first non-European and turban-wearing Sikh judge in the UK – and renowned human rights barrister Rabinder Singh, QC, UNITED SIKHS (UK/Europe), under the overall leadership of its director, Mejindarpal Kaur (barrister-at-law), has been in the forefront of litigation in the French courts for these cases. Specifically, the role of UNITED SIKHS has been to coordinate the litigation by 'instructing counsel and providing input on Sikh issues and definitions' (Mejindarpal Kaur, personal correspondence, 25 March 2007). At the time of writing, the case of the three French schoolboys expelled in 2004 is awaiting an appeal in the Conseil d'État, the highest French court, while the appeal of the fourth against his expulsion is pending in the administrative appeal court. Although Shingara Singh Mann lost his appeal in the Conseil d'État to renew his driving licence without having to take off his turban for the ID photo, appeals have been filed at the European Court of Human Rights and the UN Human Rights Committee in New York for all the photo ID cases.[14]

The cases in the European Court of Human Rights are being fought on an interpretation of Article 9 and Article 14 of the European Convention on Human Rights. The cases before the UN Human Rights Committee will be fought on the violation of Articles 18 and 26 of the International Covenant on Civil and Political Rights (ICCPR). Article 9 of the Convention and Article 18 of the ICCPR guarantee 'the right to freedom of thought, conscience and religion' for all citizens of signatory states (United Nations High Commission for Human Rights 1966). Article 14 of the Convention and Article 26 of the ICCPR provide for the right to enjoy the rights and freedoms without being discriminated against on any ground, including race or religion. Crucially, Article 9 also allows a citizen to '*manifest* his religion or belief, in worship, teaching, practice and observance' (Council of Europe 1950, emphasis mine), which would suggest that the French government is in breach of its treaty obligations. However, this right is 'subject . . . to such limitations as are prescribed by law and are necessary in a democratic society in the interests of public safety, for the protection of public order . . . or the protection of the rights and freedoms of others' (Council of Europe 1950). Consequently, the French government is able to argue that the right to manifest one's own religion is subject to considerations of 'public order' or *national* security. The turban of a French national has, thus, become 'securitized' (Buzan *et al.* 1998) by the French state and has become a crucial battleground between the nation-state and the global Sikh *qaum*.

The *globalization* of the French turban cases testifies to the *transnational* aspirations of UNITED SIKHS both to protect the rights of Sikhs throughout the globe and to further the cause of 'religious freedom'. According to ICHRA director and legal team leader Mejindarpal Kaur, it 'is necessary to appeal these cases to the international courts as if left unchecked the French law, which undermines religious freedom, will have a domino effect on religious rights globally' (UNITED SIKHS 2006). The RTT campaign, she claims, is not only for the French Sikhs, but 'for 25 million Sikhs around the globe as the French Turban problem is one that concerns the whole Sikh community' (Mejindarpal Kaur, personal correspondence, 25 March 2007). Sikhs are the only religious group fighting the French ban law and therefore they are fighting this battle for religious freedom globally. Several German states have passed similar legislation that bans the wearing of religious signs and clothing by public servants, and two Belgian Sikh schoolchildren have not been admitted to school because of their turban. Consequently, Kudrat Singh of UNITED SIKHS (France) has petitioned the European Parliament in an attempt to investigate the French law and seek France's compliance with European Union directives (UNITED SIKHS 2007d).

As a non-governmental organization, which is registered as a non-profit entity in different countries, staffed by volunteers and funded almost exclusively by volunteers and donors within the Sikh community, UNITED SIKHS has an impressive record of success in taking on developed, industrialized nation-states over the treatment of their own nationals. The fact that it has done so within a voluntary organizational hierarchy, but one that provides the Western paradigms of accountability, makes it all the more remarkable.[15] UNITED SIKHS operates as a *global* organization providing *local* support at a grassroots level. Through schemes such as Sikh with a Need (SWAN), Sikhs are encouraged to contact UNITED SIKHS if they need support, and volunteers are encouraged to run the projects themselves. Since UNITED SIKHS is a non-political organization, it works well with other groups seeking to represent the *panth*, and it is a member of both the British and the American Sikh Consultative Forum.

Although the community feels 'empowered' having such an organization, even its European director is hesitant to posit UNITED SIKHS as a paradigmatic case of a transnational religious actor operating in a post-Westphalian world. Indeed, it could be argued that the very absence of a sovereign Sikh state necessitates the existence of transnational Sikh organizations such as UNITED SIKHS. In Mejindarpal Kaur's words: '[T]he reason why organizations such as UNITED SIKHS have to exist is because we have no one in the present structure of the world powers to represent us' (Mejindarpal Kaur, interview, 25 March 2007). Although a Sikh, Manmohan Singh has a moral duty but no 'legal duty' to protect the rights of Sikhs who are non-Indian nationals. If, on the other hand, Sikhs 'had a country', then they 'would have a PM to represent' them (Mejindarpal Kaur, interview, 25 March 2007).

This, however, should *not* be taken as an endorsement of the establishment of a Sikh sovereign state for, as previously stated, UNITED SIKHS remains an apolitical organization committed to the protection of minority rights throughout the world. Their commitment to defending the rights of Sikh minorities merely highlights the difficulties transnational communities have in making their views heard on a global stage without a sovereign state to represent the interests of their members. For, as a '*qaum* without borders', its institutions have to be 'even more astute', as it does not have the power structures which territorialized nation-states have at their disposal (Mejindarpal Kaur, interview, 25 March 2007).

Beyond *Khalistan*? Voices from the diaspora

The growth of the Internet and linked technologies has facilitated and often enabled the formation of cross-border networks among individuals and groups with a shared background or interests which has engendered or strengthened alternative notions of community of membership. Although, as previously discussed, the Internet in particular has enabled the articulation of a Sikh 'nationalist' discourse in the diaspora which has instilled a sense of the global unity of all Sikhs through an involvement in 'the politics of homeland', *Khalistan* is by its very nature a *deterritorialized* imagined community described on the homepage of Khalistan.net as a 'new global reality' which anyone can visit in cyberspace. Indeed, *Khalistan* has its own constitution, flag, maps and national anthem and various competing governments in exile (in Washington, London and Birmingham). *Khalistan* is, therefore, imagined just like any other nation-state but has no territory. The global Sikh *qaum* may be seen as such a new kind of 'imagined political community'. Like the nation, the Sikh *qaum* is imagined as both *finite* and *sovereign* (Anderson 1991: 46). Membership of the Sikh *qaum* is finite in that it is limited to *Kes-dhari* Punjabi-speaking Sikhs *irrespective of their actual place of origin.* Furthermore, the Sikh *qaum* is 'imagined' as sovereign. According to Hinsley, sovereignty contains both internal and external dimensions. Internally, sovereignty entails the idea that there is a final and absolute political authority in the political community and externally that *no final and absolute authority exists elsewhere* (Hinsley 1986). The Sikh *qaum* is seen as sovereign in that all political and spiritual power is located within the *Khalsa panth*. Guru Gobind is seen to have conferred sovereignty upon the *Khalsa panth* through the proc-lamation of *Raj Karega Khalsa* ('The *Khalsa* shall rule' and, by implication, is sovereign). No territorial limits are placed on the sovereignty of the *Khalsa*.

Like the *umma*, the Sikh *qaum* challenges the Westphalian international order based on the existence of a system or society of territorialized sover-eign states in its assertion of the sovereignty of the *Khalsa panth* over the state. However, no clear distinction between 'nation' and 'diaspora' or *watan* and *umma* is possible. Sikh identity comprises three interrelated narratives of religious community, nation and diaspora. In comparison with the Muslim *umma*, the Sikh *qaum* has a strong attachment to a territorially defined ances-tral homeland in the context of territorial dispersal. It is difficult, therefore, to separate the Sikh *umma* from the *watan*. It may be possible for Sikhs to go beyond *Khalistan*, in the sense that the *Khalsa panth* does not require state-hood in order to be sovereign, but not beyond the Punjab, the ancestral homeland.

In an attempt to find out whether the Sikh diaspora had moved away from *Khalistan* or whether the nationalist discourse was still strong, I posted a questionnaire on numerous Sikh discussion groups. The question asked was as follows: 'In your opinion, is *Khalistan* desirable and/or necessary?' Furthermore, I distributed two versions of the questionnaire, one written in English and another translated into Punjabi, outside *gurdwaras* in Southall,[16] Birmingham and Manchester (UK) and Palatine, Illinois between February 2000 and March 2007. In all, I received eighty responses, and the results are illustrated in Figure 7.1. In India, copies of the questionnaire were dis-tributed to a selected group of thirty Sikhs in Chandigarh, New Delhi and Mumbai during field research in 1997 and short visits in November 2002 and March 2007.[17] A full list of questions and responses is included in the Appendix. The results on the question of *Khalistan* are illustrated in Figure 7.2.

Although the responses from the Internet questionnaires were limited owing to a variety of reasons, I had more success in eliciting opinions on the emotive issue of *Khalistan* on the anniversary of Operation Blue Star and upon the election of Manmohan Singh as prime minister of India by

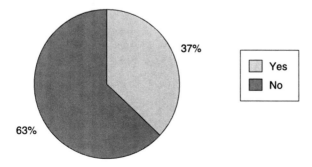

Figure 7.1 Questionnaire results (diaspora).

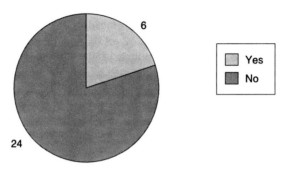

Figure 7.2 Questionnaire results (India).

initiating new discussions on the discussion groups listed in Tables 7.1 and 7.2. Online, Sikhs from the US, UK, Canada and Malaysia felt more at ease sharing their opinions upon Sikh *political* identity and whether *Khalistan* was still necessary or desirable.

In particular, I received responses from members of the following discussion groups and forums:

Table 7.1 Selected Internet discussion groups listed under the category 'Sikh'

Discussion group	Host	Country of origin (if known)	Members (31 August 2004)	Date founded (D/M/Y)
Sikh	MSN	UK	469	10/9/1999
Sikh	Yahoo	US/Canada	101	11/6/1999
Sikhism	Yahoo	US	244	7/1/1999
Sikh Agenda	Yahoo	UK	1,052	2/1/2002
Sikh Agenda 1	Yahoo	UK	206	3/8/2003
Sikh Agenda 2	Yahoo	UK	205	3/8/2003
Sikh Agenda 3	Yahoo	UK	114	3/8/2003
Sikh Agenda 4	Yahoo	UK	104	3/8/2003
Sikh Agenda 5	Yahoo	UK	91	3/8/2003
Sikh Agenda 6	Yahoo	UK	179	3/8/2003
Sikh Agenda 7	Yahoo	UK	185	3/8/2003
Sikh Americans	MSN	US	47	13/12/2001
Sikhs around the World	MSN	UK	113	20/10/2003
Sikhs' Khalistan	MSN	US	31	6/7/2002
Sikh_News_Discussion	Yahoo	UK	935	30/12/2002
Sikh Socs	Yahoo	UK	2,843	18/11/2000
UK Sikh Community	MSN	UK	114	17/12/2001
Sher-e-Punjab	Yahoo	UK	892	17/5/2003
Guru Ke Sikh	Yahoo	N/A	461	11/6/2004
International Journal of Sikh Affairs (IntJSA)	Yahoo	US/Canada	76	1/8/2000
International Sikh Youth Federation (ISYF)	Yahoo	Canada	52	2/2/2001

Table 7.2 Selected Internet discussion groups listed under the category 'Khalistan'

Discussion group	Host	Country of origin (if known)	Members (31 August 2004)	Date founded (D/M/Y)
Khalistan	Yahoo	US	508	24/4/1999
Khalistan2	Yahoo	US	21	8/12/1999
Khalistan-a Movement	MSN	US	N/A	23/5/2003
Khalistan Lionz	Yahoo	UK	8	8/8/2000
Council of Khalistan	Yahoo	US	223	24/7/2002
Punjab Forum	Yahoo	US	90	15/6/1999
Internatioanal Journal of Sikh Affairs (IntJSA)	Yahoo	US/Canada	76	1/8/2000
International Sikh Youth Federation (ISYF)	Yahoo	Canada	52	2/2/2001
Shaheed Khalsa	Yahoo	N/A	98	2/6/2004
Saint-Soldiers	MSN	Canada	30	20/11/2002
Sikh Agenda 7	Yahoo	UK	185	3/8/2003
Sikhs' Khalistan	MSN	US	31	6/7/2002

- Sikh@msn.groups.com
- Khalistan@yahoogroups.com
- Sikh Agenda@yahoo.groups.co.uk
- UK SikhCommunity@msn.groups.com
- Sikh Awareness.com
- Sikh-Diaspora@yahoogroups.com

Whilst I received a number of well-coordinated responses from representatives of *Khalistani* organizations criticizing the question in an attempt to render the issue of an independent Sikh homeland *doxic* in Bourdieu's terminology – that is belonging to 'the universe of the undiscussed' (Bourdieu 1977: 168) – the opinions of unaffiliated Sikhs were divided. Although all responses were *reflexive*, in that those who took the time to respond had clearly reflected upon whether *Khalistan* was desirable and in the best interests of the Sikh community, most operated within a hegemonic framework which can be traced to the *Tat Khalsa* understanding of Sikhism. I have included some responses below and, in most cases, only the initials of the co-respondents have been used to protect their anonymity (unless specified).

Z.R. of Khalistan@yahoogroups.com (hereafter the *Khalistan* group) thought that the appointment of Dr Manmohan Singh as prime minister would make little difference to the conditions of Sikhs in India and, therefore, that *Khalistan* was necessary. The reasons given reiterated the arguments articulated by its president, Dr Gurmit Singh Aulakh, and Dr Awtar Singh Sekhon, the editor of the Canada-based *International Journal of Sikh Affairs*. The first reason Z.R. gave was that Singh was *not* elected by the predominately Hindu electorate, but was effectively handpicked by Sonia Gandhi:

Remember also the electorate did not vote for a Sikh had he stood for election on his own merit he would have lost, his previous electoral record is far from 'shining'. The Indians voted for a Gandhi, streets were awash with people waving posters of Indira and Rajiv, both responsible respectively for the worst desecration in Sikh history and the wholesale slaughter of Sikhs in India wide pogroms. So this is the bloodline, the dynasty that was voted for, not Mr Singh.

(Z.R. 2004)

Furthermore, Z.R. correctly pointed out that it was under a 'Sikh President' (Zail Singh) that 'Blue Star was perpetrated, it was a Sikh president that for a short while held ultimate power in India whilst the mobs readied their kerosene and bicycle tyres', a reference to the anti-Sikh riots of November 1984, and 'it was a Sikh president that inaugurated a hateful son to his mothers throne and looked on whilst members of his own community burnt'. Z.R. also reminded members of the *Khalistan* group of the contributions of the Sikh police chief K.P.S. Gill to 'the tragedy of a lost generation of Sikh youth' and of the late Congress Chief Minister Beant Singh, assassinated in 1995, of 'accommodating of the central governments' Sikh *genocide*' (Z.R. 2004, italics mine). The establishment of *Khalistan* is thus, once again, legitimized by the memory of the *ghallughara* of 1984. The Sikhs are portrayed as an endangered *national* minority trapped within a Brahman-dominated 'Hindu' society and served poorly by a self-interested elite. This sentiment was expressed by J.S., who asked rhetorically:

Was President Zail Singh of any help to stop the Genocide of Sikhs in 1984? History repeats itself . . . and clever people learn from History. Will the Sikh *qaum* learn or go living in a fool's paradise. Manmohan is a complete '*chamcha*' of Sonia and under the heel of Harkrishen Singh (head of the CPM and the number one enemy of the Sikhs) . . . Still wondering if Manmohan can help the Sikhs?

(J.S. 2004)

D. S., however, was the dissenting voice challenging the nationalist orthodoxy from within the *Khalistan* group:

While I respect the opinions of all I fail to see why we as Sikhs cannot even congratulate Manmohan Singh for even becoming the first ever Sikh Prime Minister of India. That in itself says a lot for our community. As far as his politics go or if and how he is going to help the Sikh community, only time will tell. We need to give a person the chance to prove himself instead of jumping to label him '*chamcha*' and what not. Also, in 1984 Zail Singh was President who has no power in the Indian Constitution, and is far less powerful than the post of the Prime Minister.

(D.S. 2004)

D.S.'s main point that Manmohan Singh's appointment was 'at least a glimmer of hope that someone of the Sikh *panth* is at the helm now' and that 'there is at least some possibility that things might change for the better for our *panth*' was supported for different reasons particular to diaspora Sikhs by A.S. According to A.S.:

[T]he appointment of Manmohan Singh will ... lead to exposure for Sikhs worldwide, already in papers where his picture has appeared, you see the words *Sikh* Prime Minister. The more people that will see his picture and read the headline, the more Sikhs can get a much needed message across to the world as to who we are, that not all turban wearers are Arabs.

(A.S. 2004, emphasis mine)

A.S.'s reply hints at the very different problems and challenges faced by Sikhs in India and in the diaspora. Whilst it would be inconceivable to mistake a Sikh for an 'Arab' in the Punjab, in the post-9/11 US the reality of what Lacan, in a different context, termed the 'misrecognition' (*méconnaissance*) of Sikhs with the Arab/Islamic 'threatening Other' has resulted in physical attacks upon Sikhs with tragic consequences. The mistaken murder by Frank S. Roque, who claimed to be motivated by a sense of patriotism, of a Sikh man, Balbir Singh Sodhi, shot outside his gas station in the suburb of Mesa, Arizona, USA, in the wake of 9/11, illustrates the extent to which the turban and the beard of the male Sikh, shared with the radical Afghan Muslim group the Taliban and their mainly Arab Al-Qaeda backers, mark the male Sikh out in the Western popular consciousness as a 'terrorist' and, consequently, a threat to the secular institutions of the liberal-democratic nation-state. Although it was a case of mistaken identity, the murder of Sodhi was not an isolated occurrence, as recent incidents documented by the Sikh Coalition prove.[18] In India, however, the litmus test for Manmohan Singh remains the implementation of the ASR and the Rajiv–Longowal accord, which entails radically restructuring centre–state relations throughout India. In other words, Manmohan Singh will only be able to demonstrate his commitment to the *panth* by voluntarily surrendering some of the powers of the centre over which he presides to the state government, controlled by the Badal faction of the Akali Dal. For J.A.S. of the *Khalistan* group, this remains the 'only test' that Manmohan Singh needs to pass in order to prove his *panthic* credentials (J.A.S. 2004).

For members of the Sikh group (Sikh@msn.groups.com), the implementation of the Anandpur Sahib Resolution and a settlement, in Punjab's favour, to the long-running river water dispute between Haryana, Rajasthan and Punjab, will not easily wash away the 'memories' of 1984. Manmohan Singh remains for many diaspora Sikhs such as D.S. 'a Congress Party member who despite following the Sikh religion is still a member of the party which in my mind encouraged Sikh massacres during the Delhi riots. Will anything change . . . No' (D.S.S. 2004). S.S., on the other hand, feels that it is time for the Sikh community to move on:

> I think we should forgive the 1984 massacres because lets face it – what can Manmohan Singh do for those that lost their family members? money? I just hope he puts Sikhs on the world map, and stops the inno-cent killings in the present and future. We should all learn to accept each other (in terms of faith). If we pressurise him to do something about it, peace will never be achieved.
>
> (S.S. 2004)

For H.K., however, forgiveness is not so easy considering Manmohan Singh's actions since becoming prime minister. 'Forgiveness', she reminds us, 'takes place when the perpetrator seeks forgiveness.' Instead, Manmohan Singh has promoted 'perpetrators such as Jagdish Tytler', accused of organizing and coordinating the attacks upon Sikhs in Delhi in November 1984, to the Cabinet. 'This adds insult to the injury', since 'people responsible for the Sikh genocide' should 'be brought on trial and punished for their crimes' (H.K. 2004).

One can conclude that, although welcomed by most Sikhs, Manmohan Singh's appointment has been greeted with a considerable amount of scepti-cism by Sikhs in the diaspora. It was after all, as pointed out by S.S. of the UK Sikh Community, very convenient for the Indian government to 'have a turbaned Sikh' as prime minister, as they think that this will 'calm the Punjab down' (S.S. 2004). Nevertheless, as V.R. pointed out, Manmohan Singh's appointment has helped raise the Sikh profile abroad and will thus 'help Sikhs outside India more than inside' (V.R. 2004). According to H.S.:

> It is a great opportunity for the world to be taught about the Sikh *race*, and despite the injustices and cruelty of the past Indian Congress Party Governments (which should not, and will not be forgotten or forgiven), lets take this wonderful opportunity to raise the profile of *Sikhi* worldwide.
>
> (H.S. 2004)

In the diaspora, the consensus seems, in the words of Z.S. of the Sikh Agenda group, to be to 'wait and see' and 'hope for the best' whilst not *forgetting* the complicity of a Sikh president in the 'genocide' of 1984 (Z.S. 2004). Many Sikhs hope that Manmohan Singh will, in the words of A.S.S. of the Sikh group, 'speak out for the Sikh people of India, who have been cheated of their land and much more' (A.S.S. 2004).

Sikh pride at the appointment of Manmohan Singh, however, does not necessarily signal the end for *Khalistan* or the *Khalistan* movement, given its *symbolic* significance in the diaspora. For British Sikhs such as S.S, the estab-lishment of *Khalistan* would help reinforce Sikh identity over Asian/Indian identity in the diaspora. In keeping with *Tat Khalsa* orthodoxy, S.S. considers

Sikhs to have *always* been a distinct *ethno-religious* group from Hindus and Muslims. The establishment of *Khalistan* would reinforce 'the neutrality that Sikhism is suppose to have', since 'nowadays you get pro Hindu Sikhs who are also very anti Muslim mainly because of Pakistan, this is not what our Gurus wanted'. Furthermore, and again in keeping with *Tat Khalsa* orthodoxy, *Khalistan* would also 'help Sikhism to rid of the Hindu traditions and superstitions that have unfortunately clung onto the people' (S.S. 2004). In other words, the existence of *Khalistan* would facilitate the maintenance of ethnic and religious boundaries between Sikh and Hindu communities in the diaspora.

According to K.S., another British Sikh from Slough, *Khalistan* is also seen as necessary because, 'without self-determination, Punjab/Sikhs will lose everything – their rights, water, chances for economic development, spiritual/ national identity, educational opportunities etc' (K.S. 2004). This view, however, is not shared by many Sikhs who have taken advantage of the opportunities which economic globalization has afforded them and their businesses. For them, *Khalistan* remains a distant and impractical dream, which could easily turn into a nightmare if realized. According to G.S. from Malaysia, *Khalistan* was neither 'necessary nor desirable', since:

> Our numbers are too small and we lack good leadership that can face the challenges of today. Consider what is happening in Europe and why. Going on your own at a time when regional associations are growing to face global challenges, Khalistan will not benefit Sikhs.
>
> (G.S. 2004)

The appointment of Manmohan Singh as prime minister merely reinforced G.S.'s views that 'if Sikhs can stop going down the road to "self destruction" there are plenty of opportunities in India'. India, for G.S., is the 'next great economy of the world and there are plenty of opportunities if Sikhs can just look into the future'. The Sikhs, according to G.S., 'will be doing themselves and future generations a great injustice by getting out and then trying to "get in" as outsiders' – a reference to moves to strengthen the South Asian Association for Regional Cooperation (SAARC).[19] As a result of regionalization and globalization, 'Punjab is smaller that it was and it will get even smaller as *Khalistan*'. 'Our problems', G.S. concludes, 'will get bigger and our people will suffer!' (G.S 2004). It seems, therefore, that, although the dream of *Khalistan* remains alive in the diaspora, the majority of those who were prepared to share their views with me seemed to have moved *beyond Khalistan* and to have embraced a *diasporic* Sikh identity.

Concluding remarks

> Diaspora does not refer to those scattered tribes whose identity can only be secured in relation to some sacred homeland to which they must at all

> costs return . . . This is the old, the imperializing, the hegemonizing form
> of 'ethnicity' . . . The diaspora experience as I intend it here is defined not
> by essence or purity, but by the recognition of a necessary heterogeneity
> and diversity, by a conception of identity which lives with and through,
> not despite, difference.
>
> (S. Hall 1990: 235)

Applying Hall's categories to the study of the Sikh diaspora, we can distinguish between the 'old, hegemonizing form of "ethnicity" ' and newer,
more fluid identities. The 'old, hegemonizing form of "ethnicity" ' is represented by the *Khalistan* movement in the diaspora. Sikh diaspora nationalism
may be seen in Castells's terms as *resistance identity* in that 'it constructs
forms of resistance against otherwise unbearable oppression [in the case of
the Sikhs, Indian state repression in the Punjab between 1984 and 1992] on
the basis of clearly defined identities making it easier to essentialize the
boundaries of resistance' (Castells 1997: 9). This involves the building of a
defensive, masculinized, exclusionary *Kes-dhari* identity[20] which serves to
reinforce, or indeed reinvent, the boundaries between Sikhs and other South
Asian communities. It seeks, at all costs, a sovereign territorially defined state
in the ancestral homeland of the Punjab. This brings the self-appointed overseas representatives of the Sikh *qaum* into conflict with the Indian state,
which claims a monopoly of the legitimate use of force within the union state
of the Punjab. It has been argued elsewhere that this constitutes only a partial
challenge to the Westphalian international order since it reproduces its
central feature: the territorially demarcated sovereign state (Shani 2000a:
210–214).

   However, it may also be possible to speak of a 'new' counter-hegemonic
diasporic Sikh identity: an identity made possible by the nationalist project
but opposed to its territorializing, reifying imperatives. *Diasporic* here refers
to a form of community consciousness and solidarity that maintains identifications outside of the nation-state 'in order to live inside, with a difference'
(Clifford 1997: 287). This *diasporic* identity is not merely *multicultural*.
Ballard uses the adjective 'multicultural' to refer to individuals who have
acquired the competence to 'behave appropriately in a number of different
arenas, and to switch codes as appropriate' (Ballard 1994: 31). A diasporic
identity implies a *rejection* of the assimiliationist project of the nation-state.
Rather it approximates to what Castells terms a *project* identity. For Castells,
a project identity occurs when social actors, on the basis of whichever
materials are available to them, build a new identity that redefines their positions in society and, by doing so, seek the transformation of overall social
structure (Castells 1997: 8). Ballard's multicultural Sikhs may challenge
racialized notions of Britishness but they do not transform an international
society based on the sovereignty of nation-states. A Sikh project identity
could do so by constructing diasporic Sikh *subjects*: collective social actors
through which individuals reach holistic meaning (Castells 1997: 10) in their

experience of being Sikhs living in the diaspora rather than as immigrants or citizens of some imagined homeland. Globalization has brought a reconfiguration of ethnic identities within advanced capitalist societies, enabling diasporas to feel 'at home' in their places of settlement without abandoning their attachment to their communal identities or, in the case of the Sikhs, their *qaum*. For the new generation of Anglo-Sikhs, Sikh Canadians, Sikh Singaporeans or Sikh-Americans, the 'critical event' (Tatla 1999) or 'chosen trauma' (Kinvall 2002) of 1984 is but a distant memory, which can resurface at any given time. An independent homeland for the Sikhs may not be necessary, if Sikhs can feel at 'home' in Birmingham, Vancouver, Singapore, Southall or New York.

'Diasporic' political projects, as opposed to diaspora nationalism, have taken the form of a 'politics of recognition' aimed at facilitating Sikh integration into host societies whilst maintaining the external symbols of the faith: turbans and the Five Ks. As Clifford notes, the term 'diaspora' is a signifier not simply of transnationality and movement but of political struggles to define the local, as a distinctive community, in historical contexts of displacement (Clifford 1997: 287). However, the links between these local 'politics of recognition' or 'political struggles to define the local' are now globalized, and this has enabled Sikh organizations to articulate a *transnational* Sikh identity.

Immediately preceding 9/11, the Sikh Human Rights Group (SHRG), based in Ealing, West London, succeeded in getting the World Conference on Racism, Racial Discrimination, Xenophobia and Related Intolerance at Durban, South Africa (31 August to 7 September 2001) to adopt a paragraph (paragraph 73) to specifically include the Sikhs.[21] The need for a paragraph to include the Sikhs was expressed in the SHRG plenary statement:

> Existing national legislation and policies fall short of protecting the intertwined racial/cultural/ethnic/religious identity of the Sikhs. Very few groups fall into this sort of category . . . The category of religion does *not* adequately protect the Sikhs. *We call ourselves a 'Qaum' that has no translation in English.*
>
> (SHRG 2001, emphasis added)

The concept of *qaum* challenges the Westphalian order of territorialized nation-states and could well replace the nation as the basic unit of the post-national, globalized world.

SHRG's success in redefining categories of collective identities in order to include Sikhs, like the efforts of UNITED SIKHS to overturn the ban on the wearing of religious symbols in French schools, offers a glimpse into the ways in which a Sikh *diasporic* identity can go beyond *Khalistan* and actively challenge the Westphalian order by using the tools of globalization.

Conclusion

> Our world, and our lives, are being shaped by the conflicting trends of globalization and identity.
>
> (Castells 1997: 1)

> [The] Khalsa is a Global Fraternity.
>
> (Ranbir Singh 1968: 143)

This book has attempted to contribute to the further development of *critical* perspectives in both Sikh studies and international political theory.[1] A critical perspective differs from 'traditional' social science in that it is concerned with the possibilities for liberation that are *immanent* within existing political and social relations (Cox 1981; Linklater 1998). I have sought to do so by critically examining the possibilities which globalization has opened up for the articulation of a deterritorialized, *inclusive* Sikh identity *within* both South Asia and the diaspora. In so doing, I hope to have made a significant contribution to the further development of South Asian studies in two different respects.

In the first place, I have attempted to account for the construction of territorialized, nationalist narratives based on religion in contemporary South Asia. The first chapter critically examined the existing literature on ethnicity and nationalism in South Asia and argued that a revised constructivist perspective, informed by the work of Lacan (1977), Althusser (1970), Bourdieu (1977, 1990) and Anderson (1991), can best account for the construction of a Sikh nationalist identity within India. It was argued that the Sikh religious and cultural tradition is dynamic and contested by a plethora of different groups from within the *panth* but that it is not infinitely malleable as some instrumentalists have argued. Contemporary Sikh political elites, whether moderate Akali or separatist, are seen as 'unconsciously' subject to the past cultural choices of their forefathers who helped to define the 'tradition' which they are now endeavouring to defend.

Second, I have sought to illustrate how the intensification of contemporary processes of globalization has rendered territory less salient to religious and national *identity* in South Asia and the diaspora. In this book it has been argued that, contrary to neo-liberal assumptions, globalization will not lead to the creation of a 'global civil society' based upon market rationality and legitimized by a discourse of *individual* rights but to a world of deterritorialized global diasporas (Appadurai 1996; Cohen 1997). In the first chapter, it was argued instead that globalization has transformed socio-cultural identities at a local level and has made the (re-)imagination of *transnational* culturally defined identities possible. The subsequent chapters have attempted to account for the transformation of the Sikh community of the Punjab in India, from a *panth*, a 'religious' community, to a *qaum* or 'nation' during the colonial period and, finally, to a 'diaspora'.

It has been argued that, although the Sikh *panthic* tradition pre-dated the colonial encounter, the Sikh *qaum* arose as a result of the dialectical interaction between the *panthic* tradition and the colonial state. As was argued in Chapter 2, the colonial period saw a redefinition and reinterpretation of Sikh identity. Internal and external religious boundaries between Sikhs and Hindus and *Kes-dhari* and *Sahajdhari* Sikhs respectively were not so much constructed as reified by the colonial state's project of classification and enumeration as exemplified by the Census. This provided an enabling environment in which Singh Sabha reformers could articulate a *Tat Khalsa* discourse centred upon the Guru-*panth* and *Guru Granth* (Oberoi 1994). Subsequently, a more homogeneous conception of Sikh identity, which placed greater emphasis on the mythology and symbolism of the *Khalsa* and marginalized non-*Khalsa* Sikhs, arose.

After a sustained and successful mobilization which stirred *nationalist* sentiments among many Sikhs who found themselves in conflict with the colonial state, the *Tat Khalsa* definition of Sikhism was institutionalized by the Sikh Gurdwara Act of 1925 (Fox 1985; Kapur 1986). A Sikh was defined as someone who believed in the ten Gurus and the *Guru Granth Sahib* and had no *other* religious identity (SGPC 1994, 2001). Despite revisions, the basic definition of Sikhism has not changed and remains hegemonic within the *panth* today. It derives much of its symbolic power from the *embodiment* of *Khalsa* identity, and aspirations to sovereignty, in the Five Ks. They serve to *ethnicize* Sikh identity by giving (predominately but not exclusively male) Sikhs a highly visible presence within South Asia and overseas.

The Gurdwara Act, furthermore, made the *politicization* of the *Tat Khalsa* conception of Sikhism possible through the establishment of the SGPC. The SGPC and the various factions of the Akali Dal constitute a Sikh 'political system' (Wallace 1981; Gurharpal Singh 2000) which has succeeded in keeping the idea of a distinct Sikh *qaum* alive in independent, secular India through campaigns for a linguistically defined Sikh 'homeland'. The creation of a de facto Sikh-majority state through the genocidal violence of partition and, as argued in Chapter 3, the creation of a Punjabi *Suba* facilitated the *territorialization* of the Sikh *qaum*. The use, furthermore, of ethno-religious symbols to articulate the demand for a Punjabi *Suba* enabled the Indian government under Indira Gandhi to 'communalize' Punjab politics (Gupta 1985, 1997; Brass 1990, 1991) by encouraging challenges to the Sikh 'political system' from *within* the *panth*. Indira Gandhi was subsequently able to legitimize the use of force against militants who had taken (or been given) refuge in the Golden Temple complex, by depicting Sikhs as a troublesome and potentially separatist *national* minority which threatened India's territorial, and implicitly cultural, integrity defined along Hindu lines. The destruction, either by accident or – more likely – by design, of the *Akal Takht*, the site of all Sikh temporal authority, was perceived by Sikhs globally as an attack upon their *sovereignty*. This gave rise to the belief that only an independent Sikh state, *Khalistan*, could safeguard the sovereignty which Guru Gobind had bestowed upon the *Khalsa Panth* almost three centuries earlier. *Khalistan* was formally proclaimed by a *Sarbat Khalsa* on 29 April 1986, and a war of 'national self-determination' subsequently developed between armed militants and the Indian state (Pettigrew 1995) which the state won through a reassertion of 'violent control' (Gurharpal Singh 2000).

However, it was argued that the violence alone cannot explain the transformation of Sikh politics from a 'politics of identity' to a 'politics of region' in the two decades since the proclamation of *Khalistan*. As the 2007 state elections suggest, all the main political parties in the Punjab have now embraced a non-communal Punjabi identity and there is evidence to suggest that the old communal divisions between (rural) Sikhs and (urban) Hindus are breaking down, with many Sikhs voting for the INC under Captain Amarinder Singh and some Hindus voting for the SAD (Pritam Singh 2007). Although the physical elimination of militants by the Indian state has facilitated this regionalization of Punjabi politics by allowing the moderate Badal faction to reassert its hegemony within the Sikh 'political system', Chapter 4 argues that any explanation of the regionalization of Punjabi politics must also take into account the role which contemporary processes of globalization have played in the restructuring of both India's political economy and centre–state relations. At a regional level, economic globalization has exposed rural *Jat* Sikh farmers to increased competition from abroad and led to increasing inequality *within* the *panth* along class and caste lines (Jodhka 2005), which successive Akali-led governments have done little to stem. Furthermore, the chronic mismanagement of state finances by both SAD- and INC-led administrations has led to a fiscal crisis which places severe constraints on the state's ability to arrest the marked deterioration in public services and attract greater investment from the private sector (World Bank 2004). Unsurprisingly, regional development – and not *Khalistan* – remains the priority for most Sikhs in today's globalized Punjab, and those parties which have continued to espouse the cause of Sikh nationalism, such as Simranjit Singh Mann's SAD (Amritsar), have fared poorly.

At a national level, the appointment of Manmohan Singh, a respected economist credited with liberalizing India's economy, as prime minister has succeeded in convincing many Sikhs previously sympathetic to the militant cause that their best interests are served by assimilating to the 'democratic mainstream'. However, it is argued that the rise of a *Hindutva* discourse, as articulated by the BJP over the past two decades, has placed clear limits on the extent to which Sikhs can identify with 'India' as opposed to 'Punjab'. Furthermore, the existence, on the one hand, of a Sikh politico-religious establishment committed to preserving a distinct Sikh identity in India and, on the other hand, of a Hindu religio-political establishment which seeks to preserve India's cultural integrity within a framework of *Hindutva* places severe strain on the SAD–BJP electoral alliance and compromises the new coalition government's ability to represent all Punjabis.[2] A return to the militancy of the post-Blue Star period can, therefore, not be ruled out entirely, particularly given the centre's failure to implement the recommendations of the Nanavati Commission to the satisfaction of the Sikh community.

In conclusion, the failure of the movement to bring about a sovereign, Sikh state should not be interpreted as resulting from the weakness of the 'communal' ties which bind members of the Sikh *qaum* together, but points to the transformation of *national* identity under conditions of globalization. Globalization has severed the link between nation and state and facilitated the articulation of a post-national diasporic Sikh identity. The proliferation of *gurdwaras* in places of Sikh settlement, and the print and electronic media development, has facilitated the dissemination of a *diaspora consciousness* amongst Sikhs resident in advanced capitalist nation-states through a discourse of 'victimhood' articulated by organizations such as the Council of Khalistan, Khalistan Council, Khalistan Affairs Center and various branches of the Babbar Khalsa and International Sikh Youth Federation. All of these organizations maintain transnational links with one another and with Panthic Committees in the Punjab but operate *outside* of the Sikh 'political system'. In the nationalist discourse in the diaspora, Sikhs are represented as 'victims' of two twentieth-century *ghallughara* or 'genocides': partition and Operation Blue Star. How these Sikh 'holocausts' are 'remembered' and what is 'forgotten' are, it is argued in Chapter 5, central to the imagination of *both* a Sikh 'nation' and a specifically Sikh 'diaspora' (Tatla 1999; Axel 2001).

Sikh identity in the diaspora is simultaneously deterritorialized and reterritorialized (Deleuze and Guattari 1987): the 'homeland' remains central to the diasporic political imagination but, especially online, the homeland is (re-)imagined as a borderless and potentially inclusive *diaspora space* (Brah 1996), a reference point for a sovereign, transnational community rather than a specific geographical location (Axel 2001, 2002, 2005). This creates space for the articulation of post-*Khalistani* narratives by groups claiming to represent Sikhs in their places of settlement. Using case studies of Sikh communities in the United Kingdom and the United States, it was argued in Chapter 6 that the objective of Sikh political activity has been consistently to gain recognition from the state of their *difference* from other groups in the diaspora. The Five Ks, which collectively embody Sikh identity and aspirations to sovereignty, in particular has been the battleground between the *panth* and state. In the UK, Sikh mobilization led initially to some important victories which guaranteed *Kes-dhari* Sikhs the right to wear turbans and *kirpans* in the workplace. Although these localized struggles for recognition were superseded by the *Khalistan* movement, it was argued that the demand for a sovereign Sikh homeland was itself part of a broader 'politics of recognition' which sought also to gain 'acknowledgment and status' (Taylor 1994) for Sikhs in their places of settlement.

Following 9/11 in the US and 7/7 in the UK, the external symbols of Sikh identity have marked the Sikhs out as the stigmatized 'Other' against which the nation defines itself, and their manifestation has been threatened by the increasing 'securitization' of society. In response, several organizations have emerged on both sides of the Atlantic espousing an embryonic *diasporic* identity, encompassing a politics of both recognition and redistribution. Groups such as the Sikh Federation (UK), the Sikh American Legal Defense and Education Fund (SALDEF) and the Sikh Coalition in the US have sought to represent Sikh claims to 'live inside' the nation-state 'with a difference' (Clifford 1997). This 'diasporic' identity, which it is argued in Chapter 7 is best represented by transnational religious actors such as the World Sikh Council and UNITED SIKHS, is made possible by the mobilization of the Sikh community through the *Khalistan* movement. However, unlike *Khalistani* narratives, Sikh *diasporic* narratives do not attempt to place territorial limits on the sovereignty of the *qaum*.

A Sikh diasporic identity, it has also been argued, challenges the traditional constitutive narratives of international relations. As John Agnew has pointed out, these narratives rest on three assumptions: that modern state sovereignty requires clearly bounded territories, that there is a fundamental opposition between 'domestic' and 'foreign' affairs and that the territorial state is seen as acting as the geographical container of society (Agnew 1998: 50). The contemporary phase of globalization has effectively *deterritorialized* sovereignty, blurring the distinction between 'domestic' and 'foreign' affairs and unleashing the genie of national identity from the geographical bottle. This provides the Sikh *qaum* with an opportunity to adapt to the changing global reality by going beyond *Khalistan* and reasserting the *transnational* sovereignty of the *Khalsa panth*. It also affords the *Khalsa panth* an opportunity to contribute to the further globalization of international relations and human society by reaffirming the universal values and radical egalitarianism of the Sikh Gurus who, in the sacred words of Guru Gobind Singh, believed in an *Akal Purakh* (timeless being) without 'colour, mark, caste and lineage' (*Akal Ustat*, SDGS, verse 4). In short, the *Khalsa* is a 'Global Fraternity' (Ranbir Singh 1968: 143) better suited to our 'global age' than a 'timebound' (Albrow 1996) state of *Khalistan*.

Appendix

Full questionnaire results (India)

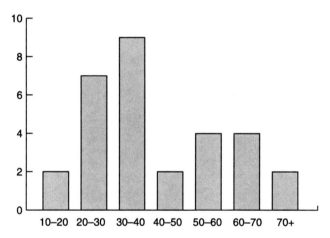

Figure A.1 Question 1) Age.

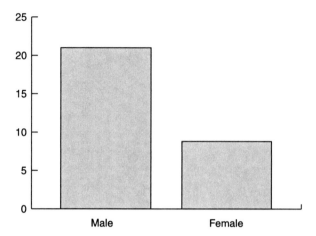

Figure A.2 Question 2) Gender.

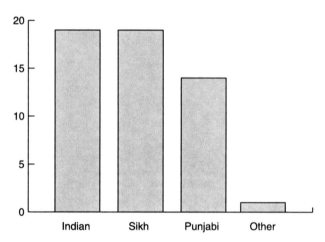

Figure A.3 Question 3) How would you categorize yourself? You are allowed to choose more than one category.

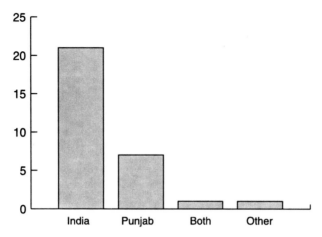

Figure A.4 Question 4) Where do you consider 'home' to be?

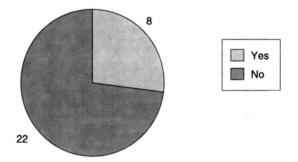

Figure A.5 Question 5) In your opinion, are Sikhs discriminated against in India?

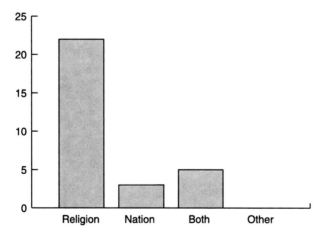

Figure A.6 Question 6) Which of the following words do you consider to best describe the *Khalsa Panth*?

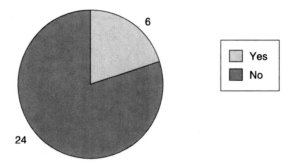

Figure A.7 Question 7) In your opinion, is *Khalistan* necessary and/or desirable?

Notes

1 Introduction: rethinking Sikh nationalism in a global age

1 See Tully and Jacob (1985) for an account of the storming of the Golden Temple complex, which is the most sacred site in Sikhism.

2 The term 'primordialism' was first applied in the social sciences by Edward Shils in reference to relationships within the family. Shils argued that the attachment one feels for one's family is 'primordial' in that it stems not from interaction but from 'a certain ineffable significance . . . attributed to the tie of blood' (Shils 1957: 142). These 'primordial attachments' were subsequently applied to the study of ethnicity in Asia and Africa by Clifford Geertz. For Geertz, 'primordial attachments' refer to 'the assumed "givens" of social existence: immediate contiguity and kin connection mainly but beyond them the *givenness that stems from being born into a particular religious community, speaking a particular language . . . and following particular social practices*' (Geertz 1973: 259, italics mine).

3 Fox argues that communalism has become assigned to South Asia in the same way as Paul Gilroy has argued that the history of slavery has been assigned to Blacks: it becomes the exclusive property of the non-West, constituting its history, rather than 'part of the ethical and intellectual heritage of the West' (Gilroy 1993: 49).

4 In *Orientalism* (1978), Said claimed that Orientalism is premised upon exteriority, that is, on the fact that 'the Orientalist poet or scholar *makes the Orient speak*, describes the Orient, renders its mysteries plain for and to the West' (Said 1978: 21, emphasis mine). The implication is that the indigenous voice of the 'oriental subject' is silenced by the power of Orientalism.

5 It is, as Fox points out, possible to argue that Welsh nationalism was initially a reaction to the 'internal colonialism' of the English bourgeoisie (Hechter 1975). However, the nature of 'colonial' rule differed to such an extent that it was possible for Wales to become a constitutive part of a 'British' nation rather than a subject territory of the English crown.

6 For an introduction to hyperglobalist, sceptic and transformationalist views of globalization, see Held *et al.* (1999: 1–30).

7 Jacobson claims that 'what we are witnessing is the development of a global (if still limited to the northern hemisphere) political culture based on human rights – which is demarcated (in principle) in non-territorial terms and, in its domain, is distinct from territorial states (the local political authorities)'. However, he acknowledges that 'it is through theses states that human rights are being institutionalized, both domestically and internationally' (Jacobson 2001: 177).

2 From *panth* to *qaum*: the construction of a Sikh 'national' identity in colonial India

1 'Sikhs' here refer to Nanak's followers, who may or may not have been conscious of the distinctiveness of their Guru's teachings.
2 *Bhallas* were descendants of Guru Amar Das's eldest son, Baba Mohan.
3 *Minas*, meaning 'dissembling rogues', contested Arjan's right to be Guru in preference to his older brother, Prithi Chand.
4 Women initiated into the new order of the *Khalsa* in the years to come similarly take a common name, Kaur, literally meaning 'princess'.
5 Bhai Gurdas, a nephew of Guru Amar Das, was a Sikh poet closely associated with Guru Arjan and Guru Hargobind. He wrote in total thirty-nine *Vars*, which, according to J.S. Grewal, have been held in esteem next only to the *Guru Granth Sahib* (Grewal 1999a: 26).
6 For a historical account of Maharajah Ranjit Singh's rule and its significance for the Sikhs, see J.S. Grewal (1994: 99–127).
7 Indeed, in the 1891 Census, which was the first to distinguish between different categories of Sikhs, 579,000 people were included under the category of 'Hindu Nanak-panthi' and 297,000 under the category of 'Sikh Nanak-panthi'. Both categories were distinguished from that of 'Sikh Kes-dhari' or 'Gobind Singhi' Sikhs (Government of India 1891).
8 The most impressive gains and losses were by the *Mazhabi*, scheduled caste Sikhs, on the one hand and Nanak-*panthis* on the other. The figures for the *Mazhabis* point to both the success of the efforts by the *Tat Khalsa* reformers to reclaim them from Hinduism and the prevalence of caste-based discrimination in the nominally egalitarian *panth*.
9 It is important to note that Oberoi's thesis has attracted vociferous and often violent criticism both from within the academic world and from the Sikh diaspora which led to attempts to remove him from his position as first Chair of Sikh Studies at the University of British Columbia, a position funded partially by the Sikh community of Canada. For a first-hand account of the controversy, see Oberoi (2001: 198–203). W.H. McLeod also provides an early sympathetic account (McLeod 1994: 121–134), whilst G.S. Dhillon offers a vigorous and personalized critique of Oberoi's attempt at 'vacuous theorising' (Dhillon 1996: 29–40). For more balanced critiques from ethno-symbolist perspectives, see Gurharpal Singh (2000: 78, 2004) and Harnik Deol (2000: 75–76).
10 See Tables 2.5 and 2.6 for numbers of *Kes-dhari* and *Sahajdari* Sikhs in the 1911 and 1921 Censuses.
11 However, a closer examination of the historical record reveals that there was little specifically 'Sikh' about Ranjit Singh's rule, apart from the religion professed by the ruler. Although Ranjit Singh nominally ruled in the name of the *Khalsa*, he made no attempt to promote Sikhism, which remained the faith of a minority, as a state ideology and chose not to draw a distinction between the faiths over those whom he governed. This was reflected in the Maharajah's pluralist state power structure: his prime minister, Dhian Singh, was a Hindu and his 'Commander and Faithful Friend' was Mian Ghausa, a Muslim.
12 E. Trumpp to Secretary of State for India, 13 January 1874, Government of India, Foreign General Proceeding, no. 34–37A of July 1873. Quoted in Kapur (1986: 19).
13 The conversion of Maharaja Duleep Singh (1838–1893), the last Sikh sovereign, who had come under British tutelage at the age of eight, to Christianity in 1853 was hailed by colonial authorities as 'the first instance of the accession of an Indian prince to the communion of the Church' (Harbans Singh 2003a).
14 For an account of the *Kuka* rebellion see Oberoi (1992).

15 Members of this elite, led by Sardar Thakur Singh Sandhanvalia (1837–1887), included the Maharaja of Faridkot, Bikram Singh (1835–1887), and Baba Khem Singh Bedi (1832–1905), a direct descendant of Guru Nanak, both of whom contributed large sums of money to the Sabha (Kapur 1986: 17).

16 A *giani* is a Sikh religious scholar.

17 Literally meaning 'brother', *bhai* is a title given to pious and learned Sikhs.

18 According to the 1881 Census, there were 784 books published in Punjabi and 745 books published in Hindi in 1880. In total, 630 new books were written in Punjabi in just five years (GOI 1881: 160).

19 Dayal Singh Majithia was a wealthy Sikh aristocrat who died leaving his fortune to a trust in his name. His widow contested the will, arguing that, since her late husband was a Sikh, the Hindu law of inheritance under which her husband had bequeathed his property to the trust did not apply. The case was taken to the Punjab High Court where it was decided that, since Sikhs *were* in fact Hindus, there were no grounds upon which to contest the will (Kapur 1986: 19).

20 A *diwan* is literally a large open meeting.

21 The *Ghadar* movement took its name from a newspaper of the same name published by the Hindustani Association of the Pacific coast of North America and edited by Lala Har Dyal. Most of the Ghadarites were Punjabis settled in North America who, politicized by their experiences of racial discrimination, returned to the Punjab in order to liberate their homeland from British colonialism. Many Sikh Ghadarites went on to play an active role in both the nationalist and the *gurdwara* reform movement during the 1920s (Puri 1993; Tatla 2001: 161–185).

22 The *Jallianwallah Bagh* massacre of 1919 is one of the most notorious incidents in the history of the British Raj, exposing the coercive nature of colonial rule. On 13 April 1919, a crowd of peaceful demonstrators gathered in the heart of Amritsar was fired upon by British troops under the command of General Dyer. According to official figures, 379 were killed and over a thousand were wounded, but unofficial figures list the number of casualties as far higher with over a thousand dead (Harbans Singh 2003b).

23 One contemporary estimate was that 30,000 Sikhs were jailed, 400 killed and 2,000 wounded during what Fox terms 'the Third Sikh War' (Fox 1985: 79; Mohinder Singh 1997: 229).

3 The territorialization of the *qaum*: Sikh 'national' identity in independent India

1 See Gurharpal Singh (2000: 100–109) for a discussion of the Sikh political system.

2 See Brass (1994: 1–28) for a detailed account of the continuities and discontinuities between pre- and post-independence India.

3 Article 25 (1) of the Constitution gives all persons 'the right to profess, propagate and practise their religion' (GOI 1949b).

4 Bhargava likens the state to a teacher forced to make a distinction between good and bad scripts in order to treat all answer scripts with equal respect and, therefore, uphold the principle of neutrality (Bhargava 1998b: 503).

5 In July 1946, Nehru stated at Calcutta during a meeting of the All India Congress Working Committee that 'the brave Sikhs of the Punjab are entitled to special consideration'. Consequently, he saw 'nothing wrong in an area and a set-up in the north wherein the Sikhs can also experience the glow of freedom' (Nehru, 1946, quoted in Surjan Singh 1982: 20).

6 See Chapter 5 for a discussion of the memory of partition on Sikh nationalist consciousness.

7 Lacan had argued that, whilst the 'specular' image was alienating, the human body

was in pieces, made up of a series of alienating images which he groups together under the term 'imagos of the fragmented body' (Lacan 1977: 11).

8 According to Purewal, the Punjab received Rs 531 per capita in the fifth (1974–1979), Rs 1,444 per capita in the sixth (1980–1985) and Rs 1,685 per capita in the seventh year plan (1986–1991) against the all-states per capita average of Rs 262, Rs 872 and Rs 1,026 respectively (Purewal 2000: 65–66).

9 Dr Chauhan was first elected to the Punjab Vidhan Sabha from Tanda as a candidate of the Republican Party of India in 1967 and later became deputy speaker when the Akali Dal-led coalition government assumed office in the state. Later, Dr Chauhan was made finance minister when Lachman Singh Gill became chief minister. In 1969, he lost the Assembly election and two years later moved to the UK, where he lived until 2001 (*Tribune* 2007a).

10 Dr Jagjit Singh Chauhan was interviewed by the author on 1 February 2000. The author is indebted to Mr Helly Chahal for setting up the interview and to the late Dr Chauhan for his time and hospitality.

11 The Congress president, D.K. Barooah, had come up with what he thought was a winning formula during the Emergency by claiming that 'India is Indira, Indira is India'. Although some commentators have argued that this contrasted unfavourably with her father's aphorism 'India is Congress, Congress is India' (Corbridge and Harriss 2000: 87), it clearly shows continuities in the symbolic language invoked by Nehru.

12 The term *qaum* was used in the Punjab version but was translated in English as 'nation'.

13 The united SAD constitution approved after the ASR was drafted committed the SAD to 'the preservation among the Sikhs of a consciousness of an independent Panthic identity and carving out a territory [*desh*] and era [*kaal*] wherein the *national sentiments and nationhood of the Sikh panth* may find the fullest embodiment and expression' (SAD 1974: 1, italics mine).

14 According to Gurharpal Singh, the Nehruvian approach consisted of 'disarticulating Sikh ethno-nationalism through accommodation, co-option, symbolic agreements, and subsequently, non-implementation of such agreements'. Indira Gandhi's 'innovations included a more overt use of violent control mechanisms with a search for an alternative hegemonizing ideology in Hindu revivalism' (Gurharpal Singh 2000: 110).

15 The Babbar Akalis were members of the Babbar Akali Jatha, a militant organization which, unlike other Akali *jathas*, sanctioned the use of violence against *mahants* and their British protectors in the *gurdwara* reform movement between 1922 and 1923.

16 See J.P.S. Uberoi (1996: 115–134) for correspondence between Gandhi and the SGPC.

17 See Pettigrew (1995: 82–102) for an account of the history and organization of the Khalistan Commando Force (KCF) and profiles of its members (Pettigrew 1995: 143–186).

18 See Gurharpal Singh (2000: 130–132) for a history of the Rajiv–Longowal accord.

19 See Human Rights Watch/Asian Physicians for Human Rights (1994) for details of atrocities carried out by the security forces under the command of Julio Ribeiro.

4 From *Khalistan* to *Punjabiat*: globalization, *Hindutva* and the decline of Sikh militancy

1 The Russian term 'kulak', meaning 'fist', is used to describe a class of rich, capitalist farmers whose economic interests extend over agricultural production and trade (Corbridge and Harriss 2000: 81).

2 According to the Economist Intelligence Unit, real GDP (at factor cost) grew by 9.3 per cent year on year in the last quarter of the fiscal 2005/6 year and by 8.4 per cent for the year as a whole (EIU 2006: 3).
3 Both Weber and more recently Huntington refer to the Christian, and specifically Protestant, origins of Western modernity. See Weber (1978) and Huntington (1996).
4 'Hindustan' literally refers to the 'land of the Hindus'.
5 See Graham (1990) for an account of the development of the Bharatiya Janata Sangh.
6 Ram is one of the most important Hindu gods.
7 Literally it means 'Ram's rule'. Advani's procession through the Hindi belt (the Hindi-speaking states of Uttar Pradesh, Madyha Pradesh, Rajasthan and Bihar) was laden with symbolism and was designed to exploit the phenomenal success of the televised version of the *Ramayana*, the epic tale of Lord Ram, which was televised throughout India by the national broadcaster Doordorshan in the 1980s and early 1990s.
8 See Nussbaum (2003) and Bhargava (2003) for a discussion of 'genocide' in Gujarat.
9 See the contributions to *Communalism Combat*, March–April 2002.
10 The use of the term 'ethnic democracy' in the Indian context, although an apt description of the post-Nehruvian period, may be seen as problematic for two reasons. First, if the term 'ethnic democracy' is used to describe the post-partition Indian state, then what term can be used to describe the genocidal settler democracies of twentieth-century South Africa, nineteenth-century USA, Australia or even Serbia under Milosevic? Perhaps the term 'ethnocracy' would have been more appropriate, given that the political culture of Nehruvian India was hardly 'participatory' – a key characteristic of any 'democratic' political culture. Second, and related to the last point, although Singh is right to point out the ideological symmetry between Congress secularism and hegemonic Hinduism, significant differences do appear to exist between the Nehruvian and post-Nehruvian periods. The post-Nehruvian period, marked by the popular rejection of the Nehruvian consensus, and the articulation of an exclusionist Hindu nationalism by Congress and BJP alike, comes closest to satisfying the criteria of being an 'ethnic democracy'.
11 Operation Woodrose refers to the combing of the Punjab villages by Indian security forces in the aftermath of Operation Blue Star. According to General Narinder Singh – a retired general, vice-chairman of the Punjab Human Rights Organization – it was 'Operation Pacification' in that everyone wearing a 'saffron *patka* or flowing beard was branded a terrorist and eliminated' by a predominately non-Sikh army (Narinder Singh, cited in Pettigrew 1995: 36).
12 Operation Black Thunder refers to the 1988 attempt to flush Sikh militants from the Golden Temple whilst avoiding damage to the *Darbar Sahib* itself. See Sarab Jit Singh (2002) for an autobiographical account of the author's role in the latter.
13 The suspension of the Jathedar of the *Akal Takht*, the custodian of the holiest shrine in the Sikh religion, Ranjit Singh, by ten members of the SGPC's fifteen-member executive committee on 10 February 1999 was widely seen as an attack upon Tohra's authority. Tohra argued, for his part, that the Jathedar could only be removed through the instrument of *Sarbat Khalsa*, a general assembly of all practising Sikhs popular during the *Khalistan* movement of the 1980s.
14 The author wishes to thank Surinder Singh Sawhney for kindly setting up the interviews.
15 See Dogra (2004).
16 See Ramesh (2004).
17 For example, Jagjit Singh Chauhan, who led the movement for *Khalistan* from

London, welcomed the appointment as 'a huge development for Sikhs' and pronounced himself 'extremely happy' since 'it has made a significant difference in the way Sikhs will be looked upon not only in India but also the world' (Dogra 2004).

18 Intervening in the discussion on the Opposition-sponsored motion in the Rajya Sabha on the Nanavati Commission report, Dr Manmohan Singh apologized 'not only to the Sikh community but to the whole nation . . . On behalf of our government, on behalf of the entire people of this country, I bow my head in shame' (*Tribune* 2005).

19 The Commission, under the direction of retired Supreme Court judge G.T. Nanavati, was appointed by the BJP-led NDA government in 2002 to investigate the 1984 anti-Sikh riots. The final report submitted to the INC government in 2005 concluded that there was evidence of INC complicity in organizing the riots, although it cleared Rajiv Gandhi or other high-ranking Congress officials of involvement. According to the Commission report, 'As the attacks on Sikhs appear to the Commission as organized, an attempt was made to see who were responsible for organizing the same. Some of the affidavits filed before the Commission generally state that the Congress Leaders/Workers were behind these riots' (Nanavati Commission 2005).

5 'The territorialization of memory': Sikh nationalism in the 'diaspora'

1 'Deterritorialized' in this context merely refers to movement from a 'homeland' irrespective of whether the migration was forced or voluntary.

2 'Transnational' in this context refers to interstate or global flows and networks.

3 Cohen, in his introduction to the series of global diasporas, had earlier distinguished between victim, labour, trade, imperial and cultural diasporas. Unlike the vast majority of South Asian diasporas, the Sikhs were not indentured labourers and therefore do not correspond to Cohen's definition of a labour diaspora.

4 The British Sikh Federation estimates that 51 per cent of all Britons of Indian origin are Sikh. See Sikh Federation (UK) (2003b). This figure is supported by the Institute of Race Relations (Institute of Race Relations 2000).

5 It must be pointed out that the caste system is against the religious doctrine of Sikhism which preaches the equality of all men, including women. However, a caste system based on hereditary occupation is a feature of Indian society, and caste divisions are reflected in the Sikh community.

6 Dr Jagjit Singh Chauhan was interviewed by the author on 1 February 2000. The author is indebted to Mr Helly Chahal for setting up the interview and to the late Dr Chauhan for his time and hospitality.

7 Basing his figures primarily on British reports, Brass, however, estimates that 'only' between 200,000 and 360,000 died as a direct result of partition violence (Brass 2003: 75). This contrasts with Butalia's higher figure of 1 million (Butalia 2000: 3).

8 According to Brass, 'the Punjab massacres precede and anticipate contemporary forms of genocide and "ethnic cleansing," retributive or otherwise, most notably in Hutu–Tutsi killings in Rwanda and the massacres and forced migrations of peoples in ex-Yugoslavia: Croatia, Bosnia and Kosovo' (Brass 2003: 73).

9 Brass suggests that the principal objective of the Sikh leadership was to maintain the solidarity and unity of the community 'by regrouping its entire populations into a compact area that included several districts where they were now in a majority' (Brass 2003: 82).

10 Tan Tai Yong argues that the Sikh leadership planned, organized and coordinated attacks upon Muslims in East Punjab. According to Yong, 'the Sikhs, enraged that the Punjab would be partitioned and half of it given to the newly created state of Pakistan, reacted with unbridled fury and plunged the province into a state of war'

(Yong 1994: 167). See also Hansen (2002) for an account of the role the Akal Fauj played in partition violence. Brass, meanwhile, concludes that, although not all the violence in East Punjab can be attributed to the Sikhs, 'there is no doubt that a large part of it was the result of deliberate actions on the part of Sikh gangs' (Brass 2003: 81).

11 In the case of Kampuchea, the term 'democide', denoting the murder of any person or people by their government, is more appropriate.

12 A prominent Congress activist, Rameshwari Nehru, visited Thoa Khalsa soon after the event and declared that a 'country that has such courageous women amongst its inhabitants can never die'. The country she was referring to was, of course, India – a new 'nation' that the women never lived to see (Pandey 2001: 87–88).

13 I interviewed thirty Sikhs from the Rawalpindi area who had lived through partition between 1997 and 2004 in India and the UK. The interviews took the form of conversations which were, for the most part, unrecorded.

14 'Witness' here refers not to a witness in a court of law but to someone 'who has lived through something, who has experienced an event from beginning to end and can therefore bear witness to it' (Agamben 2002: 17). In this sense, it shares a similar meaning to that of 'survivor' (Edkins 2003). Certainly, those 'witnesses' of the horrors of partition whom I interviewed likened themselves to 'survivors' of a great catastrophe and shared similar emotions of relief, shock and guilt.

15 For Edkins, memorialization refers to a state of 'not forgetting' (Edkins 2003: 17).

16 Preliminary fieldwork was carried out between February and June 1997 in Punjab, New Delhi and Uttar Pradesh. A total of thirty Sikhs were interviewed, including the author and Sikh historian Patwant Singh. The results of a questionnaire handed out and collected in 2002–2003 show little support for *Khalistan* amongst the politically active Sikhs I approached. Please see Figure 7.2 and the Appendix.

17 This is an approach which is also taken by instrumentalist explanations of the 'Punjab Problem'. Brass comes dangerously close to asserting that Sikh ethnonationalism may be seen almost entirely as a reaction to Indira Gandhi's centralization of power (Brass 1991). This ignores the history of Sikh nationalism as outlined in the previous chapter.

18 It is estimated that 44 per cent of the Sikh population in the UK is under 21 (Sikh Federation (UK) 2003a).

19 I interviewed many Sikh political activists in London and Birmingham between 2000 and 2001. These included Dr Jagjit Singh Chauhan, leader of the *Khalistan* movement in the UK, Ajit Singh Khera, formerly press officer of the Khalistan Council, and Dr Jasdev Singh Rai of the Sikh Human Rights Organisation. The other interviewees consented to interviews only if I did not reveal their identities.

20 Dr Chauhan, who had been campaigning for *Khalistan* since the late 1960s until his death, is an obvious exception.

21 The term *shahid*, derived from the Arabic *shahad*, literally means 'witness'.

22 *Ma boli* means 'mother tongue' or 'culture' in Punjabi.

23 Pilgrims had assembled in *Harimandir* ironically to commemorate the anniversary of Guru Arjan's martyrdom.

24 Significantly, Bhindranwale is almost always shown alive. Immediately after Operation Blue Star, the Indian government was quick to show photos of what, they claimed, was Bhindranwale's dead body. For a long time the *Khalistan* movement denied that the body exhibited was in fact Bhindranwale's, preferring to believe that he was alive and was leading the resistance to the Indian state in Pakistan. Dr Jagjit Chauhan alluded to previous 'misconceptions' when interviewed by the author on 17 February 2000.

25 The term 'chosen trauma' describes the 'mental recollection of a calamity that

once befell a group's ancestors, and includes information, fantasized expectations, intense feelings and defences against unacceptable thought' (Kinvall 2002: 86). See Kinvall (2002) for a comparative examination of Sikh and Hindu 'chosen traumas'.

6 The politics of recognition: from a Sikh 'national' to a Sikh 'diasporic' identity in a post-9/11 world?

1 This chapter builds upon, and revises some of the central assumptions of, two earlier articles published in the *International Journal of Punjab Studies* and *Studies in Ethnicity and Nationalism* (Shani 2000a, 2002). The author is grateful to Gurharpal Singh, Ian Talbot, John Sidel, Stephen Hopgood, Peter van der Veer, Partha Chatterjee, Sudipta Kaviraj and David Taylor for their comments.

2 See Shinder Singh Thandi (1996: 159–184) for an account of counterinsurgency operations in the Punjab.

3 See Gurharpal Singh (2000: 45–50) for a discussion of 'hegemonic' and 'violent' control.

4 Roger Ballard points out that an American passport has become a status symbol amongst *Jat* migrants from the Jullunder Doab region of East Punjab (Ballard 1994).

5 There are now an estimated 250 *gurdwaras* in the UK alone (Singh and Tatla 2006: 75).

6 For Avtar Brah, a 'diaspora space' is the point at which boundaries of inclusion and exclusion, of belonging and otherness, of 'us' and 'them', are contested (Brah 1996: 208–209).

7 Indeed, Sikhs have been able to attain the political power and social respectability to go with their new-found economic wealth, as the election of Ujjal Dosanjh (not a *Kes-dhari*, but ethnically a Punjabi, Sikh) as premier of British Columbia testifies. Ujjal Dosanjh was sworn in as British Columbia's thirty-third premier on 24 February 2000. He was Canada's first Indo-Canadian premier. He had previously served as attorney-general and minister responsible for multiculturalism, immigration and human rights; minister of government services; and minister responsible for multiculturalism, human rights, sports and immigration.

8 According to Buzan *et al.*, 'securitization' may be understood as an extreme form of politicization, whereby an issue comes to be either politicized or placed above politics. Securitization is simultaneously an intensification of politicization, in that it usually makes an even stronger role for the state, yet in another sense opposed to politicization in that more and more issues are removed from the political sphere by being designated 'security threats' (Buzan *et al.* 1998: 23–27). For a discussion of how 9/11 has legitimized greater securitization of society, see the contributions by Berman and Pasha to Shani *et al.* (2007).

9 The existence of 'institutional racism', as highlighted by the Macpherson Report of 1999 into the murder of black teenager Stephen Lawrence, was seen as necessitating a revision of the existing Race Relations Act and further qualified Britain's credentials as an egalitarian society.

10 In particular, the report's call for a rethinking of British identity in the light of the history of 'white colonialism' was rejected by the then British home secretary, Jack Straw, who stated that 'everyone should stand up for Britain and for British values and celebrate *the nation*'s diversity' (BBC 2000, emphasis added).

11 I use 'Sikh' in inverted commas to denote Mr Singh's ethnic descent not his religious convictions.

12 The 'Leicester Model', ironically lauded by the Cantle Report, refers to Leicester's relative success in managing ethnic diversity in a city with one of the highest, if not the highest, ethnic minority populations in the UK. However, the celebratory

narrative of multiculturalism has been abandoned in favour of a discourse of 'community cohesion' in the wake of the Cantle Report. Significantly, Labour lost control of Leicester City Council for the first time in twenty years as the Liberal Democrats, supported by Leicester's Muslim population as a result of the party's anti-Gulf war stance, joined with the Conservatives to form an alternative administration. Ethnic minority representation in the council correspondingly decreased from fourteen seats to ten (Gurharpal Singh 2003: 52).

13 For further details, see the official report by the Intelligence and Security Committee (2006).

14 See articles by William Pfaff (2005) and Martin Wolf (2005).

15 Singh and Tatla contend that this higher total includes groups and categories which either *cannot* be included for legal reasons or who have chosen to *exclude* themselves. Consequently, the Census returns are seen as providing a 'more accurate reflection of the community's strength today' (Singh and Tatla 2006: 62).

16 Indeed, the most pressing item on the Sikh Agenda, as adopted by delegates of 120 *gurdwaras* and forty Sikh organizations assembled in Guru Nanak Gurdwara in Wolverhampton in 2001, was to increase Sikh political representation with four more Sikh MPs, five new Sikh lords and an increase in the number of councillors from about 90 to 200 (Sikh Agenda 2003).

17 At the time of writing, these are Piara Singh Khabra (MP for Ealing since 1992), Marsha Singh (MP for Bradford West since 1997) and Parmjit Dhanda (MP for Gloucester since 2001). All three represent the Labour Party.

18 Indeed, the last two Lord Mayors of Leicester have been Sikh. Mr Kuldip Singh Bhatt was appointed Lord Mayor by the outgoing Labour council and was replaced by Piara Singh Clair.

19 See Bidwell (1987) and Cyber Sikh Museum (2003c) for an account of the passing of the Act.

20 I am grateful to Mr Helly Chahal for sharing this insight with me.

21 At 82 per cent, Sikhs have the highest rate of private home ownership in the UK (Singh and Tatla 2006: 67).

22 See Tatla and Singh (2006: 94–125) for a detailed analysis of the transition from a 'politics of class' to a 'politics of homeland'.

23 See for example *International Herald Tribune* (2007).

24 Agenda item number six commits the Sikh Federation to 'ensure the UK Government exert pressure on the Indian authorities to allow UN representatives and independent international human rights organisations free access to investigate and report on the widespread abuse of human rights of Sikhs and other minorities and to provide humanitarian aid to those who have suffered human rights abuses and state oppression in India' (Sikh Federation (UK) 2003h).

25 For an example of the British state's discursive use of multiculturalism, see Runnymede Trust (2000). There has been a retreat from multiculturalism in post-9/11 Britain, with the introduction of 'citizenship tests' designed to promote greater integration of ethnic and religious minorities into British society.

26 This is a phrase used by many Sikhs I have interviewed in the US, including Tejinder Singh, legal director of UNITED SIKHS, and also by R.S. Verma (2006).

27 E-mail correspondence with SALDEF, 26 February 2007.

28 See La Brack (1988) for a history of Sikh settlement in northern California.

29 Bhagat Singh Thind, a Punjabi immigrant from 1913 and a veteran of the First World War, was fighting to maintain the US citizenship he received following an honourable discharge in 1918 from the US army. The fact that Thind was awarded US citizenship in the first place was a result of American wartime imperatives, as previously a Sikh man had been denied US citizenship because he would not take off his *dastaar* (turban) while being sworn in (Mann 2000: 270).

30 Before 2000, only five ethnic categories were recognized by the US Census: African

Americans (all those with 'one drop of African blood'), Americans of Asian origin and from the Pacific Islands, Native Americans, Eskimos and residents of Alaska, and all others (Hollinger 1995).

31 Its two most important wings are the WSO-Canada, based in Ottawa, and WSO-USA, located a 'few blocks from the White House' in Washington, DC.

32 Dr Aulakh was repeatedly contacted by the author for an interview but did not reply.

33 In particular, Norman Shumway from Stockton and Wally Herger for Yuba City, California (Tatla 1999: 165).

34 Remarks included in the Congressional Record by Representative Towns are regularly posted on the Council of Khalistan website available at http://www.khalistan.com.

35 Dr Amarjit Singh was interviewed by the author on 27 February 2007. The author is grateful to Dr Swaranjeet Singh for setting up the interview.

36 Singh regards the SGPC as having been an 'extension of the government of India' since its inception in 1925, rather than as a representative body of the *Khalsa panth.*

37 The Nanavati Commission report mentioned there was 'credible evidence' that Mr Tytler 'very probably' had a hand in organizing the attacks (*Hindu*, 11 August 2005).

38 Balbir Singh Sodhi was shot dead outside his gas station in the suburb of Mesa, Arizona, USA, on 15 September 2001 by Frank S. Roque, who had mistaken him for a Muslim. See Sikh Coalition (2002) for a comprehensive list of hate crimes committed against Sikhs in the immediate aftermath of 9/11.

39 In his interview with the author, Dr Amarjit Singh recounted the example of a young Columbia University student who had become 'converted' to the *Khalistan* cause after 9/11.

40 E-mail correspondence with SALDEF, 26 February 2007. The author is grateful to associate director Rajbir Singh Datta for responding to his questions on behalf of the organization.

41 Harjinder Singh Duggal, Dhan Singh, Gurmej Singh, Mohinder Singh and Harpreet Singh Wahan were elected in September 2006 (Sikh Coalition 2006).

7 Beyond *Khalistan*? The Sikh diaspora, globalization and international relations

1 An earlier version of this chapter was published as 'Beyond Khalistan: Sikh Diasporic Identity and Critical International Theory', *Sikh Formations: Religion, Culture, Theory*, 2005, 1 (1): 57–74. It has, however, been extensively edited and revised for this volume. The comparison with Islam is further developed in Shani (2007).

2 The terms 'realism' and 'neo-realism' are used interchangeably to describe the dominant perspective in international political theory. Neo-realism, a term coined by Kenneth Waltz, may be seen as an attempt to ground realist assumptions on more 'scientific' (i.e. positivist) grounds.

3 After the Oslo Accords, Hamas replaced the PLO as the voice of the *Intifada*. See Kepel (2004: 150–158) for a discussion of the 'Islamization' of the Palestinian cause.

4 The Front Islamique du Salut (FIS) won the Algerian election in 1991 only for the army to step in (Kepel 2004: 159–176).

5 Abdurrahman Wahid, leader of the Nahdatul Ulama (Renaissance of Religious Scholars), the biggest Islamic organization in the world, became Indonesia's first directly elected president in October 1999.

6 Fukuyama had argued that secular liberal-democracy constituted the end point

of mankind's ideological evolution and the final form of human government. Consequently, the triumph of Western liberal-democracy over alternative political systems such as communism or fascism, and its gradual spread throughout the world, was seen to constitute 'the end of history' (Fukuyama 1992).

7 Indeed, many members of the WSC-AR are privately supporters of a separate Sikh homeland. The Council does not, however, take an official position on the desirability of *Khalistan* (interview with WSC-AR vice-chair Surinderpal Singh, Palatine, Illinois, 24 February 2007).

8 These questions were put to Dr Manohar Singh Grewal, chair of the WSC-AR, but unfortunately the regional committee had not approved an official response at the time of writing. The author wishes to acknowledge Dr Grewal's efforts and support for the project.

9 It must be pointed out that UNITED SIKHS does not have the same resources or enjoy the same advantages as the Red Cross.

10 *Laïcité* refers to the strict separation of religion and the state which can be traced back to the French Revolution and the founding of the First Republic. The state is required not only to remain strictly neutral in terms of religion but to actively promote secularism in the public sphere in order to guarantee freedom of thought.

11 On a visit to India, French foreign minister Dominique de Villepin stated that he was 'convinced that we are going to find a way which would be satisfactory for the Sikh community in France' (Embassy of France in India 2004).

12 Jasvir Singh, Bikramjit Singh and Ranjit Singh were expelled in 2004. They were joined in 2005 by Gurinder Singh, and by Jasmeet Singh in 2006. Maha Singh has, furthermore, not been admitted in any school since 2006 on account of his turban (Mejindarpal Kaur, personal correspondence, 25 March 2007).

13 Shingara Singh Mann was unable to renew his driver's licence and passport as he would not take off his turban for a photo ID, and Ranjit Singh, a 69-year-old political refugee, was refused a resident card in 2002 for a similar reason (Mejindarpal Kaur, personal correspondence, 25 March 2007).

14 Initially, the Conseil d'État had ruled in favour of Shingara Singh Mann, but a French government circular issued the day after the ruling made it compulsory for Sikhs to remove their turbans for their driver's licence photo, thus effectively overturning the decision. Subsequently, the Conseil d'État ruled against Shingara Singh Mann, and UNITED SIKHS in an emergency application is challenging the government circular (Mejindarpal Kaur, personal correspondence, 25 March 2007).

15 Mejindarpal Kaur regards the 'consultative coordination' of UNITED SIKHS to be its 'belief system' derived from Sikhism (Mejindarpal Kaur, interview, 25 March 2007).

16 Helly Chahal helped me to distribute the questionnaires outside the Southall Mela in August 2000.

17 In India, I was particularly indebted to the assistance of both Surinder Singh in Noida and Surinder Singh Sawhney in Chandigarh, who distributed the questionnaires for me in Chandigarh, Delhi and Uttar Pradesh.

18 The Sikh Coalition, which itself was established in the US following 9/11, has set up a 'Justice Watch Database' to monitor racially motivated crimes and incidents. See Sikh Coalition (2002).

19 The South Asian Association for Regional Cooperation (SAARC), consisting of the seven states of South Asia, officially came into existence in 1985 in an attempt to replicate the success of the European Economic Community (EEC), the forerunner of the European Union. Progress towards economic unity has, however, been slow, mainly as a result of the simmering tension between Indian and Pakistan over Kashmir, although the goal of a South Asian Free Trade Area (SAFTA) was endorsed by the tenth summit in Colombo in 1998.

20 See Nikky-Guninder Kaur Singh (2005) for a critique of 'malestream Sikh scholarship' and for an alternative account of the establishment of the *Khalsa* from a feminist perspective. Doris Jakobsh has similarly attempted to deconstruct hegemonic masculinist narratives on Sikh identity by 'relocating gender' in nineteenth-century Sikh history (Jakobsh 2003).

21 Interview with Jasdev Singh Rai, director of the Sikh Human Rights Group, Ealing, 17 September 2001.

Conclusion

1 Critical IR theory, which has both 'Gramscian' and 'Habermasian' schools, is best represented by the work of Robert Cox and Andrew Linklater. See Wyn Jones (2001) for a comprehensive survey of critical international theory. 'Critical' Sikh studies, on the other hand, refers to the work of scholars – mainly but not exclusively based in Western, academic institutions – who have been influenced not only by critical theory (Axel 2005; Gurnam Singh 2006) but also by constructivist (Oberoi 1994), post-colonial (Axel 2001; Mandair 2001), postmodern (Gurbhagat Singh 1999a, 1999b; Mandair 2001) and feminist (Jakobsh 2003; Nikky-Guninder Kaur Singh 2005) perspectives. This school is best represented by the editorial and various contributions to the inaugural volume of *Sikh Formations: Religion, Culture, Theory* (2005). See Shani (2005) for an early attempt to relate critical IR theory to Sikh studies. This forms the basis of a later article which seeks to 'provincialize' (Chakrabarty 2000) critical international theory from a post-colonial standpoint by bringing in a discussion of 'critical' Sikh and Islamic perspectives (Shani 2007).

2 The RSS regards Sikhism as a separate religion but with 'the Sikh people as belonging to our *samaj*' (RSS 2007). It is difficult to reconcile membership of the Hindu *samaj* with the *qaumic* dimensions of Sikhs identity and the duty of Sikhs to 'repudiate non-Sikh rites and ceremonies, and follow only Sikh practices' (SGPC 2001). For Sikhs, according to SGPC President Avtar Singh Makkar, 'believe only in Guru Granth Sahib and are ordered by the highest Sikh temporal seat' (*Hindustan Times* 2007).

Bibliography

Agamben, G. (2002) *Remnants of Auschwitz*, trans. D. Heller-Roazen, New York: Zone Books.

Agnew, J. (1998) *Geopolitics: Re-visioning World Politics*, London: Routledge.

Ahmed, I. (1988) *Sikh Separatism in India*, Stockholm: SAREC.

—— (1999) 'The 1947 Partition of Punjab: Arguments Put Forth before the Punjab Boundary Commission by the Parties Involved', in I. Talbot and G. Singh (eds), *Region and Partition: Bengal, Punjab and the Partition of the Subcontinent*, Karachi: Oxford University Press.

—— (2002) 'The 1947 Partition of India: A Paradigm for Pathological Politics in India and Pakistan', *Asian Ethnicity*, March, 3 (1): 9–28.

Ajrawat, P.S. (1997) 'Torture and Genocide of the Sikhs'. Online. Available http://www.khalistan.net/genocide.htm (accessed 2 February 2000).

Albrow, M. (1996) *The Global Age*, Cambridge: Polity Press.

Almond, G.A., Sivan E. and Appelby, R.S. (1995) 'Fundamentalism: Genus and Species', in Martin E. Marty and R. Scott Appelby (eds), *Fundamentalisms Comprehended*, Chicago, IL: University of Chicago Press.

Althusser, L. (1971) *Lenin and Philosophy*, trans. B. Brewster, London: New Left Books.

Amnesty International (2006) *Amnesty International Report 2006: India*. Online. Available http://web.amnesty.org/report2006/ind-summary-eng (accessed 2 October 2006).

Anderson, B. (1991 [1983]) *Imagined Communities: Reflections on the Origin and Spread of Nationalism*, rev. edn, London: Verso.

—— (1992) *Long-Distance Nationalism: World Capitalism and the Rise of Identity Politics*, Amsterdam: Centre for Asian Studies.

—— (1994) 'Exodus', *Critical Enquiry*, 20 (2): 328–342.

Appadurai, A. (1990) 'Disjuncture and Difference in the Global Cultural Economy', in M. Featherstone (ed.), *Global Culture: Nationalism, Globalization and Modernity*, London: Sage.

—— (1996) *Modernity at Large: The Cultural Dimensions of Globalization*, Minneapolis: University of Minnesota Press.

Aulakh, G.S. (2000) 'Millennium Message to the Sikh Nation'. Online. Available http://www.khalistan.com/message2000.1 (accessed 20 February 2000).

—— (2006) 'Open Letter' to Prime Minister Manmohan Singh, 10 October.

Axel, B.K. (2001) *The Nation's Tortured Body: Violence, Representation, and the*

Formation of a Sikh 'Diaspora', Durham, NC and London: Duke University Press.

—— (2002) 'The Diasporic Imaginary', *Public Culture*, 14 (2): 411–428.

—— (2005) 'Diasporic Sublime: Sikh Martyrs, Internet Mediations, and the Question of the Unimaginable', *Sikh Formations: Religion, Culture, Theory*, 1 (1): 127–154.

Balibar, E. (1991) 'Is There a Neo-Racism?', in E. Balibar and I. Wallerstein (eds), *Race, Nation, Class: Ambiguous Identities*, London: Verso.

Ballantyne, T. (1999) 'Resisting the "Boa Constrictor" of Hinduism: The Khalsa and the Raj', *International Journal of Punjab Studies*, 6 (2): 195–217.

Ballard, R. (1994) 'The Emergence of *Desh Pardesh*', in R. Ballard (ed.), *Desh Pardesh: The South Asian Presence in Britain*, London: Hurst & Co.

—— (1996) '*Panth, Kismet, Dharm, te Qaum*: Four Dimensions in Punjabi Religion', in P. Singh and S.S. Thandi (eds), *Globalisation and the Region*, Coventry: Association of Punjab Studies.

—— (1998) 'The Politicisation of Religion and the Rise of Essentialism: Sikhs, the Sikh Panth and the Construction of "Sikhism" ', unpublished paper delivered at the New Perspectives in Sikh Studies workshop, 28–29 May, School of Oriental and African Studies, University of London.

Bardhan, Pranab (1984) *The Political Economy of Development in India*, Oxford: Basil Blackwell.

Barrier, N.G. (1988) 'Sikh Politics in British Punjab prior to the Gurdwara Reform Movement', in J. O'Connell, M. Israel and W.G. Oxtoby, *Sikh History and Religion in the Twentieth Century*, Toronto: Centre for South Asian Studies, University of Toronto.

—— (2003) 'Contemporary Sikhism and the Singh Sabha Experience', paper prepared for the conference on Sikhism and Inter-religious Dialogue, Department of Theology, University of Birmingham, 25–26 October.

—— (2004a) 'Sikhism in the Light of History', in P. Singh and N. Gerald Barrier (eds), *Sikhism and History*, New Delhi: Oxford University Press.

—— (2004b) 'Authority, Politics and Contemporary Sikhism: The Akal Takht, the SGPC, and the Law', in P. Singh and N. Gerald Barrier (eds), *Sikhism and History*, New Delhi: Oxford University Press.

—— (2006) 'Trauma and Memory within the Sikh Diaspora: Internet Dialogue', *Sikh Formations: Religion, Culture, Theory*, June, 2 (1): 33–56.

Barry, B. (2001) *Culture and Equality: An Egalitarian Critique of Multiculturalism*, Cambridge: Polity Press.

Baumann, Z. (1989) *Modernity and the Holocaust*, Cambridge: Polity Press.

Baylis, J. and Smith, S. (2001) 'Introduction', in J. Baylis and S. Smith (eds), *The Globalization of World Politics*, 2nd edn, Oxford: Oxford University Press.

Benhabib, S. (2002) *The Claims of Culture: Equality and Diversity in the Global Era*, Princeton, NJ: Princeton University Press.

Bhachu, P. (1985) *Twice Migrants*, London: Tavistock.

Bhagwati, J. (1993) *India in Transition: Freeing the Economy*, Oxford: Clarendon Press.

Bharatiya Janata Party (BJP) (1996) *For a Strong and Prosperous India: Election Manifesto 1996*, New Delhi: BJP.

—— (2004) 'Our Vision, Our Will, Our Way – Election Manifesto Chapter 2: Our National Identity'. Online. Available http://www.bjp.org/manifes/chap2.htm (accessed 20 May 2004).

Bhargava, R. (1998a) 'Introduction', in R. Bhargava (ed.), *Secularism and Its Critics*, New Delhi: Oxford University Press.
—— (1998b) 'What Is Secularism For?', in R. Bhargava (ed.), *Secularism and Its Critics*, New Delhi: Oxford University Press.
—— (2003) 'The Cultural Nationalism of the New Hindu', *Dissent*, Fall. Online. Available http://www.dissentmagazine.org (accessed 1 October 2004).
Bhatt, C. (2001) *Hindu Nationalism: Origins, Ideologies and Modern Myths*, Oxford: Berg.
Bidwell, S. (1987) *The Turban Victory*, Gravesend, Kent: Sikh Missionary Society.
Biel, R. (2000) *The New Imperialism: Crisis and Contradiction in North–South Relations*, London: Zed Books.
Bourdieu, P. (1977) *Outline of a Theory of Practice*, trans. R. Nice, Cambridge: Cambridge University Press.
—— (1990) *The Logic of Practice*, Cambridge: Polity Press.
Brah, A. (1996) *Cartographies of Diaspora*, London: Routledge.
Brass, P.R. (1974) *Language, Religion and Politics in North India*, Cambridge: Cambridge University Press.
—— (1991) *Ethnicity and Nationalism: Theory and Comparison*, New Delhi: Sage.
—— (1994 [1990]) *The New Cambridge History of India: The Politics of India since Independence*, Cambridge: Cambridge University Press.
—— (2003) 'The Partition of India and Retributive Genocide in the Punjab, 1946–47: Means, Methods, and Purposes', *Journal of Genocide Research*, 5 (1): 71–101.
—— (2006) 'Victims, Heroes or Martyrs? Partition and the Problem of Memorialization in Contemporary Sikh History', *Sikh Formations: Religion, Culture, Theory*, June, 2 (1): 17–31.
British Broadcasting Corporation (BBC) (2000) BBC News UK, 'No to Rethink on British Identity'. Online. Available http://news.bbc.co.uk/1/hi/uk/966629.stm (accessed 11 October 2001).
British Sikh Federation (2003) 'Ethnic Group Monitoring Category for Sikhs'. Online. Available http://www.british-sikh-federation.org/EthnicGroup.html (accessed 2 July 2006).
Bull, H. (1977) *The Anarchical Society*, London: Macmillan.
—— (1984) 'The Revolt against the West', in H. Bull and A. Watson (eds), *The Expansion of International Society*, Oxford: Clarendon Press.
Butalia, U. (2000) *The Other Side of Silence: Voices from the Partition of India*, London: Hurst & Co.
Buzan, B., Wæver, O. and de Wilde, J. (1998) *Security: A New Framework for Analysis*, Boulder, CO: Lynne Rienner.
Carr, E.H. (1962 [1939]) *The Twenty Years' Crisis*, 2nd edn, Basingstoke: Macmillan.
Casanova, J. (1997) 'Globalizing Catholicism and the Return to a "Universal" Church', in S.H. Rudolph and J. Piscatori (eds), *Transnational Religion and Fading States*, Boulder, CO: Westview; reprinted in R. Robertson and K.E. White (eds) (2003) *Globalization: Critical Concepts in Sociology*, vol. V, London: Routledge.
Castells, M. (1996) *The Information Age*, vol. 1: *The Network Society*, Oxford: Blackwell.
—— (1997) *The Information Age*, vol. 2: *The Power of Identity*, Oxford: Blackwell.
Census India (2001) 'Indian Population by Religion'. Online. Available http://www.censusindia.net/religiondata/Summary%20Sikhs.pdf (accessed 11 October 2005).

Centre for the Study of Developing Societies (CSDS) (2004) 'How India Voted: Verdict 2004', *Hindu*, 20 May.

Chakrabarty, D. (2000) *Provincializing Europe: Postcolonial Thought and Historical Difference*, Princeton, NJ: Princeton University Press.

Chatterjee, P. (1996 [1993]) 'Whose Imagined Community?', in G. Balakrishnan (ed.), *Mapping the Nation*, London: Verso.

Clifford, J. (1994) 'Diasporas', *Cultural Anthropology*, 9 (3): 301–338; reprinted in R. Robertson and K.E. White (eds) (2003) *Globalization: Critical Concepts in Sociology*, vol. IV, London: Routledge.

—— (1997) *Routes: Travel and Translation in the Late Twentieth Century*, Cambridge, MA: Harvard University Press.

Cohen, R. (1997) *Global Diasporas: An Introduction*, London: UCL Press.

Cohn, B.S. (1996) *Colonialism and Its Forms of Knowledge*, Princeton, NJ: Princeton University Press.

Communalism Combat (2002) 'Genocide: Gujarat 2001', March–April. Online. Available http://www.sabrang.com/cc/archive/2002/marapril/index.html (accessed 1 October 2004).

Connor, W. (1994) *Ethnonationalism: The Quest for Understanding*, Princeton, NJ: Princeton University Press.

Corbridge, S. and Harriss, J. (2000) *Reinventing India: Liberalization, Hindu Nationalism and Popular Democracy*, Cambridge: Polity Press.

Council of Europe (1950) *The European Convention on Human Rights*, 4 November, Rome. Online. Available http://conventions.coe.int/Treaty/en/Treaties/Html/005.htm (accessed 26 March 2007).

Council of Khalistan (2000) 'Khalistan: The New Global Reality'. Online. Available http://www.khalistan.net/ (accessed 10 March 2002).

—— (2006) 'Open Letter to Indian Prime Minister Manmohan Singh', 10 October. Online. Available http://www.khalistan.com/OpenLetters/ol101006_OpenLetterToManmohanSingh_IndiaIsATerroristState.htm (accessed 4 April 2007).

—— (2007) 'Home'. Online. Available http://www.khalistan.com/ (accessed 4 April 2007).

Council of Sikh Affairs (1983) *Compendium of Statements and Resolutions*, Chandigarh: Council of Sikh Affairs.

Cox, R.W. (1981) 'Social Forces, States and World Orders: Beyond International Relations Theory', *Millennium: Journal of International Studies*, 10 (2): 126–155.

Cunningham, J.D. (1997 [1849]) *History of the Sikhs*, New Delhi: Low Price Publications.

Cyber Sikh Museum (2003a) 'Sikhs in British Army'. Online. Available http://www.sikhcybermuseum.org/historyarmy.htm (accessed 12 March 2004).

—— (2003b) 'First British Sikh Army'. Online. Available http://www.sikhcybermuseum.org/history/firstsikhbatalion1846.htm (accessed 12 March 2004).

—— (2003c) 'The Turban Case 1976'. Online. Available http://www.sikhcybermuseum.org/history/turbancase.htm (accessed 2 February 2004).

Das, V. (1995) *Critical Events: An Anthropological Perspective on Contemporary India*, Delhi: Oxford University Press.

Dass, N. (trans. and ed.) (2000) *Songs of the Saints from the Adi Granth*, New York: State University of New York.

Deleuze, G. and Guattari, F. (1987) *A Thousand Plateaus: Capitalism and Schizophrenia*, Minneapolis: University of Minnesota Press.

Deol, H. (2000) *Religion and Nationalism in India: The Case of the Punjab*, London: Routledge.

Dhillon, G.S. (1996) *Perspectives on Sikh Religion and History*, New Delhi: National Book Organization.

Dogra, C.S. (2004) '1984 to 2004', *Outlook India*, 14 June. Online. Available http://www.outlookindia.com/full.asp?fodname=20040614&fname=Punjab&sid=1 (accessed 14 June 2004).

Dusenbery, V.A. (1995) 'A Sikh Diaspora? Contested Identities and Constructed Realities', in P. van der Veer (ed.), *Nation and Migration*, Philadelphia: University of Pennsylvania Press.

—— (1999) ' "Nation" or "World Religion"? Master Narratives of Sikh Identity', in P. Singh and N. Gerald Barrier (eds), *Sikh Identity: Continuity and Change*, New Delhi: Manohar.

Economist Intelligence Unit (EIU) (2002) *Country Report: India*, London: EIU Publications.

—— (2003) *Country Report: India*, London: EIU Publications.

—— (2005) *Country Report: India*, London: EIU Publications.

—— (2006) *Country Report: India*, London: EIU Publications.

Edkins, J. (2003) *Trauma and the Memory of Politics*, Cambridge: Cambridge University Press.

Election Commission of India (1963) *Report on the Third General Elections in India, 1962*, Part II: *Statistical*. New Delhi: Election Commission of India.

—— (1997) *Key Highlights of General Election, 1997 to the Legislative Assembly of the Punjab*, New Delhi: Election Commission of India.

—— (2002) *State Elections 2002: State Summary for Punjab*, New Delhi: Election Commission of India. Online. Available http://archive.eci.gov.in/se2002/pollupd/ac/states/s19/AS19.htm (accessed 24 August 2005).

—— (2004) *Report on General Elections, 2004 to the 14th Lok Sabha*, New Delhi: Election Commission of India. Online. Available http://www.eci.gov.in/Statistical-Reports/LS_2004/Vol_I_LS_2004.pdf (accessed 11 November 2004).

Embassy of France in India (2004) 'Transcript of Joint Press Conference Given by Mr de Villepin and his Counterpart Mr Sinha', 13 February. Online. Available http://www.unitedsikhs.org/rtt/pdf/FrenchPrimeMinisterDominiquedeVillepin StatesSatisfactorySolutionforSikhs.pdf (accessed 20 March 2007).

Embree, A.T. (1990) *Utopias in Conflict: Religion and Nationalism in Modern India*, Berkeley: University of California Press.

Falcon, R.W. (1896) *Handbook on Sikhs for the Use of Regimental Officers*, Allahabad.

Ferguson, N. (2005) 'Sinking Globalization', *Foreign Affairs*, March/April, 84 (2): 64–78.

Fernandes, L. (2006) *India's New Middle Class: Democratic Politics in an Era of Economic Reform*, Minneapolis: University of Minnesota Press.

Foucault, M. (1991) 'Nietzsche, Genealogy, History', in M. Foucault (ed. P. Rabinow), *The Foucault Reader: An Introduction to Foucault's Thought*, London: Penguin.

Fox, R.G. (1985) *Lions of the Punjab: Culture in the Making*, Berkeley: University of California Press.

—— (1996) 'Communalism and Modernity', in D. Ludden (ed.), *Contesting the*

Nation: Religion, Community and the Politics of Democracy in India, Philadelphia: University of Pennsylvania Press.

Frank, A.G. (1969) *The Development of Underdevelopment*, Chicago, IL: University of Chicago Press.

Fraser, N. (1997) *Justice Interruptus: Critical Reflections on the 'Postsocialist' Condition*, New York: Routledge.

Fukuyama, F. (1992) *The End of History and the Last Man*, London: Penguin.

Galtung, J. (1971) 'A Structural Theory of Imperialism', *Journal of Peace Research*, 8 (2): 81–117.

Geertz, C. (1973) *The Interpretation of Cultures*, New York: Basic Books.

Gellner, E. (1983) *Nations and Nationalism*, Oxford: Blackwell.

Giddens, A. (2000) 'The Globalizing of Modernity', in D. Held and A. McGrew (eds), *The Global Transformations Reader*, Cambridge: Polity Press.

Gill, S.S. and Singhal, K.C. (1984) 'The Punjab Problem: Its Historical Roots', *Economic and Political Weekly*, 7 April: 603–609.

Gilroy, P. (1993) *The Black Atlantic: Modernity and Double Consciousness*, Cambridge, MA: Harvard University Press.

—— (1997) 'Diaspora and the Detours of Identity', in K. Woodward (ed.), *Identity and Difference*, London: Open University Press.

Glazer, N. and Moynihan, D.P. (1975) 'Introduction', in N. Glazer and D.P. Moynihan (eds), *Ethnicity: Theory and Experience*, Cambridge, MA: Harvard University Press.

Gonzales, J.L. (1986) 'Asian Indian Immigration Patterns: The Origins of the Sikh Community in California', *International Migration Review*, Spring, 20: 40–54.

Goulbourne, H. (1991) *Ethnicity and Nationalism in Post-Imperial Britain*, Cambridge: Cambridge University Press.

Government of India (GOI) (1881) *Census of India, 1881, Punjab*, vol. 1 and Abstract 63.

—— (1891) *Census of India, 1891, Punjab*, vol. 1, Calcutta.

—— (1901) *Census of India, 1901, Punjab*, vol. 1, Calcutta.

—— (1911) *Census of India, 1911, Punjab*, vols 1, 2, Delhi.

—— (1921) *Census of India, 1921, Punjab*, vol. 1, Delhi.

—— (1931) *Census of India, 1931, Punjab*, vol. 1, Delhi.

—— (1949a) *Preamble to the Indian Constitution*, New Delhi: Ministry of Law and Justice (Legislative Department). Online. Available http://indiacode.nic.in/coiweb/coifiles/preamble.htm (accessed 1 April 2004).

—— (1949b) *Right to Freedom of Religion*, New Delhi: Ministry of Law and Justice (Legislative Department).

—— (1984) *White Paper on the Punjab Agitation*, New Delhi: Government of India Press.

—— (2001) *Census India 2001*, New Delhi: Ministry of Home Affairs. Online. Available http://www.censusindia.net (accessed 11 October 2005).

Graham, B.D. (1990) *The Hindu Nationalist Movement and Indian Politics: The Origin and Development of the Bharatiya Jana Sangh*, Cambridge: Cambridge University Press.

Gramsci, A. (1991) *Selections from the Prison Notebooks*, trans. and ed. Q. Hoare, London: Lawrence & Wishart.

Grewal, J.S. (1994) *The New Cambridge History of India: The Sikhs of the Punjab*, Cambridge: Cambridge University Press.

—— (1999a) 'The Sikh Panth in the *Vars* of Bhai Gurdas', in J.S. Grewal and Indu Banga (eds), *The Khalsa over 300 Years*, New Delhi: Manohar, pp. 26–34.

—— (1999b) 'Nabha's *Ham Hindu Nahin*: A Declaration of Sikh Ethnicity', in P. Singh and N. Gerald Barrier (eds), *Sikh Identity: Continuity and Change*, New Delhi: Manohar.

Guha, R. (1988 [1983]) 'On Some Aspects of the Historiography of Colonial India' and 'The Prose of Counter-Insurgency', in R. Guha and G. Chakravorty Spivak (eds), *Selected Subaltern Studies*, New York: Oxford University Press.

Guibernau, M. (1999) *Nations without States*, Cambridge: Polity Press.

—— (2001) 'Globalization and the Nation-State', in M. Guibernau and J. Hutchinson (eds), *Understanding Nationalism*, Cambridge: Polity Press.

Gupta, D. (1985) 'Communalising of Punjab – 1980–5', *Economic and Political Weekly*, 13 July: 1184–1185.

—— (1997) *The Context of Ethnicity: Sikh Identity in a Comparative Perspective*, New Delhi: Oxford University Press.

Hall, K.D. (2002) *Lives in Translation: Sikh Youth as British Citizens*, Philadelphia: University of Pennsylvania Press.

Hall, S. (1990) 'Cultural Identity and Diaspora', in J. Rutherford (ed.), *Identity: Community, Culture and Difference*, London: Lawrence.

—— (1992) 'The Question of Cultural Identity', in S. Hall, D. Held and A.G. McGrew (eds), *Modernity and Its Futures*, Cambridge: Polity Press, pp. 274–316.

—— (1997) 'Old and New Identities', in A. King (ed.), *Culture, Globalization and the World-System*, London: Sage.

Hansen, A.B. (2002) *Partition and Genocide: Manifestation of Violence in the Punjab 1937–1947*, New Delhi: India Research Press.

Hansen, T.B. (1998) 'The Ethics of Hindutva and the Spirit of Capitalism', in T.B. Hansen and C. Jaffrelot (eds), *The BJP and the Compulsions of Politics in India*, New Delhi: Oxford University Press.

Hardt, M. and Negri, A. (2000) *Empire*, Cambridge, MA: Harvard University Press.

Harff, B. and Gurr, T.R. (1988) 'Towards Empirical Theory of Genocides and Politicides: Identification and Measurement of Cases since 1945', *International Studies Quarterly*, 32: 359–371.

Harvey, D. (2003) *The New Imperialism*, Oxford: Oxford University Press.

Haynes, J. (2001) 'Transnational Religious Actors and International Politics', *Third World Quarterly*, 22 (1): 143–158.

Hechter, M. (1975) *Internal Colonialism: The Celtic Fringe in British National Development, 1536–1966*, London: Routledge & Kegan Paul.

Held, D. and McGrew, A. (2000) 'The Great Globalization Debate', in D. Held and A. McGrew (eds), *The Global Transformations Reader*, Cambridge: Polity Press.

—— (2006) 'Introduction: Globalization at Risk?', in D. Held and A. McGrew (eds), *Globalization Theory*, Cambridge: Polity Press.

Held, D., McGrew, A., Goldblatt, D. and Peratton, J. (1999) 'Introduction', in *Global Transformations*, Cambridge: Polity Press.

Hindu (2007) 'Akali Dal Manifesto Promises to Tame Price Spiral, Generate Jobs', 4 February. Online. Available http://www.thehindu.com/2007/02/04/stories/2007020409500500.htm (accessed 21 February 2007).

Hindustan Times (2007) 'SGPC Reacts on RSS Statement on Sikh Religion', 3 May.

Online. Available http://www.hindustantimes.com/StoryPage/StoryPage.aspx-?id=00f29785-5f61-4556-adf4-184fc761ae60&&Headline=SGPC+reacts+on+RSS+statement+on+sikh+religion (accessed 3 May 2007).

Hinsley, F.R. (1986) *Sovereignty*, Cambridge: Cambridge University Press.

Hirst, P. and Thompson, S. (1996) *Globalization in Question*, Cambridge: Polity Press.

Hobsbawm, E.J. and Ranger, T. (1983) *The Invention of Tradition*, Cambridge: Cambridge University Press.

Hollinger, D. (1995) *Postethnic America: Beyond Multiculturalism*, New York: Basic Books.

Human Rights Advisory Group (HRAG) of the Panjabis in Britain All Party Parliamentary Group (2005) *Self-Determination as a Human Right and Its Applicability to the Sikhs*, Westminster: HRAG. Online. Available http://www.sikhfederation.com/pdf/self_determination_paper_2005.pdf (accessed 1 July 2007).

Human Rights Watch/Asian Physicians for Human Rights (1994) *Dead Silence: The Legacy of Human Rights Abuses in the Punjab*, New York: Human Rights Watch.

Huntington, S.P. (1996) *The Clash of Civilizations and the Remaking of the World Order*, New York: Simon & Schuster.

—— (2004) *Who Are We? The Challenges to America's National Identity*, New York: Simon & Schuster.

Ibbetson, D.C.J. (1883) *Report on the Census of the Punjab, 1881*, vol. I, Calcutta.

Inden, R.B. (1990) *Imagining India*, London: Hurst & Co.

Institute of Race Relations (2000) 'Population Statistics in the UK'. Online. Available http://www.irr.org.uk/statistics/population.html (accessed 20 March 2001).

Intelligence and Security Committee (2006) *Report into the London Terrorist Attacks on July 7 2005*. Online. Available http://www.cabinetoffice.gov.uk/publications/reports/intelligence/isc_7july_report.pdf.

International Herald Tribune (2007) 'Sikh Militant Leader Chauhan Dies of Heart Attack at 80', 4 April. Online. Available http://www.iht.com/articles/ap/2007/04/04/asia/AS-GEN-India-Obit-Jagjit-Singh-Chauhan.php (accessed 4 April 2007).

Jackson, R. (2000) *The Global Covenant: Human Conduct in a World of States*, Oxford: Oxford University Press.

Jacobson, D. (2001) 'The Global Political Culture', in M. Albert, D. Jacobson and Y. Lapid (eds), *Identities, Border, Orders: Rethinking International Relations Theory*, Minneapolis: University of Minnesota Press.

Jaffrelot, C. (1996) *The Hindu Nationalist Movement and Indian Politics, from 1925 to the 1990s*, London: Hurst & Co.

Jakobsh, D.R. (2003) *Relocating Gender in Sikh History: Transformation, Meaning and Identity*, New Delhi: Oxford University Press.

Jeffrey, R. (1985) *The Perils of Prosperity*, London: Macmillan.

—— (1986) *What's Happening to India? Punjab, Ethnic Conflict, Mrs Gandhi's Death and the Test for Federalism*, London: Macmillan.

Jodhka, S.S. (2002) 'Caste and Untouchability in Rural Punjab', *Economic and Political Weekly*, 11 May, 37 (19): 1813–1823.

—— (2005) 'Return of the Region: Identities and Electoral Politics in Punjab', *Economic and Political Weekly*, 15 January. Online. Available http://www.epw.org.in/showArticles.php?root=2005&leaf=01&filename=8163&filetype=html (accessed 22 January 2007).

—— (2006) 'The Problem', *Seminar*, 567 (Re-imagining Punjab), November. Online. Available http://www.india-seminar.com/2006/567/567_the_problem.htm (accessed 23 January 2007).

Juergensmeyer, M. (1977) 'The Ghadar Syndrome: Nationalism in an Immigrant Community', *Punjab Journal of Politics*, 1 (1): 2–17.

—— (1992) 'The Logic of Religious Violence', in T.N. Madan (ed.), *Religion in India*, Delhi: Oxford University Press, pp. 382–394.

—— (1993) *The New Cold War? Religious Nationalism Confronts the Secular State*, Berkeley: University of California Press.

Kaldor, M. (2003) *Global Civil Society: An Answer to War*, Cambridge: Polity Press.

Kapur, R.A. (1986) *Sikh Separatism: The Politics of Faith*, Oxford: Oxford University Press.

Kaviraj, S. (1986) 'Indira Gandhi and Indian Politics', *Economic and Political Weekly*, 21 (38/39): 1697–1708.

—— (1992) 'The Imaginary Institution of India', in P. Chatterjee and G. Pandey (eds), *Subaltern Studies*, VII, New Delhi: Oxford University Press.

Kepel, G. (2004) *Jihad: The Trail of Political Islam*, London: I.B. Tauris.

Kerr, I.J. (1999) 'Sikhs and State: Troublesome Relationship and a Fundamental Continuity with Particular Reference to the Period 1849–1919', in P. Singh and G.N. Barrier (eds), *Sikh Identity: Continuity and Change*, New Delhi: Manohar.

Khalistan Affairs Center (KAC) (2007) 'Home'. Online. Available http://www.khalistan-affairs.org/ (accessed 4 April 2007).

Khilnani, S. (1997) *The Idea of India*, Harmondsworth: Penguin.

Kinvall, K. (2002) 'Nationalism, Religion and the Search for Chosen Traumas: Comparing Sikh and Hindu Identity Constructions', *Ethnicities*, 2 (1): 79–107.

Kothari, R. (1964) 'The Congress "System in India" ', *Asian Survey*, December, 4 (12): 1161–1173.

—— (1998) 'The Democratic Experiment', in P. Chatterjee (ed.), *The Wages of Freedom: Fifty Years of the Nation-State*, New Delhi: Oxford University Press.

Krasner, S. (1999) *Sovereignty: Organized Hypocrisy*, Princeton, NJ: Princeton University Press.

Kumar, P. (1995) *Violence in the Punjab: Retrospect and Prognosis*, Chandigarh: Institute for Development and Communications.

Kymlicka, W. (1995) *Multicultural Citizenship*, Cambridge: Polity Press.

La Brack, B. (1988) *The Sikhs of Northern California, 1904–1975*, New York: AMS.

Lacan, J. (1977) *Écrits: A Selection*, trans. A. Sheridan, London: Tavistock/Routledge.

Lapid, Y. and Kratochwil, F. (eds) (1996) *The Return of Culture and Identity in International Relations Theory*, Boulder, CO: Lynne Rienner.

Leonard, K. (1990) 'Pioneer Voices from California: Reflections on Race, Religion and Ethnicity', in N. Gerald Barrier and V.A. Dusenbery (eds), *The Sikh Diaspora: Migration and Experience beyond the Punjab*, Delhi: Chanakya Publications.

—— (1992) *Making Ethnic Choices: California's Punjabi-Mexican Americans*, Philadelphia, PA: Temple University Press.

Linklater, A. (1998) *The Transformation of Political Community: The Ethical Foundations of the Post-Westphalian Age*, Cambridge: Polity Press.

Maboli Systems (1995) 'Picture Gallery'. Online. Available http://www.maboli.com/Sikh_HR/Picture_Gallery/index.html (accessed 2 February 2004).

Macauliffe, M.A. (1990 [1909]) *The Sikh Religion*, vols I–VI, New Delhi: Low Price Books.

McGrew, A. (2006) 'Organized Violence in the Making (and Re-making) of Globalization', in D. Held and A. McGrew (eds), *Globalization Theory*, Cambridge: Polity Press.

McLeod, W.H. (1968) *Guru Nanak and the Sikh Religion*, Oxford: Clarendon Press.

—— (1989) *Who Is a Sikh? The Problem of Sikh Identity*, Oxford: Oxford University Press.

—— (1992) 'The Sikh Struggle in the Eighteenth Century and its Relevance for Today', *History of Religions*, 31 (4): 344–362.

—— (1994) 'Cries of Outrage: History versus Tradition in the Study of the Sikh Community', *South Asia Research*, 14 (2): 121–135.

—— (2000) *Exploring Sikhism: Aspects of Sikh Identity, Culture and Thought*, Oxford: Oxford University Press.

Mahajan, G. (2002) 'Secularism as Religious Non-Discrimination: The Universal and the Particular in the Indian Context', *India Review*, 1 (1): 33–51.

Mahbub Ul Haq Human Development Centre (2002) *Human Development in South Asia 2001*, Oxford: Oxford University Press.

Mahmood, C.K. (1996) *Fighting for Faith and Nation: Dialogues with Sikh Militants*, Philadelphia: University of Pennsylvania Press.

—— (1997) 'Playing the Game of Love: Passion and Martyrdom among Khalistani Sikhs', in J. Pettigrew (ed.), *Martyrdom and Political Resistance: Essays from Asia and Europe*, Amsterdam: Centre for Asian Studies Amsterdam.

Mandair, A.S. (2001) 'Thinking Differently about Religion and History: Issues for Sikh Studies', in C. Shackle, G. Singh and A. Mandair (eds), *Sikh Religion, Culture and Ethnicity*, London: Curzon Press.

Mandaville, P. (2001) *Transnational Muslim Politics*, London: Routledge.

Mann, G.S. (1998) 'The Institution of the Khalsa', paper delivered at the New Perspectives in Sikh Studies workshop, 28–29 May, School of Oriental and African Studies, University of London.

—— (2000) 'Sikhism in the United States of America', in H. Coward, J.R. Hinnells and R.B. Williams (ed.), *The South Asian Religious Diaspora in Britain, Canada, and the United States*, Albany: State University of New York Press.

—— (2001) 'Canon Formation in the Sikh Tradition', in C. Shackle, G. Singh and A. Mandair (eds), *Sikh Religion, Culture and Ethnicity*, London: Curzon Press.

—— (2004) *Sikhism* (Religions of the World Series), London: Laurence King Publishing.

Marx, K. (1977) *Selected Writings*, ed. D. McLellan, Oxford: Oxford University Press.

Mayall, J. (1990) *Nationalism and International Society*, Cambridge: Cambridge University Press.

Meadwell, H. (1999) 'Stateless Nations and the Emerging International Order', in T.V. Paul and J.A. Hall (eds), *International Order and the Future of World Politics*, Cambridge: Cambridge University Press.

Mendus, S. (2002) 'Choice, Chance and Multiculturalism', in P. Kelly (ed.), *Multiculturalism Reconsidered*, Cambridge: Polity Press, pp. 31–45.

Modood, Tariq (2005) *Multicultural Politics: Racism, Ethnicity and Muslims in Britain*, Minneapolis: University of Minnesota Press.

Morgenthau, H. (1967) *Politics among Nations: The Struggle for Power and Peace*, New York: Alfred A. Knopf.

Nanavati Commission (2005) *Nanavati Commission Report*, Part IV: 'Assessment of Evidence and Recommendations for Action', New Delhi. Online. Available http://www.carnage84.com/homepage/nancom.htm#_H._HIGHER (accessed 1 March 2005).

Nandy, A. (1998a) 'The Politics of Secularism and the Recovery of Religious Tolerance', in R. Bhargava (ed.), *Secularism and Its Critics*, New Delhi: Oxford University Press.

—— (1998b [1995]) 'Creating a Nationality: The Ramjanmabhumi Movement and Fear of the Self', in A. Nandy, *Exiled at Home*, New Delhi: Oxford University Press.

Narang, A.S. (1983) *Storm over the Sutlej*, New Delhi: Manohar.

—— (1986) *Democracy, Development and Distortion*, New Delhi: Manohar.

—— (1997) 'The Movement for a Punjabi-Speaking State', in I. Banga (ed.), *Five Punjabi Centuries*, New Delhi: Manohar.

National Statistics Online (2001) 'Religious Populations'. Online. Available http://www.statistics.gov.uk/cci/nugget.asp?id=954 (accessed 21 July 2004).

Nayar, B.R. (1966) *Minority Politics in the Punjab*, Princeton, NJ: Princeton University Press.

Negroponte, N. (1995) 'Being Digital in a Wired World', in A. Leer (ed.), *Masters of the Wired World: Cyberspace Speaks Out*, London: Financial Times.

Nehru, J. (2003 [1945]) *Discovery of India* (Oxford India Paperbacks), New Delhi: Oxford University Press.

—— (1947) 'Speech to the Constituent Assembly', 14 August. Online. Available http://www.hindustantimes.com/news/specials/parliament/Tryst%20with%20Destiny.pdf (accessed 14 August 2006).

New York Times (1971) 'The Sikhs Demand an Independent State in India: The Only Guarantee for Peace on the Subcontinent', 12 October.

Nora, P. (1996) 'General Introduction: Between Memory and History', in P. Nora and L.D. Kirtzman (eds), *Realms of Memory: Rethinking the French Past*, New York: Columbia University Press.

Nussbaum, M. (2003) 'Genocide in Gujarat: The International Community Looks Away', *Dissent*, Summer. Online. Available http://www.dissentmagazine.org/menutest/articles/su03/nussbaum.htm (accessed 2 October 2004).

Oberoi, H.S. (1987) 'From Punjab to "Khalistan": Territoriality and Metacommentary', *Pacific Affairs*, 60 (1): 26–42.

—— (1992) 'Brotherhood of the Pure: The Poetics and Politics of Cultural Transgression', *Modern Asian Studies*, 26 (1): 157–197.

—— (1994) *The Construction of Religious Boundaries: Culture, Identity and Diversity in the Sikh Tradition*, New Delhi: Oxford University Press.

—— (2001) 'What Has a Whale Got to Do With It? A Tale of Pogroms and Biblical Allegories', in C. Shackle, G. Singh and A.S. Mandair (eds), *Sikh Religion, Culture and Ethnicity*, London: Curzon Press.

Ohmae, K. (1990) *The Borderless World*, New York: Harper Collins.

—— (1993) 'The Rise of the Region State', *Foreign Affairs*, 72 (2): 78–88.

—— (1995) *The End of the Nation State*, New York: Free Press.

Osan, Sukbhir S. (2000a) *Genocide of Sikhs*. Online. Available http://burningpunjab.com/pages/geno-1.html (accessed 1 February 2002).

—— (2000b) *Operation Blue Star*. Online. Available http://www.burningpunjab.com/pages/opera-1.htm (accessed 1 February 2002).

Pandey, G. (2001) *Remembering Partition: Violence, Nationalism and History in India*, New Delhi: Oxford University Press.

Parekh, B. (2002) 'Barry and the Dangers of Liberalism', in P. Kelly (ed.), *Multiculturalism Reconsidered*, Cambridge: Polity Press, pp. 133–151.

Pasha, M.K. (1996) 'Globalisation and Poverty in South Asia', *Millennium: Journal of International Studies*, 25 (3): 635–657.

Petito, Fabio and Hatzopoulos, Pavlos (eds) (2003) *Religion in International Relations: The Return from Exile*, New York: Palgrave.

Petrie, D. (1911) *Recent Developments in Sikh Politics, 1900–1911, a Report*, Amritsar: Chief Khalsa Diwan.

Pettigrew, J. (1995) *The Sikhs of the Punjab: Unheard Voices of the State and Guerrilla Violence* (Politics in Contemporary Asia), London: Zed Books.

Pfaff, W. (2005) 'A Monster of Our Own Making', *Observer*, 21 August. Online. Available http://www.guardian.co.uk/alqaida/story/0,12469,1553504,00.html (accessed 1 November 2006).

Pieterse, J.N. (2004) *Globalization and Culture*, Lanham, MD: Rowman & Littlefield.

Prakash, G. (1999) *Another Reason: Science and the Imagination of Modern India*, Princeton, NJ: Princeton University Press.

Price, G. (2004) 'How the 2004 Lok Sabha Election Was Lost', Chatham House Briefing Note, 23 June. Revised version. Online. Available http://www.chathamhouse.org.uk/pdf/research/asia/A-FTindia.pdf (accessed 24 July 2004).

Purewal, S. (2000) *Sikh Ethnonationalism and the Political Economy of the Punjab*, New Delhi: Oxford University Press.

Puri, H.S. (1993) *The Ghadar Movement: Ideology, Organisation and Strategy*, Amritsar: Guru Nanak Dev University Press.

Ramadan, T. (2004) *Western Muslims and the Future of Islam*, Oxford: Oxford University Press.

Ramesh, R. (2004) '20 Years after Golden Temple Killings, Sikhs Pray New PM Will Bring Justice', *Guardian*, 3 June. Online. Available http://www.guardian.co.uk/print/0,3858,4938064-111087,00.html (accessed 3 June 2004).

Rashtriya Swayamsevak Sangh (RSS) (2007) 'Mission & Vision: RSS & Minorities', 2 May. Online. Available http://www.rss.org/New_RSS/Mission_Vision/RSS_on_Minorities.jsp (accessed 3 May 2007).

Rex, J. (1991) 'The Political Sociology of a Multi-cultural Society', *European Journal of Intercultural Studies*, 2 (1): 2–17.

Riar, S. (1996) 'Khalistan: The Origins of the Demand and Its Pursuit prior to Independence, 1940–45', in P. Singh and S.S. Thandi (eds), *Globalisation and the Region: Explorations in Punjabi Identity*, Coventry: Association for Punjab Studies.

Rosenberg, J. (2005) 'Globalization Theory: A Post-Mortem', *International Politics*, 42: 2–74.

Runnymede Trust (2000) *The Future of Multiethnic Britain*, London: Profile Books.

—— (2004) *Realising the Vision*, Briefing Paper, London: Runnymede Trust.

Saffran, W. (1991) 'Diaspora in Modern Societies: Myths of Homeland and Return', *Diaspora*, 1 (1): 83–99.

—— (1999) 'Comparing Diasporas: A Review Essay', *Diaspora*, 8 (3): 255–293.

Sahni, B. (2001 [1970]) *Tamas*, Harmondsworth: Penguin.

Said, E.W. (1978) *Orientalism*, New York: Vintage Books.
—— (2000) 'Permission to Narrate', in M. Bayoumi and A. Rubin (eds), *The Edward Said Reader*, New York: Vintage.
Sardar, Z. (2003) 'Reconstructing Muslim Civilization', in Sohail Inayatullah and Gail Boxwell (eds), *A Ziauddin Sardar Reader*, London: Pluto Press, pp. 35–48.
Sassen, S. (1997) *Losing Control: Sovereignty in an Age of Globalization*, New York: Columbia University Press.
Savarkar, V.D. (1923) *Hindutva*, Bombay: Veer Savarkar Prakashan.
—— (1998) 'Some of the Basic Principles and Tenets of the Hindu Movement', in F. Dallmayr and G.N. Devy (eds), *Between Tradition and Modernity: India's Search for Identity*, Delhi: Sage Publications, pp. 114–120.
Sayyid, S. (2001) 'Beyond Westphalia: Nations and Diasporas – The Case of the Muslim *Umma*', in Barnor Hesse (ed.), *Un/settled Multiculturalisms: Diasporas, Entanglements, Transruptions*, London: Zed Books.
Scholte, Jan Aart (2005) *Globalisation: A Critical Introduction*, 2nd edn, Basingstoke: Palgrave Macmillan.
Sekhon, A.S. and Dilgeer, H.S. (2006) *A White Paper on Khalistan (A True Story): The Sikh Nation* (ed. A.T. Kerr), Edmonton, AB: Sikh Educational Trust.
Sen, A. and Drèze, J. (1999) 'India: Economic Development and Social Opportunity', in A. Sen and J. Drèze, *The Amartya Sen and Jean Drèze Omnibus*, Oxford: Oxford University Press.
Shani, G. (2000a) 'The Politics of Recognition: Sikh Diasporic Nationalism and the International Order', *International Journal of Punjab Studies*, 7 (2): 193–223.
—— (2000b) 'The Construction of a Sikh National Identity', *South Asia Research*, 20 (1): 3–18.
—— (2002) 'The Territorialization of Identity: Sikh Nationalism in the Diaspora', *Studies in Ethnicity and Nationalism*, 2 (1): 11–20.
—— (2005) 'Beyond Khalistan: Sikh Diasporic Identity and Critical International Theory', *Sikh Formations: Religion, Culture, Theory*, 1 (1): 57–74.
—— (2007) 'Provincialising Critical Theory: Islam, Sikhism and International Relations', *Cambridge Review of International Affairs*, May, 20 (2).
Shani, G., Sato, M. and Pasha, M.K. (eds) (2007) *Protecting Human Security in a Post 9/11 World: Critical and Global Insights*, Basingstoke: Palgrave Macmillan.
Shils, E. (1957) 'Personal, Primordial, Sacred and Civil Ties', *British Journal of Sociology*, 8: 130–145.
Shiromani Akali Dal (SAD) (1961) *Constitution of the Shiromani Akali Dal*, Amritsar: SGPC Publications.
—— (1973) *The Anandpur Sahib Resolution* (16–17 October 1973), Amritsar: SGPC Publications.
—— (1974) *Constitution of the United Shiromani Akali Dal*, Amritsar: SGPC Publications.
—— (1978) *The Anandpur Sahib Resolution* (28–29 October 1978), Amritsar: SGPC Publications.
—— (2004) 'Aims of Shiromani Akali Dal'. Online. Available http://www.akali-dal.com/aims.htm (accessed 15 May 2004).
Shiromani Gurdwara Prabandhak Committee (SGPC) (1946) *Resolution of Sikh State*, Amritsar: SGPC Publications. Online. Available http://www.maboli.com/sikh_hr/pages/documents/1946resolution.html (accessed 2 February 2004).
—— (1994) *The Sikh Reht Maryada*, Amritsar: SGPC Publications.

—— (2001) 'Sikhism'. Available http://www.sgpc.net/sikhism/index.html (accessed 2 February 2002).

—— (2007) 'Home'. Available http://www.sgpc.net (accessed 27 April 2007).

Shiva, V. (1997) *The Violence of the Green Revolution: Third World Agriculture, Ecology and Politics*, London: Zed Books.

Sikh Agenda (2003) *Sikh Agenda 1*. Online. Available http://groups.yahoo.com/group/sikhagenda1/ (accessed 21 March 2004).

Sikh American Legal Defense and Education Fund (SALDEF) (2007) 'Home'. Online. Available http://www.saldef.org/ (accessed 25 February 2007).

Sikh Coalition (2001) 'Senate Unanimously Passes Resolution on Hate Crimes against Sikh-Americans', 18 October. Online. Available http://www.sikhcoalition.org/pr.asp?mainaction=viewpr&prid=28 (accessed 21 April 2007).

—— (2002) 'Incidents and Hate Crimes'. Online. Available http://www.sikhcoalition.org/ListReports.asp?mainaction=LIST&listwhat=Reports&select=US&select4=&imageField22.x=18&imageField22.y=15 (accessed 31 August 2004).

—— (2005) *Sikh Coalition: Annual Report 2004–5*, 23 August, New York: Sikh Coalition.

—— (2006) 'First Sikhs Elected in New York', 18 September. Online. Available http://www.sikhcoalition.org/advisories/sikhs_elected.htm (accessed 24 January 2007).

—— (2007a) 'Home'. Online. Available http://www.sikhcoalition.org/ (accessed 24 January 2007).

—— (2007b) 'History'. Online. Available http://www.sikhcoalition.org/History.asp (accessed 24 January 2007).

—— (2007c) 'Mission'. Online. Available http://www.sikhcoalition.org/Mission.asp (accessed 24 January 2007).

—— (2007d) 'Sikhism at a Glance'. Online. Available http://www.sikhcoalition.org/SikhismGlance.asp (accessed 20 February 2007).

Sikh Federation (UK) (2003a) 'About Us'. Online. Available http://www.sikhfederation.com/aboutus.htm (accessed 31 April 2006).

—— (2003b) 'Policies'. Online. Available http://www.sikhfederation.com/policy.htm (accessed 1 July 2006).

—— (2003c) 'Sikhs and the British Establishment'. Online. Available http://www.sikhfederation.com/sikh_agenda_1_british_sikhs_and_establishment.htm (accessed 3 July 2006).

—— (2003d) 'Government Funding for Sikh Organisations'. Online. Available http://www.sikhfederation.com/sikh_agenda_2_government_funding_sikh_organisations.htm (accessed 7 July 2006).

—— (2003e) 'Promotion of Sikh Identity and Panjabi Language'. Online. Available http://www.sikhfederation.com/sikh_agenda_3_promotion_sikh_identity_panjabi_language.htm (accessed 8 July 2006).

—— (2003f) 'Establishment of State Funded Sikh Schools'. Online. Available http://www.sikhfederation.com/sikh_agenda_4_establishment_state_funded%20_sikh_schools.htm (accessed 8 July 2006).

—— (2003g) 'Preserving Sikh Heritage'. Online. Available http://www.sikhfederation.com/sikh_agenda_5_preserving_sikh_heritage.htm (accessed 9 July 2006).

—— (2003h) 'Protecting Human Rights of Sikhs and Humanitarian Aid'. Online.

Available http://www.sikhfederation.com/sikh_agenda_6_protecting_human_rights_sikhs_humanitarian_aid.htm (accessed 9 July 2006).

—— (2003i) 'Self-Determination for the Sikh Nation'. Online. Available http://www.sikhfederation.com/sikh_agenda_7_self_determination_sikh_nation.htm (accessed 1 July 2006).

Sikh Human Rights Group (SHRG) (2001) 'Plenary Statement to World Conference against Racism, Racial Discrimination, Xenophobia and Related Intolerance', Durban, South Africa, 31 August – 7 September.

Sikh Pride (2001) *Sikhs in Census*. Online. Available http://www.sikhpride.com/census/census.htm (accessed 2 December 2003).

Singh, A. (1988) 'The Shiromani Gurdwara Prabandhak Committee and the Politicisation of the Sikhs', in J. O'Connell, M. Israel and W.G. Oxtoby (eds), *Sikh History and Religion in the Twentieth Century*, Toronto: University of Toronto Press.

Singh, Gopal (1984) 'Socio-economic Basis of the Punjab Crisis', *Economic and Political Weekly*, 19 (1): 1111–1125.

Singh, Gurbhagat (1999a) 'Vaisakhi of 1699: Rupture of the Indian Grand Narratives', *International Journal of Punjab Studies*, July–December, 6 (2): 187–194.

—— (1999b) 'Sikhism and Postmodernism', *Sikh Review*, November. Online. Available http://www.sikhreview.org/november1999/philosophy.htm (accessed 23 April 2003).

Singh, Gurbux (2001) 'New Year's Wishes', *Guardian*, 31 December. Online. Available http://www.guardian.co.uk/g2/story/0,,626043,00.html (accessed 1 December 2002).

Singh, Gurharpal (1992) 'The Punjab Elections of 1992', *Asian Survey*, 32 (11): 988–999.

—— (1998) 'The Akalis and the BJP in the Punjab: From Ayodhya to the 1997 Legislative Assembly Election', in T.B. Hansen and C. Jaffrelot (eds), *The BJP and the Compulsions of Politics in India*, New Delhi: Oxford University Press.

—— (1999) 'A Victim Diaspora? The Case of the Sikhs', *Diaspora: Journal of Transnational Studies*, 8 (3): 293–309.

—— (2000) *Ethnic Conflict in India: A Case Study of the Punjab*, London: Palgrave Macmillan.

—— (2003) 'Multiculturalism in Contemporary Britain: Reflections on the "Leicester Model" ', *International Journal on Multicultural Societies*, September, 5 (1): 40–54.

—— (2004) 'The Strange Death of Sikh Ethno-nationalism: Reassessing Operation Blue Star and Its Aftermath,' paper prepared for 'Remembering and Forgetting: Memory and Trauma in Contemporary Sikh and Punjabi Experience', 3rd International Conference organized by Sardarni Kuljit Kaur Bindra, Chair in Sikh Studies, Hofstra University, New York, 9 May.

Singh, Gurharpal and Rex, J. (2003) 'Multiculturalism and Political Integration in Modern Nation-States: Thematic Introduction', *International Journal on Multicultural Societies*, September, 5 (1): 3–19.

Singh, Gurharpal and Tatla, D.S. (2006) *Sikhs in Britain: The Making of a Community*, London: Zed Books.

Singh, Gurjeet (2007) 'First World Sikh Lobby – Geneva, Switzerland', *Panthic Weekly*, 4 April. Online. Available http://www.panthkhalsa.org/panth/index.php (accessed 6 April 2007).

Singh, Gurnam (1960) *A Unilingual Punjabi State and Sikh Unrest*, New Delhi: Super Press.

Singh, Gurnam (2006) 'Sikhism's Emancipatory Discourses: Some Critical Perspectives', *Sikh Formations: Religion, Culture, Theory*, 2 (2):135–151.

Singh, Harbans (2003a) 'The Singh Sabha Movement', *The Encyclopedia of Sikhism*. Online. Available http://www.sikhcybermuseum.org/history/SinghSabha1870.htm (accessed 20 January 2004).

—— (2003b) 'The *Jallianwallah Bagh* Massacre', *The Encyclopedia of Sikhism*. Online. Available http://www.sikhcybermuseum.org/history/SinghSabha1870.htm (accessed 20 January 2004).

Singh, K. (1966) *A History of the Sikhs*, vol. 2: *1839–1964*, Princeton, NJ: Princeton University Press.

—— (2006) *An Illustrated History of the Sikhs*, New Delhi: Oxford University Press.

Singh, Manmohan (2006) 'Independence Day: Text of PM's Address to the Nation', 15 August. Online. Available http://www.hindu.com/nic/independence.htm (accessed 15 August 2006).

Singh, Mohinder (1997) 'Akalis and the Nationalist Politics', in I. Banga (ed.), *Five Punjabi Centuries*, New Delhi: Manohar.

Singh, Nikky-Guninder Kaur (2005) *The Birth of the Khalsa: A Feminist Re-memory of Sikh Identity*, New York: State University of New York.

Singh, Pashaura (2000) *The Guru Granth Sahib: Canon, Meaning and Authority*, New Delhi: Oxford University Press.

—— (2004) 'Sikh Identity in the Light of History', in Pashaura Singh and N. Gerald Barrier (eds), *Sikhism and History*, New Delhi: Oxford University Press.

Singh, Pritam (2007) 'Punjab's Electoral Competition', *Economic and Political Weekly*, 10 February: 466–467.

Singh, Ranbir (1968) *The Sikh Way of Life*, New Delhi: Caxton Press.

Singh, Sarab Jit (2002) *Operation Black Thunder: An Eyewitness Account of Terrorism in the Punjab*, New Delhi: Sage.

Singh, Sri Guru Gobind, '*Akal Ustat*', *Sri Dasam Granth Sahib*. Online. Available http://www.sridasam.org/dasam?Action=Page&p=34 (accessed 1 April 2007).

Singh, Surjan (1982) *Case for the Republic of Khalistan*, Vancouver, BC: Babbar Khalsa Press.

Singh, Tara (1946) 'Foreword' to L. Sarsfield, *Betrayal of the Sikhs*, Lahore: Lahore Book Shop.

Singh, Teja (1988) *The Religion of the Sikh Gurus*, Santa Fe, NM: Sun Books.

Smith, A.D. (1996) 'Memory and Modernity: Reflections on Ernest Gellner's Theory of Nationalism', *Nations and Nationalism*, 2 (3): 371–388.

—— (1999) *Myths and Memories of the Nation*, Oxford: Oxford University Press.

Smith, D.E. (1963) *India as a Secular State*, Princeton, NJ: Princeton University Press.

Strange, S. (1996) *The Retreat of the State: The Diffusion of Power in the World Economy*, Cambridge: Cambridge University Press.

Talbot, I. (1996) 'The British Punjab, 1875–1937', in G. Singh and I. Talbot (eds), *Punjabi Identity: Continuity and Change*, Delhi: Oxford University Press.

Talib, Gurbacharan Singh (comp.) (1991 [1950]) *Muslim League Attacks on Sikhs and Hindus in the Punjab*, Amritsar: SGPC Publications.

Tambiah, S.J. (2000) 'Transnational Movements, Diasporas and Multiple Modernities', *Daedalus*, 129: 163–194.

Tatla, D.S. (1999) *The Sikh Diaspora: The Search for Statehood*, London: UCL Press.

—— (2001) 'Imagining Punjab: Narratives of Nationhood and Homeland among the Sikh Diaspora', in C. Shackle, G. Singh and A.S. Mandair (eds), *Sikh Religion, Culture and Ethnicity*, London: Curzon Press.

—— (2006) 'The Morning After: Trauma, Memory and the Sikh Predicament since 1984', *Sikh Formations: Religion, Culture, Theory*, June, 2 (1): 57–88.

Taylor, C. (1994) 'The Politics of Recognition', in A. Gutman (ed.), *Multiculturalism: Examining the Politics of Recognition*, Princeton, NJ: Princeton University Press.

Thandi, S.S. (1996) 'Counterinsurgency and Political Violence in the Punjab', in G. Singh and I. Talbot (eds), *Punjabi Identity: Continuity and Change*, New Delhi: Manohar.

Thapar, R. (1989) 'Imagined Religious Communities? Ancient History and the Modern Search for a Hindu Identity', *Modern Asian Studies*, 23 (2): 209–231.

Thomas, S.M. (2000) 'Taking Religious and Cultural Pluralism Seriously: The Global Resurgence of Religion and the Transformation of International Society', *Millennium: Journal of International Studies*, 29 (3): 815–842.

—— (2005) *The Global Resurgence of Religion and the Transformation of International Relations*, New York and Basingstoke: Palgrave Macmillan.

Tölölyan, K. (1991) 'The Nation State and Its Others: In Lieu of a Preface', *Diaspora*, 1 (1): 1–10.

Tonnies, F. (1955) *Community and Association* [Gemeinschaft und Gesellschaft], trans. C.P. Loomis, London: Routledge & Kegan Paul.

Tribune (1998–2007) Online. Available http://www.tribuneindia.com.

—— (2002) 'Tohra Wiped Out in His Bastion', 24 February. Online. Available http://www.tribuneindia.com/2002/20020225/main1.htm (accessed 25 May 2002).

—— (2004a) 'Impact of Tohra's Death on Punjab Politics', 1 April. Online. Available http://www.tribuneindia.com/2004/20040401/main1.htm (accessed 1 April 2004).

—— (2004b) 'SAD–BJP Alliance Sweeps Punjab', 13 May. Online. Available http://www.tribuneindia.com/2004/20040513/main10.htm (accessed 13 May 2004).

—— (2004c) 'Sonia Emerging Front Runner', 15 May. Online. Available http://www.tribuneindia.com/2004/20040515/main1.htm (accessed 15 May 2004).

—— (2005) 'Manmohan Apologises to Sikhs for '84 Riots', 11 August. Online. Available http://www.tribuneindia.com/2005/20050812/main1.htm (accessed 12 August 2005).

—— (2007a) 'Chohan Dead', 4 April. Online. Available http://www.tribuneindia.com/2007/20070405/main5.htm (accessed 4 April 2007).

—— (2007b) 'SAD–BJP Got 45.37% Votes, Cong 40.9%', 2 March. Online. Available http://www.tribuneindia.com/2007/20070302/punjab1.htm#1 (accessed 2 March 2007).

—— (2007c) 'Elated, Badal Buries Bitter Past', 1 March. Online. Available http://www.tribuneindia.com/2007/20070301punjab1.htm#1 (accessed 2 March 2007).

—— (2007d) 'Punjab Votes 07: Fiercest Poll Battle Ever', 11 February. Online. Available http://www.tribuneindia.com/2007/20070212/main1.htm (accessed 12 February 2007).

Trumpp, E. (1979 [1887]) *The Adi Granth or Holy Scriptures of the Sikhs*, New Delhi: Munshiram Manoharlal Publishers.

Tully, M. and Jacob, S. (1985) *Amritsar: Mrs Gandhi's Last Battle*, London: Pan Books.

Uberoi, J.P.S. (1996) *Religion, Civil Society and the State: A Study of Sikhism*, Delhi: Oxford University Press.

United Kingdom Government Home Office (2001) *Community Cohesion: A Report of the Independent Review Team Chaired by Ted Cantle*, London: UK Government Home Office.

—— (2002a) *Secure Border, Safe Havens: White Paper on Immigration 2002*, London: UK Government Home Office.

—— (2002b) *Nationality, Immigration and Asylum Act 2002*, London: UK Government Home Office.

United Nations Development Programme (UNDP) (2003) *Human Development Report 2003: Millennium Development Goals – A Compact among Nations to End Human Poverty*, New York: Oxford University Press.

—— (2005) *Human Development Report 2005: International Cooperation at a Crossroads*, New York: Oxford University Press.

United Nations General Assembly (1948) Resolution 260 (III), 'Official Records of the General Assembly', Third Session, Part I (A-810), 1948:174. Online. Available http://ods-dds-ny.un.org/doc/RESOLUTION/GEN/NR0/044/31/IMG/NR004431.pdf?OpenElement (accessed 31 March 2003).

—— (1960) 'Declaration on the Granting of Independence to Colonial Countries and Peoples Adopted by General Assembly Resolution 1514 (XV) of 14 December 1960'. Online. Available http://www.unhchr.ch/html/menu3/b/c_coloni.htm (accessed 20 April 2003).

United Nations High Commission for Human Rights (1966) 'International Covenant on Civil and Political Rights', 16 December. Online. Available http://www.ohchr.org/english/law/ccpr.htm (accessed 24 April 2007).

UNITED SIKHS (2006) 'French Turban Campaign Continues in Earnest as More Sikh Students Face Expulsion'. Press Release, 18 November. Online. Available http://unitedsikhs.org/PressReleases/PRSRLS-18-11-2006-00.htm (accessed 25 February 2007).

—— (2007a) 'About'. Online. Available http://www.unitedsikhs.org/about.htm (accessed 21 February 2007).

—— (2007b) 'Projects'. Online. Available http://www.unitedsikhs.org/projects.htm (accessed 21 February 2007).

—— (2007c) 'Right to Turban'. Online. Available http://www.unitedsikhs.org/rtt/ (accessed 22 February 2007).

—— (2007d) 'Euro Campaign for Right to Difference and Diversity'. Online. Available http://www.unitedsikhs.org/euro_campaign/ (accessed 22 February 2007).

Upadhyaya, P.C. (1992) 'The Politics of Indian Secularism', *Modern Asian Studies*, 26 (4): 815–853.

Veer, P. van der (1994) *Religious Nationalism: Hindus and Muslims in India*, Princeton, NJ: Princeton University Press.

—— (1999) 'Hindus: A Superior Race', *Nations and Nationalism*, 5 (3): 419–430.

Verma, P.S. (1987) 'Akali Dal: History, Electoral Performance and Leadership Profile', in G. Singh (ed.), *Punjab Today*, Chandigarh: Panjab University Press.

Verma, R.S. (2006) 'Trauma, Cultural Survival and Identity Politics in a Post 9/11 Era: Reflections of Sikh Youth', *Sikh Formations: Religion, Culture, Theory*, 2 (1): 89–101.

Walker, R.B.J. (1993) *Inside/Outside: International Relations as Political Theory*, Cambridge: Cambridge University Press.

Wallace, P. (1981) 'Religious and Secular Politics in Punjab: The Sikh Dilemma in Competing Political Systems', in P. Wallace and S. Chopra (eds), *Political Dynamics of the Punjab*, Amritsar: Guru Nanak Dev University Press.

Wallerstein, I. (1974) 'The Rise and Future Demise of the World Capitalist System', *Comparative Studies in Society and History*, September, 16 (4): 387–415.

Waltz, K. (1979) *Theory of International Politics*, Reading, MA: Addison-Wesley.

—— (1986) 'Systemic and Reductionist Theories', in R.O. Keohane (ed.), *Neorealism and Its Critics*, New York: Columbia University Press.

—— (1990) 'Realist Thought and Neo-realist Theory', *Journal of International Affairs*, 44 (1): 20–40.

Walzer, M. (1995) 'The Concept of Civil Society', in M. Walzer (ed.), *Toward a Global Civil Society*, Providence, RI: Berghahn Books.

Weber, M. (1978) *Selections in Translation*, trans. E. Matthews and ed. W.G. Runciman, Cambridge: Cambridge University Press.

—— (1991) *From Max Weber*, trans. and ed. H.H. Gerth and C. Wright Mills, London: Routledge.

Wendt, A. (1996) 'Identity and Structural Change in International Politics', in Y. Lapid and F. Kratochwil (eds), *The Return of Culture and Identity in International Relations Theory*, Boulder, CO: Lynne Rienner.

Witness 84 (2004) 'Home'. Online. Available http://www.witness84.com/site/ (accessed 6 June 2004).

Wolf, M. (2005) 'When Multiculturalism Is Nonsense', *Financial Times*, 31 August. Online. Available http://www.ft.com/cms/s/4c751acc-19bc-11da-804e-00000e2511c8.html (accessed 1 November 2006).

World Bank (2004) *Resuming Punjab's Prosperity: The Opportunities and Challenges Ahead*, Washington, DC: Poverty Reduction and Economic Management Sector Unit (South Asia Region).

World Sikh Council (WSC) (2007) 'Home', 'Aims and Objectives' and 'History'. Online. Available http://www.worldsikhcouncil.org/ (accessed 1 February 2007).

World Sikh Organization (WSO) (2007) 'Aims and Objectives', 'History' and 'Constitution'. Online. Available http://www.worldsikh.org (accessed 19 February 2007).

Wyn Jones, R. (ed.) (2001) *Critical Theory and World Politics*, Boulder, CO: Lynne Rienner.

Yong, T.T. (1994) 'Prelude to Partition: Sikh Responses to the Demand for Pakistan', *International Journal of Punjab Studies*, July–December, 1 (2): 167–196.

Young, T. (1995) 'A Project to Be Realised: Global Liberalism and Contemporary Africa', *Millennium: Journal of International Studies*, 24 (3): 527–546.

Interviews

Mr Patwant Singh, Author of *The Sikhs* (London: John Murray, 1999), Private Residence, New Delhi, 27 March 1997.

Dr Jagjit Singh Chauhan, ex-President of Khalistan, Private Residence, London, 1 February 2000.

Mr Ajit Singh Khera, ex-Press Secretary, Khalistan Council, Private Residence, London, 1 October 2000.

Mr Bhupinder Singh, Managing Director, Sikh Pride website, via e-mail, 13 July 2001.

Dr Jasdev Singh Rai, Director of Sikh Human Rights Group, Ealing, 17 September 2001.

Mr Amardeep Singh, Executive Director of the Sikh Coalition, Sikh Religious Society, Palatine, IL, USA, 24 February 2007.

Mr Tejinder Singh, Legal Adviser to UNITED SIKHS, Sikh Religious Society, Palatine, IL, USA, 24 February 2007.

Mr Surinderpal Singh, Vice-Chair of World Sikh Council, Sikh Religious Society, Palatine, IL, USA, 24 February 2007.

Dr Swaranjeet Singh, Director of Institute for Conflict and Peace Studies, Sikh Religious Society, Palatine, IL, USA, 24 February 2007.

Dr Balwant Singh Hansra, Council of Parliament of World Religions, Palatine, IL, USA, 25 February 2007.

Dr Amarjit Singh, Director, Khalistan Affairs Center, Washington, DC, by phone, 27 February 2007.

Ms Mejindarpal Kaur, Director, UNITED SIKHS UK/Europe, London, by phone, 25 March 2007.

Discussion groups

A.S. (2004) 'Is Khalistan Still Necessary?', Khalistan discussion group. Online posting. Available e-mail: Khalistan@yahoogroups.com (20 May 2004).

A.S.S. (2004) 'Is Khalistan Still Necessary?', Sikh discussion group. Online posting. Available e-mail: Sikh@msn.groups.com (20 May 2004).

D.S. (2004) 'Is Khalistan Still Necessary?', Khalistan discussion group. Online posting. Available e-mail: Khalistan@yahoogroups.com (20 May 2004).

D.S.S. (2004) 'Is Khalistan Still Necessary?', Sikh discussion group. Online posting. Available e-mail: Sikh@msn.groups.com (22 May 2004).

G.S. (2004) 'Is Khalistan Still Necessary?', Sikh discussion group. Online posting. Available e-mail: Sikh@msn.groups.com (31 August 2004).

H.K. (2004) 'Is Khalistan Still Necessary?', Sikh discussion group. Online posting. Available e-mail: Sikh@msn.groups.com (26 May 2004).

H.S. (2004) 'Is Khalistan Still Necessary?', UK Sikh Community discussion group. Online posting. Available e-mail: UKSikhCommunity@msn.groups.com (22 May 2004).

J.A.S. (2004) 'Is Khalistan Still Necessary?', Khalistan discussion group. Online posting. Available e-mail: Khalistan@yahoogroups.com (20 May 2004).

J.S. (2004) 'Is Khalistan Still Necessary?', Khalistan discussion group. Online posting. Available e-mail: Khalistan@yahoogroups.com (21 May 2004).

J.S.S. (2004) 'Is Khalistan Still Necessary?', UK Sikh Community discussion Group. Online posting. Available e-mail: UKSikhCommunity@msn.groups.com (31 August 2004).

K.S. (2004) 'Is Khalistan Still Necessary?', UK Sikh Community discussion group. Online posting. Available e-mail: UKSikhCommunity@msn.groups.com (31 August 2004).

S.S. (2004) 'Is Khalistan Still Necessary?', UK Sikh Community discussion group. Online posting. Available e-mail: UKSikhCommunity@msn.groups.com (31 August 2004).

V.R. (2004) 'Is Khalistan Still Necessary?', UK Sikh Community discussion group. Online posting. Available e-mail: UKSikhCommunity@msn.groups.com (21 May 2004).

Z.R. (2004) 'Is Khalistan Still Necessary?', Khalistan discussion group. Online posting. Available e-mail: Khalistan@yahoogroups.com (20 May 2004).

Z.S. (2004) 'Is Khalistan Still Necessary?', Sikh Agenda discussion group. Online posting. Available e-mail: SikhAgenda@yahoogroups.com (20 May 2004).

Index

Lightning Source UK Ltd.
Milton Keynes UK
26 June 2010

156124UK00003B/17/P

9 780415 586108